JUNGLE FEVER

JUNGLE FEVER

Exploring Madness and Medicine in Twentieth-Century Tropical Narratives

Charlotte Rogers

Vanderbilt University Press
Nashville

© 2012 by Vanderbilt University Press
Nashville, Tennessee 37235
All rights reserved
First printing 2012

This book is printed on acid-free paper.
Manufactured in the United States of America

Library of Congress Cataloging-in-Publication Data on file

ISBN 978-0-8265-1831-6 (cloth)
ISBN 978-0-8265-1833-0 (e-book)

Contents

Acknowledgments

THIS BOOK HAS COME TO BE MY OWN ADVENTURE IN THE LITERARY jungles of novels, manuscripts, historical treatises, and medical texts—writings in three languages about tropical lands on three continents. Most of my research was conducted during my time in the doctoral program of the Department of Spanish and Portuguese at Yale University, in the holdings of the Cushing/Whitney Medical Library, the Sterling Memorial Library, and the Beinecke Rare Book and Manuscript Library. I thank their respective staff members for their invaluable assistance over the years. A generous fellowship from the Beinecke Rare Book and Manuscript Library made it possible for me in 2007 to study the unpublished works of Conrad housed at the Beinecke and in the Berg Collection of the New York Public Library. Portions of Chapter 3 were published in my article "Medicine, Madness, and Writing in *La vorágine*" in the *Bulletin of Hispanic Studies* in January 2010.

Like all travelers in the wilderness who inevitably lose their way and require external guidance, I benefited immeasurably from scholars whose comments and expertise pointed me in the right direction, especially Rolena Adorno, Christopher L. Miller, Gustavo Pérez Firmat, and Vera Kutzinski. I owe a special debt of gratitude to Roberto González Echevarría, whose graduate course "The Jungle Books" first set me on this adventure, and whose unflagging enthusiasm for my work has resulted in the present volume. I also thank Eli Bortz at Vanderbilt University Press for being an excellent guide to the process of publication. Finally, I thank my husband, Richard, for his support of my scholarly quests, and for never minding that our home occasionally resembled an ever-encroaching jungle of books.

A Note on Translations

In translating French and Spanish texts into English, I have used existing translations whenever possible. All renderings of previously untranslated materials into English are my own, though I would like to thank Julie-Françoise Kruidenier Tolliver for her advice in translating French medical texts from the early twentieth century. When a published translation of a particular work exists, I have generally used only the English-language version and corresponding page numbers. In the cases in which a published translation is nonexistent, I maintain the original language's title and page numbers, with a translation of the title into English in parentheses.

JUNGLE FEVER

Introduction

Tales of men going mad in the wilderness have been popular in novels and films for over a century, from the initial appearance of Joseph Conrad's *Heart of Darkness* (1899) to its reinvention in Francis Ford Coppola's *Apocalypse Now* (1979). The popular imagination, now as it was then, is fascinated by the story of a seemingly rational individual who ventures into the forest, loses his mind, lives among "the natives," and turns his back on society for good. This book explores five such tales: Conrad's *Heart of Darkness*, *The Way of the Kings* (*La voie royale*) by André Malraux, *The Vortex* (*La vorágine*) by José Eustasio Rivera, *Canaima* by Rómulo Gallegos, and *The Lost Steps* (*Los pasos perdidos*) by Alejo Carpentier. These novels from disparate regions, historical moments, and linguistic traditions ascribe the madness of their protagonists to a single cause: a foray into the wilderness. In each work, the main character goes into the undomesticated rainforest in search of the financial and spiritual riches that he has found Western civilization to be lacking. While there, he loses himself both literally and metaphorically. Freed from societal restraints, the civilized, rational protagonist becomes increasingly less so. The descent into madness experienced by these characters indicates their twentieth-century creators' disenchantment with narratives of imperial expansion and their ostensible rationality. A deep undercurrent of pessimism runs beneath the surface of these adventure novels. They go far beyond a critique of colonialism; the fates of their protagonists undermine the Cartesian tenets of modern society and question the notion of progress on which it is founded.

This skepticism regarding Western civilization is also played out on a deeper linguistic level within the texts. Indeed, the most important element of madness in these works is that all the protagonists try to narrate their lunacy and find that the attempts bring them to the boundaries of conventional literary language. To narrate their madness, they must make sense out of non-sense, and in doing so they create a new mode of expression. The fragmentary and unruly nature of the protagonists' disturbed minds is reflected in the prose of the novels, and in the wilderness each narrator describes. These adventure novels thus derive their literary modernism—their new mode of expression—from their main characters' struggles to narrate madness.

The literary history of the twentieth century is awash with stories of dramatic adventures in the tropical wilderness. In addition to the five principal novels examined here, we can count Edgar Rice Burroughs's *Tarzan of the Apes*, Arthur Conan Doyle's *The Lost World* (and Michael Crichton's 1995 novel and movie of the same name), W. H. Hudson's *Green Mansions*, Horacio Quiroga's Misiones stories, Virginia Woolf's *The Voyage Out*, selections from Louis-Ferdinand Céline's *Journey to the End of the Night*, Severo Sarduy's *Colibrí* (The hummingbird), Wilson Harris's *Palace of the Peacock*, Mario Vargas Llosa's *The Storyteller* and *The Green House*, and Álvaro Mutis's *Amirbar* and *The Snow of the Admiral*.[1] Many films seek to portray their adventurous heroes' mental unraveling on the big screen: the aforementioned *Apocalypse Now*, Werner Herzog's *Aguirre, Wrath of God* (*Aguirre, der Zorn Gottes*), and Peter Weir's *The Mosquito Coast* are only a few examples.[2]

Amid the profusion of twentieth-century works set in the wilderness, the narratives that constitute the essence of this study stand out because, in each novel, medical theories play a major role in shaping the portrayal of madness in the tropics. In each case, a medical lexicon informs the way in which the tale is told.[3] The selected texts also mark the transition in literary history from Romanticism to modernism. Throughout this book, I argue that their modernism is due precisely to their struggle to narrate lunacy without resorting to Romantic or classical imagery. They turn, instead, to medical terminology and the nascent science of psychology to explain their protagonists' erratic behavior in the tropics. Their literary modernism spans continents and linguistic and national boundaries. It is unified by the refusal to be bound to conventional literary language about the tropics, and takes advantage of a new medical lexicon to portray madness.

Most of these tropical adventure stories share a narrative trajectory similar to that of travelogues, as defined by Ottmar Ette: each tale is marked by the protagonist's departure from society, the encounter with a new culture and environment (which Ette calls "the climax"), the arrival at the goal of his journey, and the return to civilization (32–38). This voyage has its roots in the genre of quest romance as defined by Northrop Frye (to which I will return shortly), as well as in the adventure novel tradition. In each novel studied in this work, a parallel process of introspection mirrors the physical voyage, whereby these four steps occur in the protagonist's internal life, and in which his arrival at the goal of the journey, the innermost part of the wilderness, coincides with his loss of sanity. In this sense, these tropical narratives are equal parts psychological and physical adventure tales in which each protagonist glimpses madness when he peers into his own soul. The sensational narration of this harrowing experience and the dangers faced by the travelers in remote locales have made the tropical adventure tale a vibrant literary and film subgenre through much of the twentieth century. Indeed, the tropics were *created* as much as discovered by explorers, soldiers, writers, scientists, and artists as a site of adventure from the advent of European imperialism to today's tropical tourism industry.[4]

The five novels explored in this book have their roots in centuries of depictions of the interaction between exploratory or colonizing forces and indigenous peoples, flora, and fauna in diverse writings and pictorial representations. Before delving into the literary antecedents to these twentieth-century works, it is essential to consider the way in which European societies created their myth of the tropics. At the heart of this confection is the dynamic relationship between humans and their environment, the familiar and the foreign, self and other. The recent development of ecocriticism has been useful in illustrating the extent to which descriptions of the earth's ecology in writing are highly mediated constructions. In a word, depictions of "nature" are decidedly unnatural. A premise elucidated by ecocriticism that is central to this work is the idea that, as William Cronon argues, wilderness "is quite profoundly a human creation—indeed, the creation of very particular human cultures at very particular moments in human history" ("Trouble" 69). This observation is clearly borne out by the changing descriptions of flora and fauna by Europeans as they extended the bounds of their empires.

The following sketch of tropical myth creation from the sixteenth to the early twentieth centuries is selective rather than comprehensive. Its purpose is to underscore the development and permutations of Western attitudes toward tropical climates that were independent of—and indeed sometimes contrary to—historical and geographical realities. Among the territories located between the Tropics of Cancer and Capricorn, those that have an average monthly temperature above 18º C (64.4º F) and precipitation over 5.3 centimeters (2.1 inches) are considered tropical.[5] Historically, these regions have been placed on the margins of Western traditions and considerations.[6] This relegation of the tropics to the cultural periphery is highly ironic given that those same regions occupy the central portion of the earth in cartographical representations. Indeed, the tropics are marginal spaces not in a geographic sense, but in terms of what Rob Shields has called "the periphery of cultural systems of space in which places are ranked relative to each other" (5).[7] According to Shields, the "place-myth" of a region contributes to the formation of an "imaginary geography" in which notions of space are neither static nor universal (7). Like the topographical features of physical geographies, these imagined geographies are created slowly over time, but the forces that shape them are historical and cultural rather than geological and climatological. The creation of stereotypes and associations that enable an individual to draw a mental image of a place even if he or she has never been there is part of what sociologists have called *mental mapping* or *cognitive mapping* (Shields 29; Gould and White). A culture's collective imaginary geography or mental map of a location is generated through the accumulation of images, anecdotes, and descriptions found in high and low sources—from advertising campaigns, news footage, artwork, journalism, and fiction.

Geographic locations remote from Western metropoles are most frequently subject to the creation of a place-myth precisely because of their relative physical inaccessibility to the native of Europe or the United States. This physical remove is complemented and compounded by a cultural one, as many distant regions often have racial, linguistic, social, sartorial, and religious traditions different from those of the Western observer. In this sense, the tropics are located on the periphery of the Western imagined geography, despite their central position on the globe. This imaginary geography is a prerequisite for the creation of the *exotic* (from the Greek *exotikos*, or "foreign"), a term that intrinsically and significantly refers to a quality of being outside of or unfamiliar to the observer.[8] An object, person, or location is not exotic in itself; rather, it only becomes exotic in the moment of discovery by another (Mason 1). Similarly, a place is never inherently remote or foreign; it is made distant and strange by the vantage point of the observer.[9] In this way, "the tropics" become an imagined geography as they are relayed from the periphery to the center in the form of story, picture, or artifact. At the core of the denomination of an object, person, or landscape as exotic is the observer's recognition of its foreignness. The exotic, therefore, is less a quality of being than a momentary reaction or feeling provoked in the viewer.

This moment of the exotic occurs when the physical distance between the observer and the exotic object has collapsed but the imaginary distance remains intact. Perhaps the most elegant definition of the exotic is that coined by Victor Segalen, whose unfinished essay *The Exotic: An Aesthetics of Discovery* was published posthumously in 1955. He envisioned the exotic as "the rapture of the subject conceiving its object, recognizing its own difference from itself, sensing Diversity" (20). His vision sought to distance the word *exotic* from notions of place, commercialization, and colonialism—in other words, to strip it of its "cheap finery" and "its camels and coconuts," which he saw as diluting the purely aesthetic recognition of diversity (18).[10] The meandering and at times self-contradictory quality of Segalen's essay works against his stated purpose. For the exotic is, after all, tied to geography, race, commerce, and imperialism. Segalen's essay inadvertently underscores the impossibility of separating the notion of the exotic from ideas of place, as Segalen himself noted in a diary entry: "Exoticism is willingly 'tropical.' Coconut trees and torrid skies. Not much Arctic exoticism" (13). How did the exotic, the tropics, and colonialism become linked in a common place-myth? The roots of this relationship stretch back to the very lexicon used to describe previously unknown lands and peoples in several European languages.

The words *woodland* and *forest*, both known in Latin as *silva forestis*, have an etymology whose evolutions reflect the perceived divide between humanity and the natural world. In the transition to Romance languages, the Latin *forestis*—derived from *foris*, or "outside"—was transformed into the Spanish *afuera* and the French *dehors*, later giving rise to the French *forêt* and English *forest*. In the twelfth century AD, the term came to signify those peoples and things that came from afar, or that did not form part of a particular society: thus, the French *forestier*, the Italian *forestiero*, the Spanish *forastero*, and the English *foreigner* (Rey

1107; Bloch and von Wartburg 270).[11] In several European languages, therefore, the forest is inherently associated with the undomesticated and the foreign.

The development of the English and French *jungle* and Spanish *jungla* occurred more recently. The word, derived from the Hindi *jangal*, originally meant "dry ground, wasteland, desert, which is of uncertain origin" when it was first used in English in 1776 (Klein 836). Over time, it came to signify a densely wooded area rather than a desert or wasteland, though it maintained its connotations of the unknown, the uncultivated, and the uncertain (Skeat 275).[12] More figuratively, the *Oxford English Dictionary* defines it as "a wild, tangled mass. Also, a place of bewildering complexity or confusion" ("Jungle"). Scientific terms such as *rainforest* or *tropical savannah* have described climatic and geographical conditions more precisely in recent times; the word *rainforest* did not appear in English dictionaries until the 1970s and 1980s (Slater, "Amazonia" 126). The term *jungle*, in contrast, enjoyed and still enjoys widespread use. Thanks in large part to Rudyard Kipling's *The Jungle Books*, it conjures up associations of danger, hot lands, exotic peoples, and adventure for the Anglophone world.[13]

The first component of the Latin term *silva forestis* became *selva* in Spanish. The Real Academia Española defines *selva* as "an extensive terrain, uncultivated and heavily populated with trees."[14] Juan Corominas notes that the first use of *selva* occurred in 1275 in the *Primera crónica general* (First general chronicle of Spain) in reference to the mythical *selva Nemea*, or "Nemean forest" (Corominas 179). The word was later used in Juan Ruiz's 1330 *The Book of Good Love*. The text reads:

> A group of timid rabbits once upon a forest lighted.
> But there, at every little sound, the creatures grew affrighted. (206)
>
> (Andávanse las liebres en la selva allegadas
> sonó un poco la selva, e fueron espantadas.) (qtd. in Corominas 179)

Corominas's etymological history demonstrates that *selva* quickly became an arcane, literary word that was replaced in common usage by the more pedestrian *bosque* (179–80). *Selva* was therefore a poetic and noble term (*una voz poética y noble*) found mainly in the novels of chivalry and the works of Miguel de Cervantes, Juan de Mena, and Luis de Góngora.[15] The historical usage of *selva* reveals two traits that endure in twentieth-century tropical adventure novels in Spanish. The first is the clearly literary quality of a supposedly natural word. Second, Corominas cites Juan Ruiz's employment of *selva* as a proactive agent: it "sounds" or makes noise, thus frightening the hares. The ability of the selva to startle and provoke fear in those who venture into it is therefore established nearly from its first use. Most important, even in this early appearance, the selva was not a passive background but rather an actor in the narrative. From its earliest manifestations, the selva is personified and imbued with the capacity to be either noble or menacing. This Janus-faced aspect of the wilderness has endured into the twenty-first century.

Long before the divisions of the globe into climatic zones, the natural world was often aligned with the *locus amoenus* of Virgil's classical pastoral poetry, a trope that enjoyed a revival in the Spanish Golden Age, such as in the *Églogas* (Ecologues) of Garcilaso de la Vega; it is for this reason that Corominas calls the term *selva* "noble" even though it has the power to frighten. Its use resonated with the biblical depiction of the Garden of Eden as a place of ecological splendor and bounty that was free from human sin.[16] The idyllic notion of a terrestrial paradise was inaugurated on the American continents when Christopher Columbus declared on his third voyage that he had discovered paradise on earth. While Columbus's original assessment of the flora and fauna was limited by his lack of botanical knowledge and his obsession with finding gold, he nevertheless praised the verdant climate on October 15, 1492: "These islands are very green and fertile and with sweet-smelling breezes; and there may be many things that I do not know about because I do not want to stop, so I can investigate and go to many islands in order to find gold" (83). Columbus's reaction anticipates the attitude of many explorers who would follow him: an admiration for the unfamiliar landscape, the desire to exploit natural resources for financial gain, and what Antonello Gerbi calls "a vague feeling that such a climate and such a land must produce creatures and plants of extraordinary powers" (15). Every traveler's description of a previously unknown land reveals as much about the writer, his or her place of origin, and his or her expectations as it does about the place being described. Indeed, as is widely known, Columbus maintained throughout his lifetime that he had landed in Asia rather than on a new land mass.[17] To a great extent, Columbus's expectations were colored by his biblical readings, as was the case for subsequent writers about the tropics. As Elizabeth DeLoughrey, Renée Gosson, and George Handley note, "This led to the reconfiguration of the region through classical and Christian toponyms such as the Virgin Islands, the Antilles, and Brazil" (11). Later writers were not immune to this tendency to view new territory through old textual lenses. In fact, their reactions to the contrast between bucolic literary representations of the tropics and their own perceptions of the rainforest would magnify the legacy of these literary recreations of ecological realities.

The notion that traveling to warm climates was a journey to a biblical origin, stretching beyond the limits of Western history, is a hallmark of European writings about the tropics.[18] Uncolonized lands on several continents were frequently depicted as spaces devoid of history, thereby justifying colonization. The idea of Africa as a place lacking in history was popularized by the German philosopher Georg Hegel in his "Geographical Basis of History": "Africa proper, as far as History goes back, has remained—for all purposes of connection with the rest of the World—shut up; it is the Gold-land compressed within itself,—the land of childhood, which lying beyond the day of self-conscious history, is enveloped in the dark mantle of Night" (109).[19] This erasure of non-Western history is reflected cartographically in the colonial-era maps that show territory uncharted by Europeans as blank spaces. These regions were often embellished with imaginative drawings, thereby documenting their imagined geographies. As Jonathan Swift wrote in 1733:

> So geographers, in Afric maps,
> With savage pictures fill their gaps,
> And o'er unhabitable downs
> Place elephants for want of towns. (151)

In this way, Europeans projected their own ignorance on the regions unknown to them, transferring the blank space in their minds onto the geographical and historical realities about which they knew nothing.

The Americas were similarly subjected to a process of European projection and reinvention. Despite increasing identification of the Americas as a biblical paradise, the continents were (and are) still referred to as "new." Indeed, newness was a key component of the depictions of the American tropics in their literary and scientific incarnations from the first encounter through the twentieth century. Each writer posited himself as the earliest explorer, allowing the reader to experience the natural world as "new" over and over again. In order for the tropics to be thought of as a blank slate ready for a European imprimatur, it was necessary for them to be devoid of prior civilizations. The early decimation of the indigenous Caribbean populations and importation of African slave labor facilitated this process. In many discussions of the Americas, advanced civilizations such as the Mayas or the Incas were dismissed and discounted as either anomalous or not truly advanced because of a lack of writing.[20] The central focus of European writings came to rest not on peoples but on plants and animals. As Mary Louise Pratt has noted, explorers "wrote America as a primal world of nature, an unclaimed and timeless space occupied by plants and creatures (some of them human), but not organized by societies and economies; a world whose only history was the one about to begin" (126). The Americas were therefore continually recast as recently discovered in an imagined geography that paradoxically based its newness on previous descriptions of the continents.

Even in regions that were colonized well into the modern era, such as Cambodia (the setting for Malraux's *The Way of the Kings*, which I will study in Chapter 2), the distinctions between a wide range of ethnic groups (including the ancient Khmer society) were effaced in order to form an artificial tabula rasa for the French *mission civilisatrice*, as Pierre Brocheux and Daniel Hémery show in *Indochina: An Ambiguous Colonization* (198). Once the non-Western world had been constituted in the European imagination as an empty vessel, it became an imperial imperative to fill that vessel with European values and customs. The erasure of tropical history and geography was thus a necessary prerequisite for colonization, and offered writers a fertile imaginative terrain on which their own fantasies, fears, and assumptions about non-Western cultures could be played out. As Nancy Leys Stepan shows in *Picturing Tropical Nature*, "The 'tropical' came to constitute more than a geographical concept; it signified a place of radical otherness to the temperate world, with which it contrasted and which it helped constitute. Descriptions and pictures of the tropics in this way contributed to the formation of European identity, as distinct from that of the tropical zone, where the superabundance of nature was believed to overwhelm the human endeavor and reduce the place to nature itself" (17–18). The lack of geographical and historical specificity extends from early encounters to twentieth-century tropical adventure narratives.

With the advent of the sixteenth century, the image of the tropical New World was shaped by—if not directly culled from—accounts of shipwrecks and voyages into the interior of barely colonized lands. Enterprising Europeans often looked to the tropical sojourn as a means of making money through the exploitation of natural resources such as the precious metals in the mines of Potosí, the extraction of *Caesalpinia echinata* (Brazilwood), and the manpower of the enslaved indigenous population. Their accounts ranged from Hernán Cortés's descriptions of Tenochtitlan (1522–1525) to the story of the English seaman Alexander Selkirk, which inspired Daniel Defoe's *Robinson Crusoe* (1719). These tales of transatlantic crossings, shipwrecks, armed conflict, and the subjugation of foreign peoples present engaging, carefully crafted narratives that fueled interest in further colonization and laid the foundations for the adventure narrative tradition. One such tale, however, writes a counternarrative of imperial expansion, and therefore anticipates the twentieth-century tropical adventure narratives examined in detail in this book. The narrative of Alvar Núñez Cabeza de Vaca (1542) contradicts Columbus's earlier utopian vision of the Caribbean (carefully tailored to procure funding for further voyages) by depicting the hot, wet tropics as a site of natural and human disaster. In contrast to Edenic notions of the New World, Cabeza de Vaca's infernal journey repeatedly belies many suppositions about Europeans in the Americas. The account tells of Spaniards as slaves rather than slave drivers, demonstrates the inefficacy of Western tools and technology, reverses stereotypes about cannibalism, and advocates for the peaceful colonization and evangelization of the indigenous population.[21] Cabeza de Vaca's account is a significant counterweight to the representation of Spanish America as a realm of natural beauty and easy bounty.[22] His narrative, originally known as the *Relación*, was later rechristened *Naufragios*—meaning "shipwrecks," or, more broadly, "calamities"—to evoke the hardships he and his three surviving companions had endured. His work is important to the dialectical representation of the tropical world as being by turns "paradisiacal and pestilential" (Arnold 8). Another major figure on the negative side of this dichotomy is the Spanish priest Bartolomé de Las Casas. Las Casas's condemnation of the abuse suffered by the native residents of Hispaniola from Spaniards and his advocacy for reform of the colonial system fueled the so-called *leyenda negra* (Black Legend), which conceived of the Americas as a place of suffering, injustice, and misery. The early duality of meaning ascribed to the natural world—the tropics were both idyllic and threatening, idealized and vilified—was in these ways transferred to the Americas and perpetuated for centuries.

Romantic writers of the eighteenth and nineteenth centuries reinterpreted this dialectical pattern of description by aligning nature with the Sublime. During the nineteenth century, the prolific writings of Baron Alexander von Humboldt, who had traveled through Latin America from 1799 to 1804, defined European interpretations of the American tropics. Of particular interest to this study is Humboldt's account of his river and land voyages up and down the Orinoco River and its tributaries as related in his *Personal Narrative of Travels to the Equinoctial Regions of the New Continent*, published from 1807 to 1834. Humboldt's extensive scientific training and Romantic literary formation are evident in his minutely detailed and ecstatic portraits of the Venezuelan tropical interior. In keeping with his Romantic sensibility, Humboldt sought to comprehend the sublime harmonies of nature, but he also set out to categorize and classify them. His account unifies the binary presentation of the tropics as a place of simultaneous natural splendor and unhealthy peril into an experience made sublime by the juxtaposition of beauty and danger. For example, in describing his travels on the Río Negro, Humboldt recounts that tigers frequently came to the shores of the river to drink, despite the proximity of his canoe:

> I confess that these often repeated scenes greatly appeal to me. The pleasure comes not solely from the curiosity a naturalist feels for the objects of his studies, but also to a feeling common to all men brought up in the customs of civilization. You find yourself in a new world, in a wild, untamed nature. . . . "Es como en el paraíso" ("It is like paradise") our old Indian pilot said. Everything here reminds you of that state of the ancient world revealed in venerable traditions about the innocence and happiness of all people; but when carefully observing the relationships between the animals you see how they avoid and fear each other. The golden age has ended. In this paradise of American jungles, as everywhere else, a long, sad experience has taught all living beings that gentleness is rarely linked to might. (178–79)

In passages such as this excerpt, Humboldt merges the technical and the philosophical by playing both naturalist and Romantic writer intent on evoking aesthetic pleasure in his reader. Rather than opposing each other, scientific specificity and florid description are complementary.[23] The menacing presence of the tiger simultaneously enhances the thrilling fear of death and leads Humboldt to a scientific reflection on the relations between animal species. While Humboldt did partially ascribe to a paradisiacal view of the American wilderness, he also wrote at length about the ill health and discomfort he had endured while traveling up and down the Orinoco. His botanist companion, Aimé Bonpland, had nearly died from malarial fever. This combination of geography and climate-borne illness was, in Humboldt's mind, the central impediment to Western-style cultural and economic development in the region:

> In the impenetrable jungle of the torrid zone rivers increase the dismemberment of great nations, favor the transition of dialects into separate languages, and nourish distrust and national hatred. . . . When we carefully examine this wild part of America we imagine how it was in primitive times when the land was peopled in stages, and seem to be present at the birth of human societies. In the New World we do not see the progressive developments of civilization, those moments of rest, those stations in the lives of a people. (229)

Nearly every adventure writer glorifies the voyage to the tropics as an opportunity to be present at the origin of human society while, like Humboldt, simultaneously confronting dangers such as tigers and swarms of mosquitoes. Yet as Nigel Leask, Vera Kutzinski, and Ottmar Ette have shown, Humboldt did not dismiss the New World as being irredeemably barbarous.[24] He ultimately harmonized the beauty and perils of the Americas under the rubric of sublime scientific adventure. This fusion of paradise and pestilence would mark later European writings about the region through the twentieth century.

Humboldt had received permission to travel in the Americas from King Carlos IV of Spain, even though the Spanish colonies were in obvious and near total revolt. His expedition was presented as a service to economic and scientific imperialism despite Humboldt's critique of the Spanish treatment of Cuba and his low opinion of Spanish missionaries living in the Amazon. While Spain's imperial might was extinguished late in the eighteenth century, the British Empire continued its colonization of Africa and Asia. For this reason, the fictional tropical adventure tradition is strongest in the Anglophone canon.

The literary genre of the nineteenth century that most contributed to the image of empire in the tropics was the adventure novel. Adventure narratives have a long pedigree, going back as far as the *Odyssey*, but in the nineteenth century they took on a fixed, formulaic shape and became vehicles for the drama and conflict of imperial expansion. These narratives belong to the genre of what Northrop Frye has denominated the *quest romance*, in which the protagonist has a series of adventures involving travel, danger, and battle that culminate in the death of the protagonist or his foe. According to Frye, "The complete form of the romance is clearly the successful quest, and such a complicated form has three main stages: the stage of the perilous journey and the preliminary minor adventures; the crucial struggle, usually some kind of battle in which either the hero or his foe, or both, must die; and the exaltation of the hero" (187). The core concept behind Frye's definition of quest romance can be traced back to Joseph Campbell's study of the figure of the Hero in myth, fairy tales, literature, and film. In its most reductive form, Campbell's argument maintains that the Hero's life consists of three phases similar to those put forth by Frye: the departure of the Hero from society, the rite of initiation or triumph in trial, and the final reintegration into society. The Hero, like the adventure novel protagonist, is invariably male. He triumphs in adversity by virtue of his strength or cunning, and returns to his homeland in order to claim his reward, which is frequently a bride, material wealth, or domestic comfort. Campbell notes that it is the third stage, the Return, that may be the most difficult for the Hero, because his experiences away from society have profoundly changed him (36). This classical narrative was revived in nineteenth-century adventure novels such as Jules Verne's *Around the World in Eighty Days* (1863) and H. Rider Haggard's *King Solomon's Mines* (1885).

The protagonists of adventure novels are, like Frye's searchers, usually post-adolescent males who, either by choice or by chance, travel away from the metropolis and into the wilderness, surviving by dint of their own courage and pluck. The young male reader could escape from his modern domestic softness by immersing himself in tales set in wild environments in which manhood was demonstrated through physical strength, aggression, and cunning.[25] In these narratives, nature is consistently forced into submission by the white man's intelligence and power. The effect of the adventure on the protagonist is twofold and paradoxical: on one hand, the young man imposes Western mores and rationality on the wilderness and its inhabitants; on the other, it offers him an opportunity to shed the trappings of civilization and resort to brute force, thereby enhancing his virility. The protagonist eventually returns to marry the sweetheart he has left at home, or he embarks on new adventures.

These stories narrate rites of passage much like bildungsromans in the wilderness.[26] Arnold Van Gennep delineates a similar process of separation, transition, and reintegration in non-Western societies in his 1908 *Rites of Passage*, though the young men he describes undergo initiation rites close to the age of puberty, while adventure novel protagonists are usually white males in their late twenties. Despite their relatively advanced ages, these protagonists seem to be in need of initiations into manhood, having been denied opportunities to forge their own in their increasingly automated, industrialized worlds and their hierarchical social situations. The young men revel in the liberty they find away from the confines of civilization, but consistently return to the society they had left once their quests are fulfilled.

Notably, the tropical forest is a space almost entirely devoid of European women. One of the few female protagonists of novels set in the tropics is found in Virginia Woolf's *The Voyage Out*, which I will discuss in Chapter 1. Throughout the genre, women are portrayed as the arbiters of domestic life; their presence in the forest would make it tame. Instead, they remain home, serving as rewards for successful quests or as unwanted fates from which the heroes flee. The protagonist of W. H. Hudson's *Green Mansions* explains the supposedly inherent unsuitability of women to tropical adventure thus: "A daughter of civilization and of that artificial life, she could never experience such feelings as these and return to nature as I was doing. For women, though within narrow limits more plastic than men, are yet without that larger adaptiveness which can take us back to the sources of life, which they have left eternally behind" (135). In Arthur Conan Doyle's *The Lost World*, Gladys, the love interest of the adventurer-journalist Malone, is an unvarnished plot motivator denied any level of introspection or exposition. She is relegated to serving as the ostensible cause of adventure for which Malone must risk everything, and she is ultimately abandoned by him when he embarks on another adventure with a fellow male traveler. Actual women are replaced by the earth itself, which is consistently depicted as a closed feminine space that yields only to forced male penetration. It is in the tales of violent domestication—of bending the laws of nature and other peoples to the will of the adventurer—that the adventure novel genre reinforces the goals of the imperial project.[27] The increase in the popularity of adventure narratives coincides with the intensification of imperial expansion, as Martin Green demonstrates in his *Dreams of Adventure, Deeds of Empire*. For the British and American reading publics at the end of the nineteenth century, the allure of the colonial adventure narrative was particularly captured by Rudyard Kipling, in his *Plain Tales from the Hills* (1899) and, more important for this book, *The Jungle Books* (1894–1895). Though later writers were quick to criticize Kipling, mostly because of his political views, his work shaped both popular and erudite interpretations of the wilderness in print, film, music, and theater.[28] *The Jungle Books* are a collection of animal fables, many of them interlinked by the presence of Mowgli, a boy raised by wolves. Most scholars agree that *The Jungle Books* are an allegory of empire in which the British tame and subjugate "The Jungle." The animal kingdom serves as a metaphor for human civilization in which rank and hierarchy dictate behavior and maintain order in the service of colonial rule.[29] The song "The Law of the Jungle" imposes the imperial mandate on an unruly native population:

> Now these are the Laws of the Jungle, and many and mighty are they;
> But the head and the hoof of the Law and the haunch and the hump
> is—Obey! (*Jungle Books* 172)

As Mowgli comes of age, he learns from forest animals to follow these codes of conduct. Various battles between the animal species demonstrate that the strong have a moral imperative and duty to rule over the weak, thus foreshadowing the message of Kipling's "The White Man's Burden" (1899) in allegorical terms. The boy raised by wolves eventually becomes a forest guard for the British government in "In the Rukh." Mowgli's transformation both revels in the untamed aspect of the wilderness and shows the necessity of domesticating it. The stories alternate between demonstrating the destructive power of the unrestrained wilderness and illustrating the beneficial effects of British rule on India and the importance of following the rules. In this way, Kipling's work advances the goals of the British Empire.[30] Kipling thus forms part of a constellation of writers who depicted the colonial struggle in terms of adventure. His work marks the end of the era in which tropical narratives uniformly supported the imperial project. Kipling's stories also mark the transition from the nineteenth-century's Romantic evocations of the wilderness as sublime to the twentieth-century's conception of the tropics as dangerous sites of disease, decay, and madness. During the late nineteenth and early twentieth centuries, the waning of imperial powers led to an increase in questioning justifications of colonialism. This trend was paralleled by the rise of novels that interrogated the natural superiority of the Western adventurer in the tropics and raised doubts about his inherent rationality. Five such novels are the topic of this book.

Tropical quest narratives of the twentieth century share several characteristics that identify them as a subgenre of the adventure novel. Each male protagonist flees civilization to prove himself in the wilderness. The depiction of nature in these novels repeats common assumptions about the tropics I have traced in the preceding pages. At first, nature is awe-inspiring and refreshing, but it quickly becomes menacing, cruel, and overpowering, thus perpetuating the dialectical representation of nature begun centuries earlier. The protagonist inevitably gets lost and undergoes a transformative experience. Very often, this life-altering rite is associated with madness provoked by nature. In each novel, the moment of return and reintegration, as identified by Campbell, is made problematic. In the novels discussed in *Jungle Fever*, the quest is ultimately a failure, and this failure is what sets them apart from earlier tropical adventure novels. A brief look at several tropical adventure novels of the early twentieth century will demonstrate this formula and place the novels I examine in detail in later chapters in a broad literary and historical context.

The naturalist W. H. Hudson's 1904 novel *Green Mansions* merges Romantic images of tropical nature with a doomed love story in which a Venezuelan protagonist, Abel, falls in love with a forest nymph. In a style similar to Humboldt's writing a century earlier, the natural world is at first depicted as a site of natural beauty and spiritual ecstasy. Once in the forest, Abel feels "purified and had a strange sense and apprehension of a secret innocence and spirituality in nature" (21). Abel lives among the "Guyanese savages," and attempts to become like them: "By an effort of the will I emptied myself of my life experience and knowledge—or as much of it as possible—and thought only of the generations of my dead imaginary progenitors, who had ranged these woods back to the dim forgotten years before Columbus" (57). At first, Abel revels in "that luxuriant tropical nature, its green clouds and illusive aerial spaces, full of mystery . . . a half-way heaven" (34). As the narrative progresses, however, this portrait of the wilderness as a tropical Eden is consistently eroded. By the conclusion of the novel, the rainforest has morphed into the sickening cesspool that marks the opposite end of the dialectical representation of nature: "The impressions of nature received during that sick period are blurred, or else so colored and exaggerated by perpetual torturing anxiety, mixed with half-delirious night-fancies, that I can only think of that country as an earthly inferno, where I fought against every imaginable obstacle, alternately sweating and freezing, toiling as no man ever toiled before" (309). The reference to malaria and fever-induced delirium are archetypes of twentieth-century tropical adventure novels. In later texts, medical terms play an increasingly important role in the description of the wilderness.

Abel's beloved Rima, a half-human sprite who lives in harmony with nature, is burned alive by the indigenous group with whom Abel had been staying. Rima's death drives Abel insane, which leads him to murder the Guyanese men who killed her. He hears voices talking to him: "A torturing voice would whisper in my ear: 'Yes, you are evidently going mad. By-and-by you will rush howling through the forest, only to drop down at last and die: and no person will ever find and bury *your* bones'" (290). Abel mourns the loss of Rima by living alone in the wood she frequented, surviving by eating grubs and berries for several months. While he seems to have "gone native" in habit, dress, and diet, his mad ravings are peppered with Romantic exclamations such as "O cruel Nature!" and show that his insanity is due, paradoxically, to his refinement and intelligence. Indeed, unlike later novelists, Hudson maintains the superiority of his criollo protagonist over the Guyanese forest-dwellers despite his erratic, illogical behavior. Abel tells himself: "The low-minded savage, cut off from all human fellowship, keeps his faculties to the end, while your finer brain proves your ruin" (291). This refusal to concede a common humanity between urban sophisticates and indigenous peoples is what separates novels such as *Green Mansions* from those discussed at length in the following chapters of this book.

A more famous tropical adventure novel of the early twentieth century is also set in Venezuela, specifically on Mount Roraima.[31] Arthur Conan Doyle's *The Lost World* (1912) is mostly written in the form of an epistolary diary kept by reporter Edward Malone, who chronicles the voyage of archenemies Professor Challenger and Professor Summerlee to the summit of Mount Roraima. On scaling the mountain, they discover a prehistoric world overrun by dinosaurs, "ape-men," and "Indians," all of whom are subsequently dominated and pacified by the Western explorers. Like previous descriptions of the tropics, the diary portrays Mount Roraima as both idyllic and diabolical; it is alternately a "fairyland" (114) and one of Dante's seven circles of hell (216). Unlike *Green Mansions*, however, *The Lost World* casts scientists rather than geographers or conquistadores as the new adventurers. Accordingly, the novel is sprinkled with the scientific theories of the era, including phrenology, Darwinism, the theory of degeneration, eugenics, and the diagnoses of various types of fevers. The Darwinian overtones are strongest, of course: Doyle playfully presents the "ape-men" as the missing link between modern man and his simian ancestors. As in *Green Mansions*, the narrator invokes "race memory" to demonstrate the Europeans' superior level of evolution and consequent moral imperative to explore, discover, and conquer (10).

Just as in Humboldt's comparison of the Orinoco river basin to the ancient world (179), the natural course of evolution has been halted on Doyle's novelistic Mount Roraima. This pseudoscientific plot twist is a reincarnation of the entrenched perception of the tropics as a place devoid of history. To Malone, it seems that the group had "by some magic been conveyed to some raw planet in its earliest and wildest state" (180). Professor Challenger makes it clear that "the ordinary laws of nature are suspended. The various checks which influence the struggle for existence in the world at large are all neutralized or altered. Creatures survive which would otherwise disappear.... The dinosaurs have been artificially conserved by those strange accidental conditions" (59–60). The tropics appealed to the average nineteenth- and twentieth-century reader as sites of adventure because they offered the possibility of traveling through time by traveling geographically, just as *The Lost World* provides the opportunity to see human life at an early stage when the drama of evolution was playing itself out. Following World War I, however, the sprites, dinosaurs, and other fantastical creatures in adventure tales vanished along with the protagonists' cavalier attitudes. They were replaced by tales that identified the tropics as an extension of the battlefield, on which white Europe showed itself to be exceedingly savage.

In the Francophone tradition, the exemplary postwar novel that excoriates both Europe and its colonies is Louis-Ferdinand Céline's vituperative *Journey to the End of the Night* (1932). Published just two years after André Malraux's *The Way of the Kings*, Céline's work is a venomous first-person narration of the protagonist Bardamu's peripatetic travails, which range from the French countryside during World War I to colonial French West Africa, Detroit, New York, and Paris. The novel breaks countless moral taboos and adventure novel conventions, such as depicting a wholly irredeemable narrator-protagonist and refusing to wrap up the adventure in a satisfying denouement. In the portions of the work devoted to Bardamu's travels in West Africa, the tropics are entirely devoid of the paradisiacal resonances so common to other European adventure narratives. Instead, they are purely pestilential, and serve only to emphasize the wretchedness of all humans. Once Bardamu's French ship enters the tropical climate, all pretense of civility disappears from those onboard:

> From that moment on we saw, rising to the surface, the terrifying nature
> of white men, exasperated, freed from constraint, absolutely unbuttoned,
> their true nature, same as in the war. That tropical steam bath called
> forth instincts as August breeds toads and snakes on the fissured walls of
> prisons. In the European cold, under gray, puritanical northern skies, we
> seldom get to see our brothers' festering cruelty except in times of car-
> nage, but when roused by the foul fevers of the tropics, their rottenness
> rises to the surface. That's when the frantic unbuttoning sets in, when

> filth triumphs and covers us entirely. It's a biological confession. Once
> work and cold weather cease to constrain us, once they relax their grip,
> the white man shows you the same spectacle as a beautiful beach when
> the tide goes out: the truth, fetid pools, crabs, carrion, and turds. (95)

Céline explicitly locates the tropics as a site of moral and physical degeneracy
for all people. His novel is similar to those of other authors discussed in this
book in that he recognizes that the illogical, barbarous nature of the white man
does not originate in the tropics, but rather that it arrives with him and that it
flourishes once European codes of conduct are no longer in effect. While imperial expansion fed stereotypes about European superiority, the trauma of "world"
war (another phrase that conjures up an imagined geography) reversed that trend
and made many European authors question their supposed moral and biological
superiority.

The first two chapters of *Jungle Fever* trace the European paradigm shift
regarding the myth of the tropics. The last three chapters explore the ways in
which Latin American authors reacted to European constructions of the tropics in their own work. This latter portion of the book poses the question: how
did authors and intellectuals born in the tropics confront so many centuries of
cultural assumptions and stereotypes? How did they react to imagined geographies that classified them as racial degenerates and labeled their places of origin
as wild paradises and unhealthy backwaters? During the post-Independence era,
Latin American intellectual debates centered on European-style modernization
of the tropics. This process included adopting European farming and ranching
techniques, as well as enacting educational reforms and public hygiene campaigns. In short, Latin American progressive reformers sought to domesticate
the landscape and its peoples. These principles were generally adopted by early
nineteenth-century writers, whose vision of their own birthplace was, ironically,
frequently informed by the interpretations of foreigners. Among Latin American
literary figures, Andrés Bello embodies the links between the Europeanizing,
liberal drive toward modernity, Romantic poetics, and the domination of the
wilderness. His "Ode to Tropical Agriculture" was written in 1826 in London,
several years after he reportedly met Humboldt in Caracas. Bello had previously
translated and published the portions of Humboldt's work regarding Venezuela
in *El censor americano* (London, 1816), and his "Ode" contains much of the same
vocabulary and phrasing as his rendition of Humboldt's words (Durán Luzio
141).[32] In the "Ode," Bello employs the form and imagery of Virgilian Georgic
poetics in exhorting Latin Americans to found post-Independence Latin America
by working the land:

> Oh, youthful nations, with early laurels crowned,
> who rise before the West's astonished gaze!
> Honor the fields, honor the simple life,

and the farmer's frugal simplicity.
Thus freedom will dwell in you forever,
ambition be restrained, law have its temple. (37)[33]

For Bello, the cities of Latin America offered vice and ill health, while fecund nature could be tamed for the well-being of each nation. Working the land would not only provide food and products for exportation, but it would also dampen political and social unrest. Twenty years later, Domingo Faustino Sarmiento's *Facundo* (1845) would prescribe the same remedy to harness the unruly (and non-tropical) Argentine pampas, gauchos, and caudillos. Rómulo Gallegos recast this political goal for the Venezuelan plains in literary terms in *Doña Bárbara* (1929), in which the eponymous protagonist and the country's landscape are both eventually subdued by the urban, urbane Santos Luzardo. The drama of the struggle to dominate nature was therefore posited by post-Independence intellectuals as the central literary narrative of Latin America. Among the Spanish-language novels studied in this book, *The Vortex* and *Canaima* both narrate the attempt by urban modernizing forces to subdue Latin American nature; in both instances, however, the forest dominates the individual, thereby debunking the myth of nation formation through nature domination.

The major predecessor to Rómulo Gallegos and José Eustasio Rivera in the Latin American tradition is the Uruguayan writer Horacio Quiroga (1878–1937), who first dramatized the physical and psychological challenges of the wilderness in the Latin American short story. Quiroga is often hailed as the first "regionalist" writer in Spanish America. His stories in *Cuentos de amor de locura y de muerte* (Stories of love of madness and of death, 1917) and *Cuentos de la selva* (Stories of the forest, 1918), many of which are collected in English in *The Decapitated Chicken and Other Tales*, are of great importance to later writers of rainforest narratives for two reasons: first, the wilderness is itself a protagonist in each narrative, rather than merely a backdrop against which the story unfolds; and second, madness, illness, and the specter of death dominate the tales.

Quiroga, like most writers of tropical adventure tales, first traveled into the wilderness in short jaunts as part of an organized expedition. In 1903, Quiroga accompanied his mentor Leopoldo Lugones to the Jesuit ruins of Misiones, Argentina, as a photographer and diarist. This first voyage up the Paraná River may have inspired Quiroga's story "La miel silvestre" (Wild honey), in which an inexperienced dandy plays at being *un robinson* (after *Robinson Crusoe*) and quickly finds his urban dress and habits to be unsuited to his new environment. Unlike Conrad, Malraux, Rivera, Gallegos, and Carpentier, however, Quiroga became a resident of the forest, first in El Chaco and later in Misiones, rather than a transitory visitor.

Sadly, Quiroga's biography is a tragic tropical narrative in itself. His life was marked by death: Quiroga witnessed his father's accidental death as an infant and his stepfather's suicide as an adolescent; he inadvertently shot and killed his best friend while toying with a gun in his twenties; his first wife, Ana María, killed herself in the wilderness of El Saladito after several years of solitary living and childrearing; and Quiroga himself committed suicide after learning that he was suffering from cancer.

Seeking refuge from the early death of his friend, Quiroga used his inheritance from his father to buy several acres in the nearby region of El Saladito, with the idea of growing cotton in the wilderness. Although he produced little cotton, the literary harvest from his tropical sojourn was significant. In stories such as "Los mensú" (The monthly wage earners), Quiroga evokes the brutality inherent in the natural world and the individuals who inhabit it. Although his letters frequently aimed to convince friends and relatives to join him in the forest, his stories tell of a far less tranquil and restorative atmosphere. Instead, man's unsuccessful struggle to survive in the wilderness makes up the dramatic core of most of Quiroga's Misiones stories.[34] Unlike most novels set in the tropics, Quiroga's short stories do not contain quest narratives; rather, they alternately present parables for children or portray the immense challenges that the harsh climate and exploitative working conditions present to pioneers, settlers, and laborers in the rainforest. With their portrayals of psychological introspection deep in the wilderness, stories such as "The Son" and "Drifting" form the foundation of the Latin American regional novel (*novela de la tierra*) of the 1920s and 1930s.

"Drifting" ("A la deriva") chronicles the delirium and death of Paulino, a peon of Misiones who has been bitten by a snake. After killing the snake, Paulino uses his machete to quickly cut around the wound in an effort to remove the poison, and then sets off in a canoe in hopes of reaching a settlement downriver before the poison kills him. The tale is chilling in its near total lack of emotion. Rather than evoke the suffering endured by the victim before death, the story unflinchingly narrates the swift progression of the venom and its symptoms from the victim's point of view. The victim's wandering hallucinations mimic the trajectory of the canoe: both are *a la deriva*, adrift in the current that is also a metaphor for human existence, always ending in death. "The Son" ("El hijo") is a similarly brief story that examines the delusions and the psychological torment of a father whose thirteen-year-old son accidentally shoots himself while hunting alone. "The Son" explores the mental as much as the physical dangers of the wilderness. It, more than any other Quiroga tale, encompasses the title of the collection in which it was first published (Stories of love of madness and of death): it is concerned with a father's love for his son, his madness in the form of hallucinations, and death, in his son's tragic and unnecessary end. The protagonist's alternately terrifying and reassuring hallucinations about his son's activities are belied by the narrator's cutting final line: "Because behind him, at the foot of a fence post, with his legs higher than his body, caught in a wire fence, his beloved son, dead since ten o'clock in the morning, lies in the sun" (*Decapitated Chicken* 166). One's own actions and thoughts, Quiroga implies, can do as much damage as any violence found in the wilderness. Moreover, both "Drifting" and "The Son" debunk the paradisiacal vision of Latin American nature imposed by European observers. There are no florid descriptions of the verdant foliage, but rather terse evocations of dark river canyons, unbearable heat, and the dangers of solitude. Quiroga's life and work inaugurate the twentieth-century Latin American narrative formula of a protagonist who flees modern society in search of wealth and equanimity, and who finds that the solitude of the forest cannot silence his inner demons.

The five modern and modernist quest narratives I explore in *Jungle Fever* mimic the format of the nineteenth-century adventure novel, and yet they also mock and ultimately reverse the outcomes of the works that came before them. They all imitate the traditional Hero narrative, but their protagonists are decidedly unheroic. While, like Campbell's heroes, they feel the "call to adventure" and participate in initiation rites, the issue of the Return becomes conflicted and complex (49). The five novels narrate the failure of the antihero's quest rather than his successful return to society. To wit, Conrad's Kurtz expires far from Europe; Malraux's Perken dies of syphilis and fever without ever returning to Paris; Rivera's Cova never emerges from the wilderness; Gallegos's Marcos Vargas embraces his initiation into indigenous life and never fulfills his civic duty; and Carpentier's narrator-protagonist fails both to stay forever in the tropical environment and to reintegrate himself into the nameless Northern city. All the works I examine in detail are posterior permutations of the adventure novel tradition that, in an oedipal fashion, seek to debunk the very foundations of the genre from which they spring. While eighteenth- and nineteenth-century adventure novels extol the virtues of empire and rationality embodied in their heroes, their twentieth-century counterparts probe the premise of the genre and question the inherent "civility" of the Western world.

The thorny negotiation with colonialism and its legacy lies at the heart of the depiction of the tropical forest as a green prison (*cárcel verde*), in José Eustasio Rivera's words (*Vortex* 127; *La vorágine* 189).[35] The adventure novels analyzed in this book contain dark subtexts that reflect the authors' growing ambivalence toward Europe's colonization of large swaths of the globe.[36] Much of "the horror" (as Conrad's Kurtz puts it) of the tropical forest is triggered by the abuses of the colonial system that are evident in the tropics. As DeLoughrey, Gosson, and Handley argue: "Addressing the historical and racial violence of the Caribbean is integral to understanding literary representations of its geography" (2). In this book, I expand DeLoughrey, Gosson, and Handley's emphasis on the Caribbean to include tropical Africa and Southeast Asia, because all the regions depicted in *Jungle Fever* demonstrate varying levels of engagement with the historical and racial violence perpetrated in the tropics. Some writers, like Malraux and Rivera, were politically active in denouncing the financial and human exploitation of colonial and postcolonial territories.[37] In particular, *The Vortex* is in many respects a strident protest novel that condemns the abuses of the rubber plantations, whose products were exported to Britain and the United States.[38] For all the novels examined here, the authors' complex relationship to colonialism and postcolonialism contributes to the broader questions regarding the supremacy of Western rationality raised by the protagonists' madness in the tropics. While the European authors grappled with the ramifications of their nations' colonial projects, Latin American writers were involved in a process of self-consciously establishing their own autochthonous literary identity in the face of imported colonial theories that often depicted them as inferior to their European counterparts. The broadest aim of this work is to examine the ways in which Latin American authors appropriated European theories about them for their own aesthetic purposes. For Rivera, Gallegos, and Carpentier, as for Horacio Quiroga before them, the vast South American wilderness provided a source of artistic inspiration and originality and a novelistic arena in which Latin America and its literature could be defined on their terms.

The tropical colonial outposts of interest for this work are the Belgian Congo of *Heart of Darkness*, the Indochina of *The Way of the Kings*, and the Amazonian region of Venezuela and Colombia where *The Vortex*, *Canaima*, and *The Lost Steps* are set.[39] Yet, as with earlier creators of popular depictions of the tropics, the authors of these five adventure tales are purposefully elusive when it comes to the geographical specificity of their stories. Conrad refuses to name the Belgian Congo or the river up which Marlow travels in all of *Heart of Darkness*. Malraux, too, is geographically evasive, perhaps for reasons relating to his trial for unlawful removal of stone carvings during his real-life adventure in Cambodia, but he also collapses geographical distances for narrative convenience.[40] Among the Latin American writers, this trait is strongest in Carpentier, but even for Gallegos and Rivera, who consciously sought to produce novels that were regional (*de la tierra*), their depictions of the wilderness lose geographical relevance in the most lyrical passages. In all five novels, the authors sacrifice specificity for the sake of symbolism. They continue to mythologize the rainforest—to infuse it with a timeless, mysterious quality. The concrete specificity of the wilderness is exchanged for the aura of a monolithic space that is defined only by its negative; the jungle, an imaginary geography *par excellence*, is the antithesis of the metropolis from which the protagonists have fled. This characterization makes the tropical voyage seem to the protagonist to be a trip outside of history, and it contributes to the metaphorical value of the journey as an introspective passage into the past and the psyche of the protagonist. In this way, the five novels perpetuate the myth of the tropics as established in previous centuries. They depart from that myth, however, in their refusal to portray the wilderness as a site of bucolic tranquillity. Instead, it is a site of violence and misery. Indeed, an essential element of these authors' modernism stems from their insistence that nature is not sublime, amenable, or pleasing, but rather a nightmarish, diseased wilderness, albeit a literary one.

How did the literary presentation of the rainforest shift from a realm of bucolic tranquillity to a source of terror, madness, and death? The major cause of this change was the rise of intertwined concerns about racial mixing and tropical disease that were spurred by colonialism, as I will show throughout this work. Race and racial essentializing played a major role in shaping the portrayal of tropics in twentieth-century literature. DeLoughrey, Gosson, and Handley explicitly link "the shift from utopian representation of tropical nature to concerns about its generation of hypersexuality, disease, and moral decay" and "the increased transplantation of Africans to the American neotropics" (7). Similarly, in the works considered here, the sexual mixing of white male colonists and indigenous Amazonian, African, and Cambodian women is reflected in the depiction of the environment. From Conrad to Carpentier, the possibility of racial miscegenation is presented as a significant outcome—be it a menace (in Conrad and Rivera) or an idealized aesthetic (in Carpentier)—in these tropical adventure narratives. As I will argue, the literary forest remains a creation largely populated by the protagonists' own fears, misgivings, and interpretations. In this sense, the authors are not unique; as Felix Driver and Luciana Martins have stated: "The tropics …have long been the site for European fantasies of self-realization, projects of cultural imperialism, or the politics of human or environmental salvage" (4). As a European creation, the forest was formed by historical, scientific, and literary forces at the turn of the twentieth century: the zenith of colonialism, the eugenics movement, and the adventure novel. The combination of these elements resulted in the depiction of the tropical forest as an environment home to the morally deficient, the degenerate, and the racially undesirable.[41]

The primary result of colonialism that will be studied at length here is the diffusion of Western scientific knowledge throughout the world.[42] Spurred by the incursion of people of European descent into what had previously been the "blank spaces on the earth," advances in medical science gave rise to new theories regarding race, climate, and illness.[43] As Rod Edmond shows, the fear that diseases acquired in the tropics could affect the metropolitan populace became widespread as Europeans colonized ever-larger portions of the earth ("Returning Fears" 175–94). This pseudoscientific fearmongering manifested itself in popular culture and medical texts alike. In her work on pictorial representations of the tropics, Stepan shows that interpretations of the natural world were affected by deep-seated assumptions about race, disease, and sexuality: "Even within European representations, tropical nature stood for many different values—for heat and warmth but also for a dangerous and diseased environment; for superabundant fertility but also for fatal excess; for species novelty but also for the bizarre and deadly; for lazy sensuality and sexuality but also for impermissible racial mixings and degeneration" (*Picturing* 21). As I will argue throughout this work, these sociomedical theories profoundly shape the ways in which these five novelists conceive and depict their protagonists' sojourns in the wilderness.

During the latter half of the nineteenth century and the early years of the twentieth, European medical discourse implied that an extended period of time spent in the tropics was detrimental to colonists' mental and physical health. The linguistic manifestation of this association between ill health and the tropics is the term *jungle fever*, which inspired the title of this work.[44] Before Spike Lee's 1991 film popularized the phrase in reference to interracial sex, *jungle fever* was "a form of remittent fever caused by the miasma of the jungle; the hill-fever of India" ("Jungle fever"). The two meanings of the word have come to share connotations of the perceived dangers of interracial desire. Prior to the twentieth century, however, *miasma* was thought to be a poisonous mist of putrid materials that caused disease, in particular cholera. Miasmatic theory was eclipsed by the rise of germ theory around the turn of the twentieth century, but the sense that the very air of the rainforest could lead to sickness resonated in popular culture long after scientific theory changed course.

Nonfiction travel narratives from the nineteenth century amply demonstrate that this deeply rooted association of warm climates with the possibility of decline and death was projected onto the indigenous inhabitants of each region in the form of their laziness and lack of self-determination (Stepan, *Picturing* 54). In this sense, indigenous peoples were thought to be inferior based on climatic conditions and inherent racial characteristics. Yet Johannes Fabian's *Out of Our Minds: Reason and Madness in the Exploration of Central Africa* provides documentary evidence that it was in fact the European explorers and ethnographers of Central Africa in the late nineteenth century and early twentieth century who behaved in ways that were far from the rational, civilized instruments of colonial improvement they were supposed to be: "More often than not, [the explorers] too were 'out of their minds' with extreme fatigue, fear, delusions of grandeur, and feelings ranking from anger to contempt. Much of the time they were in the thralls of 'fever' and other tropical diseases, under the influence of alcohol or opiates (laudanum, a tincture of alcohol and opium, was the principal drug used to control acute and chronic dysentery), high doses of quinine, arsenic, and other ingredients from the expedition's medicine chest" (3). Fabian's research was not conducted in the regions depicted in the novels considered here, but his work is valuable for this study because it belies the ostensibly inherent rationalism of colonialism and its basis in the notions of European progress, science, and superiority. The tropical wilderness is construed as a place that bred sick individuals and also contaminated healthy ones. Fabian shows that the encounters between explorers and Central Africans that

> paved the way for imperial rule or established it in embryonic form were often inherently contradictory—indeed, anarchic—so much so that their true nature had to be concealed or, better, negated by projecting to the world images of a purposeful *oeuvre civilisatrice*: intrepid explorers zapping the unknown; saintly missionaries offering their lives for the salvation of pagans; heroic military men vanquishing an enemy that always outnumbered them; unselfish administrators toiling for the public good; and so forth. This colonial hagiography cannot simply be

dismissed as pious legend. It represents a discourse that must be interpreted by reading it backward—from the rationalizations and glorifica-
tions to that which was thought to be in need of rationalization and
glorification. (4–5)

The tropical adventure tales examined in this work have subtexts of irrationality
that reveal much the same behavior as that meticulously laid bare by Fabian.
Conrad and Malraux both heighten the drama of their novels by incorporating
destabilizing elements of madness, sickness, and intoxication into their tales
of exploration and adventure. Similarly, Fabian debunks the representation of
colonial exploration disseminated by travelogues in which "the myth of science as an arduous battle for victory over self and nature has been condensed
and concentrated" (5). Instead, he argues, colonial explorers existed "for long
periods outside the rationalized frames of exploration, be they faith, knowledge, profit, or domination" (8).[45] Fabian's exemplary work reveals a current
of irrationality and inherent anarchy in the Western explorer that calls into
question the supposed rational justifications of imperialist expansion. *Heart of
Darkness* and *The Way of the Kings* likewise expose the fissures in the veneer of
imperial rationality. The Latin American authors, however, go beyond simply
including instances of madness in their texts. For them, the link between madness and literature is not merely a reaction against colonialism, but rather an
exploration of the origins of poetic creation first mentioned by Plato and reborn
in Romanticism.

In *Heart of Darkness* and *The Way of the Kings*, fears regarding the health
dangers of the tropics manifest themselves in fever-induced delirium, oppressive heat, and unruly vegetation, which drive the main characters mad. In both
novels, medical discourse regarding the insalubrious qualities of the jungle affects
the vocabulary that the authors use to describe the protagonists' inner lives. Most
important, this scientific lexicon affects the ways in which the stories themselves
are told. The narrators of the tales struggle to describe and contain the non-sense,
in the most fundamental meaning of the word, of the protagonists' irrational
ravings, and are ultimately forced to confront it. In the first chapter, I will show
how Marlow's narration confines and effaces Kurtz's maddened speech, thereby
contributing to the famous allusiveness of Conrad's modernist prose in *Heart of
Darkness*. In the second chapter, I will examine medical pamphlets distributed at
the Exposition Coloniale Internationale in Paris in 1931 and show how medical
writings about health and climate in France and its overseas possessions inform
the mental and physical decay of the main character in Malraux's philosophical
adventure novel *The Way of the Kings*. In both European novels, the tropical rainforest is depicted as a threat to sanity and to the ordered logic of the written word.
In the wilderness of the colonial outpost known as the Inner Station, Kurtz's
eloquent colonial treatise devolves into the primal scrawl "Exterminate all the
brutes!" (Conrad, *Heart* 155) while in *The Way of the Kings* the disfigurement and

mental deterioration of the protagonist can be described only through his *langage de chair* (language of the flesh; Malraux, *La voie* 122).

In the European texts, the tropical environment is thus presented as having solely deleterious effects on the protagonists. The Latin American works, however, share the notion that the unbridled wilderness can be both a menace to sanity and a source of literary and artistic inspiration. Indeed, each Latin American protagonist finds his creative powers heightened into an artistic frenzy by the unruly surroundings. In the last three chapters, I will show how medical terminology is used to demonstrate the Latin American authors' cultural modernity and how it becomes the source of their literary originality. Rivera, Gallegos, and Carpentier reject bucolic, Romantic European visions of the rainforest as artificial. Instead, medical terms are an essential component of the way in which these authors sought to create their own autochthonous literary tradition based in the Latin American selva. Most important of all, the madness of each protagonist is reflected in the narrative form itself. Rivera's novel is the most famously ragged, but Gallegos's chapter "The Storm" and Carpentier's baroque prose also reflect the unruly and prolific nature of their settings. As I will show in Chapter 4, Gallegos uses early psychological terms to chronicle the transformation of Marcos Vargas from a potential savior and leader of Venezuela to a broken, shoeless individual living in the wild with an indigenous family. In Chapter 5, I will illustrate the ways in which Carpentier's involvement with medicine and surrealism affect his portrayal of the Venezuelan interior as the only viable source for artistic inspiration.

The significant difference between the European and the Latin American texts is that once the Latin American protagonists are in the wilderness, they *write*. Unlike the European characters, they novelize the struggle between rational and irrational modes of thought rather than containing it within the narration. Ultimately, the Latin American characters celebrate both the exuberant foliage and their own encroaching madness as elements of a new path to literary expression. This conclusion has wide ramifications in terms of understanding the way in which these Latin American novelists view their own roles in literary history. The two European texts throw the innovations of the Latin American regional novel into relief. The literary fruit of the protagonist's madness has important consequences for later Latin American novels set in the tropics: in all of them, the earth itself becomes a catalyst for artistic and literary expression.

This book seeks to explore several questions raised by the presence of medical terminology in tropical adventure novels: Why were these authors interested and well-versed in contemporary medical theories? How and why do they incorporate scientific terminology into their fiction? How does the medical lexicon inform their attempts to narrate madness? More broadly, how does medical writing influence literature?

I argue that the novels examined here employ medical knowledge popular at the time to further their authors' artistic purposes rather than to illustrate specific medical conditions in literary characters. As a result, the use of medical terms in these adventure narratives ranges from evocative and allusive to clinically precise. I analyze the climate of contemporary medical theories in which each novel was written to illuminate each author's dramatization of madness. I do not propose that any of these authors necessarily incorporated his own medical history into the novel in a conscious fashion, nor do I read the narrative of each protagonist's descent into madness as a thinly veiled autobiography. Instead, I have found that each novelist's experiences filtered into his fiction in both expected and surprising ways. Similarly, I do not attempt to translate ailments such as "tropical neurasthenia" into modern-day pathological language, but rather to examine the rhetoric of disease itself and how it shapes each novel's narrative form.

Twentieth-century scholars and historians have examined a given society's classifications of and reactions to madness as cultural signposts that indicate shifts in a culture's self-definition rather than any concrete change in the behavior of the insane themselves. This concept is most thoroughly explored in Michel Foucault's *History of Madness* (originally published in French in 1961 as *Folie et déraison: Histoire de la folie à l'âge classique*). I follow him in arguing that in any culture there can be no reason without madness, and that consequently the different ways of viewing, approaching, expressing, and treating madness throughout human history reveal more about society than about any inherent characteristics of the condition itself.[46] According to Foucault, the history of insanity in the Western world is marked by the progression from a classical period, in which madness and sanity were undifferentiated, to the modern era, in which scientific discourse effectively silenced the mad in the eighteenth century by making madness the object of medical inquiry.[47] Foucault is nostalgic for what he believes to be a premodern era in which madness was not objectified, pathologized, or medicalized by society.[48] Foucault and the authors of the tropical narratives examined here share the idea that the pre-Cartesian era was a site of a now "inaccessible primitive purity" in which reason and nonreason were intermingled, and nonreason retained its own language and "all the marvellous secrets of Knowledge" (*History of Madness* xxxiii–xxxiv). Likewise, the adventure tales examined here also narrate a search for the mythical moment in which madness and sanity, civilization and barbarism, were not separate entities.[49] In that sense, both Foucault and the tropical narrative authors are marked by nostalgia for a prehistoric and perhaps apocryphal moment of linguistic unity.

If Foucault delineated the process of confining madness, the novels studied here explore what happens when madness is *not* confined; they pose a "what if" scenario in which the madman is allowed to express himself outside the borders of Cartesian society. In each case, the author appropriates medical language to depict the madness of the protagonist; the medical terminology once used to confine the mad is now employed to give a voice to the narrating madman. He thus restores the voice of the insane, who have been "robbed of subjectivity," as Shoshana Felman, following Foucault, has put it (*Writing* 3). In an ironic twist, the mad use the very medical terms previously used to contain them to best express their budding irrationality.

In much modern fiction, madness—particularly neurasthenia—is associated with hysteria and the female body, such as that of the protagonist of Charlotte Perkins Gilman's "The Yellow Wallpaper" and Bertha in Jean Rhys's *Wide Sargasso Sea*. Scholarly treatments of this topic generally articulate and refute the pathologization of female behavior by the male medical establishment. As Barbara Rigney states, "A greater part of the feminist movement has considered modern psychology to be both a product and a defense of the status quo—a patriarchal society" (3). Marginalized peoples—be they women, or colonial subjects of both genders—are frequently diagnosed by dominant ones as aberrant, deviant, or mad.[50] Fewer scholars have focused on madness in white males. This book seeks to fill that lacuna by showing that hysteria, neurasthenia, and neurosis were significant health concerns among men as well, especially during the early part of the twentieth century. In this respect, works such as Martin Bock's *Joseph Conrad and Psychological Medicine*, Valerie Pedlar's "*The Most Dreadful Visitation*": *Male Madness in Victorian Fiction*, and Gabriella Nouzeilles's *Ficciones somáticas* (Somatic fictions) are exemplary works. The protagonists of all the novels discussed in *Jungle Fever* are elite European or creole white men who have been made neurotic by the frenetic pace and artificiality of modern life. Once in the wilderness, this debility leaves them unprepared for the challenges they face. Their weakness soon changes into complete mental unraveling.

Like Fabian's historical explorers, all the protagonists in these tropical tales link their incipient madness to their surroundings, particularly to the dizzying abundance of plant life and to their time spent among the indigenous residents of the tropics. This attribution of illness to climate and personal contact is rooted in then-widely accepted European suppositions regarding the influence of the tropics on colonists' health. In the late nineteenth and early twentieth centuries, European doctors and medical professionals working in and on the colonies were concerned with several health issues: the impact of foreign climates on colonists, the eradication of diseases that afflicted both colonists and the indigenous population, and the effect of racial miscegenation on the future European citizenry. These topics are reflected in European travel and medical writings of the time. In Chapters 1 and 2, I will show how Conrad and Malraux's statements and travel arrangements while in the colonies indicate common suppositions about the health dangers presented by warm climates. The reception and interpretation of European scientific theories in Latin America naturally differed significantly from that of their points of origin for many reasons. During the nineteenth century and the first decades of the twentieth, medical information arrived in Latin America principally from Paris, and the best Latin American doctors traveled to France to attend medical school and to bring home the latest in medical science.[51] The diffusion of this knowledge throughout the continent, however, proceeded at a glacial pace, thus making the state of Colombian and Venezuelan medicine lag behind that of Europe and larger Latin American countries such as Mexico, Argentina, and Brazil. Latin American intellectuals and doctors debated the application of European theories to their own unique situations. What was one to make of medical texts that defined the region as degenerate and backward?[52] Writers such as José Vasconcelos reconceptualized the medical and philosophical impact of *mestizaje* (miscegenation) on Latin American nations, while others, such as Sarmiento, called for a racial "whitening" of Latin America.

In a parallel fashion, authors of regional novels during the first half of the twentieth century often addressed contemporary political situations and consciously strove to present a new form of modern Latin American literature strongly rooted in the region itself rather than in European models. As a result, nonliterary writings such as those of the legal and scientific disciplines permeate telluric novels in order to demonstrate Latin America's engagement with modernity.[53] Indeed, medical terminology has played an important and largely unexplored role in this process of the literary construction of the nation.[54] Stepan has written that Latin America "was involved in nationalist self-making, in which the setting of boundaries between self and other and the creation of identities were increasingly carried out by and through scientific and medical discourses" (*Hour* 7). For writers such as Rivera, Gallegos, and Carpentier, Latin America's literary identity would be forged in the overlap between imported theories about their nations and their real and fictional explorations of the wilderness.

In both Europe and Latin America, popular medical connections between climate, racial degeneration, and mental and physical collapse offered fertile ground for the imaginations of writers exploring the intersections of vastly different cultures and the inner workings of the human psyche. For the authors examined here, tropically induced madness becomes akin to "going native," or relinquishing Western customs and adopting the habits of the native population—a prospect both terrifying and seductive to the reader and protagonist alike. The association of the madman with "primitive" man runs through Western science, art, and literature.[55] Long before the modern era, Plato maintained that lunacy offers the possibility of access to the pure, primordial essence of man "untouched by the evils that awaited us in a later time" (30). As I mentioned previously, Foucault seems obsessed by the "primitive" quality of madness, as he wants to "approach more closely these primitively tangled words" of the mad (*History of Madness* xxxv). Richard C. Keller has noted that during the nineteenth and twentieth centuries, madness was often attributed to the postcolonial subject for his or her failure to conform to Western standards (4). Madness, it seems, is not merely an act of "going native," but also of *being* native.

The authors of these wilderness adventure narratives shared a profound disillusionment with modern life, and at times even viewed each other as companions in their disappointment. For example, in an article written shortly after the publication of *The Way of the Kings*, Alejo Carpentier sympathized with André Malraux's rebellion against "a society that imprisons us, that relegates us to the gray and amorphous masses" ("André Malraux" 37). In fact, all these tropical narratives turn away from rationalism and science even as they appropriate their terminology for literary use: Conrad's Marlow scoffs at the "alienist" who examines him before he departs for Africa, and Malraux's Claude is disgusted with the practice of colonial medicine. Despite his unique incorporation of medical terminology in *The Vortex*, Rivera's Arturo Cova perishes in the forest. Even though Gallegos was known in Venezuela as El Maestro (the Teacher), in *Canaima* he disparages Western education as useless for life in the jungle. Carpentier's rejection of science is bound up in his disillusionment with civilization in the wake of World War II, but its roots extend to his early interest in surrealism and the occult. Rather than exporting the virtues of order, progress, and rationality to the wilderness, as previous adventure tales such as *Robinson Crusoe* had done, these adventure novels revel in the supposed barbarity and irrationality of the rainforest.

Madness in these five novels is subversive and seductive to both reader and protagonist because it erodes the distinctions between the colonizer and the colonized, between sanity and insanity, between civilized and savage. The tropical wilderness becomes the site where these dichotomies converge, because in it the protagonist is removed from the supposedly civilizing effects of hierarchical society. In these narratives, the forest is thus an imagined palimpsest on which the protagonist's unacceptable irrational desires can be inscribed and indulged; it becomes a moral as well as physical jungle. On a linguistic level, these books are similarly destabilizing because they seek to express the madness of each protagonist in his own terms; they write against what Foucault called psychiatry's "monologue by reason *about* madness" and use medical terms intended to harness madness as a means of linguistic liberation and literary originality (*History of Madness* xxviii). Rivera's *The Vortex* is the most daring and modern work in this respect, as the narrative form of the novel cannot contain the wild speech of Arturo Cova when he loses his mind in an equally wild natural environment. At their core, these tropical adventure narratives are subversive texts because they demonstrate that all that separates the mad from the sane is the veneer of rationality afforded by human society. As Hayden White has written, "Instead of the relatively comforting thought that the Wild Man may exist *out there* and can be contained by some kind of physical action, it is now thought … that the Wild Man is lurking within every man, is clamoring for release within us all" (7). By erasing the neat, artificial barriers between reason and nonreason in the wilderness, these novels reveal that an uneasy coexistence between the rational and the irrational, the civilized and the barbarous, lies at the heart of human existence. These novels capture the popular imagination and stoke critical debate precisely because they pose the possibility of madness in the civilized; they suggest that the reader, too, might go crazy in the jungle.

Chapter 1

Medical Discourse and Modernist Prose in *Heart of Darkness*

"It makes one awfully queer, don't you find?" St. John Hirst complained. "These trees get on one's nerves—it's all so crazy. God's undoubtedly mad. What sane person could have conceived a wilderness like this, and peopled it with apes and alligators? I should go mad if I lived here—raving mad."

—Virginia Woolf, *The Voyage Out* (348)

INCIDENTS OF MADNESS AMONG EUROPEAN CITIZENS IN THE TROPICS WERE common enough in the late nineteenth and early twentieth centuries that the Dutch language contains a word for it: *tropenkollered* (maddened by the tropics).[1] Like the term *jungle fever*, the existence of the expression *tropenkollered* is a linguistic manifestation of European fears and fantasies surrounding the colonial wilderness. While the phenomenon appears in many literary works, it plays a central role in *Heart of Darkness*, afflicting not only the novel's famous protagonist, Kurtz, but also a Swedish colonist who takes his own life without apparent provocation other than the hot, humid climate (116).[2] The word encapsulates Conrad's conception of the tropics, which had a profound impact on twentieth century depictions of the undomesticated rainforest in popular culture. Like Kipling before him, Conrad bequeathed a literary legacy that transcended the English language and became a touchstone for other writers of tropical narratives. His portrayal of a specific tropical place—in his case, the region then known as the Belgian Congo—became the archetype of colonized tropical spaces. While *Heart of Darkness* was not heralded as Conrad's greatest work immediately following its publication, its depiction of the river voyage undertaken by the protagonist, Marlow, reverberates in later writings about the tropics throughout the twentieth century by authors as diverse as Virginia Woolf and André Malraux, and in popular media such as the film *Apocalypse Now*. This chapter examines the presentation of madness of Europeans in *Heart of Darkness*. It then places *Heart of Darkness* within the context of British colonial tropical fiction by underscoring the role the climate plays in the death of the protagonist in Woolf's *The Voyage Out* (1915).

Conrad scholars have generally glossed Kurtz's behavior in the wilderness in two ways. Those in the first camp situate Kurtz's degeneration within the array of medical theories of the time that were concerned with the decline and fall of the European race. In those readings, Kurtz's demise and death are a symptom of this decline and an allegory for the fate of British imperialism in Africa.[3] Many of these discussions link sociomedical concepts to a Victorian anthropological discourse that offered a scientific veneer to racial essentializing and justifications of discrimination, slavery, and subjugation of the colonized.[4] In general, this sub-set of Conrad scholars depicts Kurtz's process of "going native" as a product of racist Victorian medico-anthropological theories; some condemn him as a white supremacist (Ogede 131), while others absolve him as a product of his time.[5] The second group of scholars reads Kurtz's behavior from a narratological perspective, arguing that Kurtz, like the narrative, is "hollow at the core" (Conrad, *Heart* 165). They read the framed tale as an exemplary achievement of high modernism and frequently discount the historical, racial, and medical contexts of Marlow's river voyage (Brooks 238; Todorov 167). Most of these scholars speak of Conrad's genius and his timelessness as a modernist author rather than his rootedness in his own epoch and artistic movement. Others tend to defend Conrad from charges of racism or ignore those charges altogether (McClure 137–38; Hawkins 169). My own work builds on both of these divergent strains in the extensive body of Conrad criticism. It goes beyond them in connecting the madness provoked by Kurtz's degeneration to Conrad's narrative style. To this end, I examine Conrad's edits to the handwritten manuscript of *Heart of Darkness* to show how Kurtz's lunacy is shaped into an allusive, modernist style. In short, Marlow's attempt to narrate madness is at once based in Victorian medicine *and* forms the essential component of *Heart of Darkness*'s modernism.

Patrick Parrinder calls *Heart of Darkness* "the most over-interpreted literary text of the last one hundred years" (85). Conrad has been so repeatedly glossed because his impact on later writings set in the colonial tropics has been so great. Several tropes elaborated by Conrad become commonplace in later narratives set in the tropics and make *Heart of Darkness* key to understanding the French- and Spanish-language novels I will discuss in the later chapters of this book. Conrad's most important contribution to the literary portrait of the colonial wilderness consists of three elements: he depicts the tropics as an immutable, prehistoric, and unknowable place; a region unfettered by societal constraints; and most important, an environment capable of causing both mental and physical illness. This combination of characteristics makes the Congolese wilderness at once attractive and repellent to the protagonists. In *Heart of Darkness*, the tropical environment embodies Freud's definition of the uncanny: the forest seems to be the antithesis of European life, and yet it simultaneously provokes an uneasy and often sublimated shock of self-recognition.

For Conrad's Marlow, as for European colonists of previous centuries, the utter strangeness of the environment transforms a specific geographical location into a universal screen on which previously hidden desires and fears are projected and played out.[6] Faced with the specter of what he deems the unknown and the unknowable, the European imbues the wilderness with facets of himself that remain taboo in Western society. The undomesticated tropics thus form a pillar of the dialectic of civilization: the British can only be civilized, sane, and healthy if the colonial environment is presented as unrestrained, maddening, and infectiously malevolent. This gesture forcibly obscures the realities of a colonized territory and remakes it according to the Westerner's imagination. As Nancy Stepan has noted: "Tropical nature was ... part of the formation of Europe's identity as a place of temperateness, control, hard work and thriftiness as opposed to the humidity, heat, extravagance and superfluity of the Torrid Zone" (*Picturing* 36). Conrad and later European and Latin American adventure novelists participate in the formation and perpetuation of this dialectic between cold, imperial centers and warm, permissive peripheries by creating protagonists who attribute to the tropics the characteristics found within themselves that have no place in the drawing room. The wilderness, at first seen by these outsiders as a historical and cultural empty vessel, becomes the repository of the base, the sexual, the suicidal, the irrational, and the repressed.

As I noted in the Introduction, Kipling's colonial fiction is a clear forerunner to later Anglophone tropical novels, although his views on the viability and morality of the imperial project differ greatly from Conrad's. The central difference between the two is precisely what separates the novels discussed in *Jungle Fever* from previous tropical adventure narratives. Kipling believed firmly in the imperial mandate and merely advocated for changes in the system. Conrad, however, demonstrated the fallibility of British imperialism, even though he had earned his living as a sea captain in the British Navy.[7]

Despite their points of divergence, Kipling's portrayal of the madness of British subjects in India anticipates the lunacy of Conrad's tropical fiction protagonists. Both authors have a keen eye for the absurdities of colonial life, the brutal effects of the tropical climate on their protagonists, and the madness of colonial officers in the wilderness. In Kipling's stories, these elements combine to imbue India with an aura of stultifying heat, frustrating bureaucracy, superstitious soldiers, and incipient madness. For example, in "The Madness of Private Ortheris," the eponymous soldier suffers a psychotic fit after spending an extended amount of time in India. He nearly deserts his post and threatens suicide, saying, "I ain't 'fraid o' dyin' 'fore I gets my discharge paipers" (*Plain Tales* 278). The protagonist of Kipling's "At the End of the Passage" also suffers from hallucinations and commits suicide. As Conrad would later suggest with some of his own characters, Kipling implies that the madness of both men is provoked by their disenchantment with their role in the British imperial machine.[8] The combination of oppressive heat, homesickness, frustration with colonial bureaucracy, and proximity to the native population overcomes their faculties and they seek refuge in the club, opium, or death, and sometimes all three.[9] As John McClure argues in his insightful study of Kipling and Conrad, both men chronicle the transformations of the European in the colonies, yet their purposes in doing so could not be more different. He shows that Kipling sought to reform the practices of the British colonial administration so that officers would feel neither isolated from the British community nor unprepared for their responsibilities; Kipling ultimately sought to "eliminate the flaws in the imperial mold" (McClure 81). Kipling, therefore, presented madness as a natural reaction to the absurdities of life and as a critique of the colonial system without advocating its overthrow.

McClure shows that while the madness of Kipling's characters is a reaction of logical individuals to an unfair system, that of Conrad's characters is a response to the revelation that all humanity is morally bankrupt. Moreover, I argue that while *Heart of Darkness* follows Kipling in depicting the colonial tropics as a maddening space, the threat of insanity in Conrad's work is more psychologically complex and literarily significant because it affects the way the tale itself is narrated. Conrad's mad characters gain insights into human nature that they are unable to articulate. Indeed, the author portrays Kurtz's experience as an unnarratable occurrence specifically because the madness it provokes and the self-knowledge thereby attained cannot be expressed in words. The meaning of the experience is rendered illegible because it unleashes in Kurtz thoughts and feelings that are presented as extralinguistic, prehistoric, and outside the bounds of experience containable by language. The story is literally unintelligible because of the current of insanity, or non-sense, that runs through the work. In this way, *Heart of Darkness* is a tale of a failed narration caused by the incommunicability of the madness and dark self-knowledge attained by Kurtz in the wilderness. The attempts to narrate this unnarratable madness result in Conrad's modernist prose style: the fragmentary, allusive, nonlinear, and impressionistic depiction of events within the work.[10] In turn, madness in *Heart of Darkness* is based on contemporary theories regarding sickness and mental illness in the tropics that shaped Conrad's opinion of the colonial environment in both his life and his literature.[11]

Medical writings regarding the relationship between climate and inherent mental and physical human characteristics play a key role in all the tropical quest narratives under discussion in this book. While the theories I analyze here reached the zenith of their popularity at the turn of the twentieth century, their origins stretch back to the 1700s. For example, in *The Spirit of the Laws* (1748), Montesquieu expounds contemporary hypotheses regarding physiological differences between inhabitants of warm and cold climates. His conclusions regarding the slackening of nerve elasticity in hot, humid climates in the mid-eighteenth century reinforce beliefs in European superiority and seem to give biological justifications for them, thereby perpetuating slavery and colonization (231). According to his argument, peoples of warm climates were thought to be weaker, more sensual and criminal, and less ordered and restrained than those of cold climates. Montesquieu writes:

> You will find in the northern climates people who have few vices, enough virtues, and much sincerity and frankness. As you move toward the countries of the south, you will believe you have moved away from morality itself: the liveliest passions will increase crime; each will seek to take from others all the advantages that can favor these same passions. In temperate countries, you will see peoples whose manners, and even their vices and virtues are inconstant; the climate is not sufficiently settled to fix them. (234)

Montesquieu consequently condones (though he also laments) both slavery and colonization by showing that residents of warm climates are unable to control their passions, and thus are unable to rule themselves. He also finds them unfit for self-rule, accusing them of cowardice: "The peoples in hot climates are timid like old men; those in cold countries are courageous like young men" (232). European judgments and suppositions regarding inhabitants of the tropics changed surprising little between Montesquieu's work and Conrad's publication of *Heart of Darkness* a century and a half later. Changes in medical opinion and scientific discoveries were interpreted in ways that confirmed and perpetuated racial and geographical stereotypes. For example, Montesquieu's theory that increased nerve elasticity in tropical residents resulted in sensuality, vice, and weakness was reconstituted by phrenologists and eugenicists who repeated similar claims and stipulated that the average African adult was only as intelligent and developed as a European child (Veit-Wild 13).

Colonial and postcolonial scholarship from the second half of the twentieth century to the present has examined the practice of colonial medicine—specifically psychiatry—and its complicity in identifying the colonial subject as inherently pathological. Beginning with Frantz Fanon's seminal text, *Black Skin, White Masks* (1952), psychologists and scholars have analyzed the effects of subjugation and colonization on the psyches of individuals living under imperial rule. As Flora Veit-Wild points out, "The problem the colonial observer of mental illness had was that ... for them the African was a priori 'the other'" (13). As an example, Veit-Wild notes that H. L. Gordon, the superintendent of the Mathari Mental Hospital of Nairobi during the 1930s, "found it difficult to distinguish in Africans between normal and abnormal behavior" (13). Gordon claimed that "the African had no regard for the sanctity of life, no sense of decency; by European standards he was simply abnormal" (qtd. in Veit-Wild 13). Similarly, as Richard C. Keller notes in *Colonial Madness: Psychiatry in French North Africa*, French psychiatrists in Algeria pathologized their patients based on race, place of origin, and religion: "Psychiatrists proposed that the consciousness of the 'normal' North African Muslim represented 'a mixture of insanity in varying doses'" (7).

Fanon was quick to decry this mental as well as physical colonization as a form of violence perpetrated in the name of science. Colonial physicians, however, prided themselves on bringing European customs, medical practices, and standards of hygiene to the newly conquered territories. Their explicit goal of bringing these values to the colonies defined the colonial subject as inherently unhealthy, unsanitary, and insane.

Most discussions of colonial madness examine the historical and cultural causes and ramifications of the ways in which European doctors diagnosed non-European subjects as mad. Keller, for example, explores how psychiatry informed the colonial encounter, particularly by analyzing the activities of French-trained doctors and their North African patients. This chapter examines the flip side of that coin—namely, the perceived madness among the *colonizing* forces in warm climates. According to the colonial medical profession, if warm climates produced weak, indulgent, and inferior humans, Europeans venturing into these areas risked the same fate, even though they were supposedly superior by nature. Colonial physicians were therefore preoccupied with madness among colonists as well as colonial subjects; at times, colonists made up half of the North African psychiatric hospital population (Keller 13). While dangers posed to physical health by dysentery and malaria were substantial, the psychological impact of high mortality rates and constant fevers suffered by the Europeans in the colonies was even more wide-ranging and long-lasting.[12] As I illustrated in the Introduction, Johannes Fabian has shown that European explorers in central Africa during the second half of the nineteenth century were plagued by fears of fever, madness, and enervation. Accordingly, the notion of hygiene took on mythic proportions; it became not just a means of feeling physically clean, but also a talisman for warding off mental and physical illnesses: "Hygiene meant something that was both much deeper and more encompassing than what went later by that name" (Fabian 59). Constant activity, wearing flannel, and frequent bathing, all activities practiced at home, could keep one safe.[13] Fabian quotes the explorer Joseph Thomson to illustrate the connection between physical and mental uncleanliness:

> It is a well-known fact that the only way to resist successfully the enervating effects of a humid tropical climate is by constant exertion, and by manfully fighting the baleful influence. The man who has nothing to do, or won't do what he has to do, is sure to succumb in a few months, and degenerate into an idiot or a baby. He becomes the helpless victim of manifold bilious troubles, and is continually open to attacks of fever, diarrhea, or dysentery. His mental energy flies with his physical, till any sustained thought is impossible, and to pass the time he must dose night and day, except when he is grumbling and defaming the climate. Hard constant work is the great preserver. Sweat out the malaria and germs

of disease, and less will be heard of the energy-destroying climate of the tropics. (58)

Thomson makes it clear that physical exertion was thought to stave off mental decay. The Protestant work ethic and European virility were thus contrasted with native indolence and mental degeneracy, neatly meshing centuries-old suppositions regarding the perceived laziness of tropical residents with contemporary scientific theories regarding the spread of malaria and germ-driven diseases. The unquestioned connection between the climate and illness, without an understanding of the exact methods of virus and germ transmission, resulted in a plethora of supposed causes of fevers: "All authors were convinced that fever could be brought about, not only by psychosomatic states such as fatigue caused by overexertion, but also by overexcitement and excessive anger and aggravation" (Fabian 61–62). Given the myriad causes of fevers, their source is vaguely defined by Thomson as the "energy-destroying climate"; the root of the malady was not microbial or biological, but rather meteorological.

What, precisely, made the tropical environment dangerous for the European colonist? After Montesquieu's eighteenth-century theories regarding nerve elasticity fell from favor, they were replaced by newer scientific statements that attributed physical and mental disintegration to warm climates. The mental disturbances that afflicted Europeans in tropical climes were known by a variety of terms as ambiguous as their ostensible causes, including *African spleen*, *tropical neurasthenia*, *degeneration*, and, of course, *jungle fever*. Before germ theory gained credence among doctors and scientists, the notion that conditions such as fever, dysentery, and tropical neurasthenia were caused by the heat and rays of the sun held sway in both popular and medical writing. According to doctors such as Charles E. Woodruff, these "actinic" rays were harmful only to light-skinned Europeans, who needed to wear protective clothing (such as the sola topi) and to live in darkened quarters with large verandas (*Tropical Light*).[14] Even more prevalent than concerns about the rays of the sun was the theory that time spent in the tropics led to the physical and mental "degeneration" of European citizens.

Originally expounded by Bénédict-Augustin Morel in 1857 and popularized by Max Nordau forty years later, *degeneration* was a general medical and anthropological hypothesis to explain the decline of people of European descent, as evidenced by a series of symptoms ranging from fatigue to nervous disorders and culminating in insanity. It is this final result that will be significant in this study.[15] Degeneration, an amorphous and vast "condition," has been analyzed in both medical and literary disciplines as a manifestation of cultural and social anxiety in the face of immigration, colonization, and the growing modernization of society, as well as a significant literary motif.[16] All these perceived ills were linked to the fear of a weakened, largely white ruling class being overthrown by the nonwhite masses. These concerns meshed with a philosophy of environmental determinism derived from Darwinian evolution, in which people with dark complexions were naturally healthy (though indolent and unintelligent) in tropical climates, while whites became ill in warm weather and could thrive only in temperate climes.[17]

Patrick Manson's *Tropical Diseases* was first published in 1898; revised since, it is still a standard medical text today. In his preface, Manson underscored the danger of the tropical climate to the light-skinned European and its benign effect on the indigenous population:

> Speaking generally, the natives of tropical countries are not injuriously affected by the meteorological conditions of the climates they live in, any more than are the inhabitants of more temperate climates; their physiological activities are attuned by custom and habit to the conditions they were born into. The European, it may be, on his first entering the tropics, and until his machinery has adjusted itself to the altered meteorological circumstances, is liable to slight physiological irregularities, and this more especially if he persists in the dietetic habits appropriate to his native land. A predisposition to certain diseases, and a tendency to degenerative changes, may be brought about in this way. (xii)

Even as the medical community gradually reached consensus about the cause of illness—that germs were responsible, rather than the sun or meteorological conditions—the general public did not relinquish popular assumptions about the physical and psychological menace presented by the wilderness. Fabian argues that fever was "the most formidable threat to the scientific enterprise of exploration" (62), but the question of contagious mental illness triggered by the tropics is even more significant than the physical ailments induced by the environment. The danger is alluded to in Manson's warning about "a tendency to degenerative changes" and illustrated by the epigraph to this chapter, in which Woolf's character declares that he would go "raving mad" if he lived in the tropics.

Colonial anxieties about the effects of the wilderness on mental health have culturally complex roots. They were often based on popular fears that were presented as medical fact. Fabian cites Portuguese explorers Herminigildo Capelo and Roberto Ivens, who describe experiencing "African spleen": in 1888, after several months in central Africa, they are afflicted by "a state of irritability, and nervous excitement closely allied to derangement. The extravagance of gesture, precipitating of every act, abruptness in issuing orders, baseless fears, and a desire to rush along the road, as though pursued by some phantom, all are evidence of the change that is being wrought, and are symptoms of the malady known as African Spleen" (qtd. in Fabian 64). In their journals, the explorers asked themselves, "Did these strange vagaries … these fixed prepossessions portend the dawn of madness?" (64). The profusion of names for states of mental perturbation, their symptoms, and their ostensible causes reveals both how widespread and how biologically unfounded these conditions were among Europeans in the tropics. While the symptoms were palpable, the causes were psychological rather than biological.

Madness in the colonies was also thought to be a result of "tropical neurasthenia," an offshoot of the theory of degeneration. Its variety of names, such as the aforementioned "African Spleen," and its nebulous symptoms—"fatigue, irritability, loss of concentration, loss of memory, hypochondria, loss of appetite, diarrhea, insomnia, headaches, depression, palpitations, ulcers, alcoholism, anemia, sexual profligacy, sexual debility, premature and prolonged menstruation, insanity, and suicide"—became a catchall label for the result of Westerners coming into contact with an alien climate and society (Kennedy 123). The threat of suicide posed by this malady was of special concern to the government and military officials who administered the colonial presence in tropical climates. For example, in an article published in the *Philadelphia Medical Journal* on April 7, 1900, the army doctor Charles E. Woodruff notes that among the U.S. troops in the Philippines, "when there is a tendency to insanity it often happens that the extra nervous exhaustion is due to hot weather. It is the final determining cause of the mental breakdown" ("Tropical Subjects" 773). To support his conclusion, Woodruff exhibits a table compiled by the Italian criminologist Cesare Lombroso in which mental cases and suicides were shown to increase in warm months and decline in cold ones. Without any empirical evidence of the direct cause, such cases were attributed to the climate as a whole, and specifically to the heat and the sun. The broad symptoms bolstered general fears about the causal relationship between madness and the environment, which in turn informed the literary portrayal of the tropics as a mysteriously dangerous place for Westerners.

Many of these turn-of-the-century medical opinions find a deep and psychologically complicated resonance in Conrad's fiction. Apart from his literary genius, Conrad was uniquely positioned to explore the relationship between popular medicine and the tropics: he both engaged in the colonial enterprise as a sailor in the British Navy and sought medical treatment for the fashionable ills of the day (such as neurasthenia, gout, and nervous collapse) at various spas in Europe. Martin Bock has proved that Conrad's life and literary works were permeated by medical discourse, particularly following his trip through the Congo.[18] Late Victorian England and the United States were particularly concerned with the effects of the tropics on their colonial residents. For example, Dr. Woodruff notes that among American troops in the Philippines, "the insanities are more numerous than at home" (*Tropical Light* 194). Indeed, Woodruff's observations are of particular importance to my study of Conrad because they focus specifically on sea captains of the British fleet, and his diagnoses reflect the general atmosphere of medical thought both during the time Conrad spent in Africa and while he was writing *Heart of Darkness*. According to Woodruff's *The Effects of Tropical Light on White Men* (1905), "It is reported that neurasthenia is becoming a serious matter among the officers in the British Navy, so many of whom are being disabled by it" (203). Woodruff further states, "In medical and popular literature there is a wealth of data on the neurasthenic conditions coming on in the tropics and it would be a waste of time to mention even the sources. Kipling's stories of India contain very clear pictures of neurasthenia, but he did not know the nature of the condition he described" (202). Kipling did suffer from mental breakdowns while in the colonial service, as well as following the abuse he had suffered as a child, but he did not seek medical treatment for any psychological distress provoked by serving the empire (McClure 16–17). Conrad, on the other hand, frequently sought out medical advice and avoided warm climates whenever possible. In a letter written between his return from Malaysia and his departure for the Congo, Conrad begged off a trip to Mexico and the West Indies because he feared the warm climate would damage his health: "I think that, given my prolonged stay in the warm countries (from which I have recently returned) and my probable departure for Africa in less that a month, it would be prudent for me to benefit from the European climate for as long as possible."[19]

Like many travelers of his era, Conrad was clearly concerned about the debilitating effects of hot climates on his mental and physical health. In a letter to his cousin Charles Zagórski, written when Conrad was in port in Sierra Leone, he remarked, "What makes me rather uneasy is the information that 60 per cent of our Company's employés [*sic*] return to Europe before they have completed even six months' service. Fever and dysentery! There are others who are sent home in a hurry at the end of a year, so that they shouldn't die in the Congo. God forbid!"[20] In addition, the correspondence between Conrad and Marguerite Poradowska shows that Conrad experienced both mental and physical ailments during his time as a ship captain, suffering from tropical fever on three separate occasions.[21] Like the members of the expeditions in central Africa examined by Fabian, Conrad found himself obligated to diagnose and medicate other Europeans in the tropics. In his "Congo Diary," Conrad recounts how he nursed a fellow employee of the Société, Prosper Harou, through a "billious [*sic*] attack and fever," administering "1 gramme of quinine and lots of hot tea" to stop him from "vomiting bile in enormous quantities" (108). The maladies often suffered by colonists in tropical climes included fever and insanity, which were commonly attributed to neurasthenia exacerbated by the climate. The most advanced stage of neurasthenia resulted in suicide, according to medical communities both in Europe and the United States.[22] Conrad thus hoped to avoid the incursion of tropically induced ailments, such as those suffered by Harou, by remaining in a temperate climate.

Conrad later incorporated the prevailing medical theories regarding mental illness and the infectious diseases of tropical regions into his narratives. Many of Conrad's stories and novels depict the mental and moral decay of white men in the tropics in ways that reflect Manson's assertions of 1898. In addition to the impact of tropical disease specialists such as Manson, Conrad was heavily influenced by Nordau's *Degeneration*, which first appeared in English in 1895. In the year prior to the publication of *Heart of Darkness*, Conrad wrote to an acquaintance, thanking her for passing along a letter and autograph from Nordau. In a possible reference to his recently published *The Nigger of the Narcissus*, Conrad writes: "There is not the slightest doubt MN has understood my intention. He has absolutely detected the whole idea: This to me is so startling that I do not know what to think of myself now.... He is wondrous kind."[23] This letter makes it clear that Conrad knew Nordau's work and felt that it bore an affinity to his own. In the month following this correspondence, Conrad began work on *Heart of Darkness*; yet even before he received the letter from Nordau, Conrad's fiction depicted Europeans who decline, go mad, and die in warm climates. In Conrad's first novel, *Almayer's Folly* (1895), Kaspar Almayer, the son of Dutch colonials born in Java, slowly wastes away in a remote Malay river camp. Almayer's "folly" refers to the unfinished construction of a large house he had begun to build in the expectation of becoming a prosperous businessman. More broadly, his "folly" is his aspiration to improve his situation, escape the tropics, and live in Europe (a place he has never visited) with his mixed-race daughter, Nina. From the opening lines of the novel, Almayer's ultimate decline is presented as inevitable. Nina, whom he has had educated in Singapore, dashes his hopes that she will rise above her station in life when she marries a Malay chief named Dain. Almayer's own Malay wife is described as "betel-nut chewing … squatting in a dark hut, disordered, half naked, and sulky," and Nina's marriage implies she will share her mother's fate (81). In an expression of maddened despair, Almayer sets fire to his office and retreats to the house to smoke opium and await "forgetfulness and oblivion," his only companion a pet monkey (201). His death in the final pages of the novel is a deliverance "from the trammels of his earthly folly" (208). The novel is a minute and pessimistic description of the process of degeneration suffered by people of European stock who remain in the tropics. As Rod Edmond has shown, *Almayer's Folly* "dramatizes the notion that civilization is skin deep, that Europeans cut off from the roots that nurtured them are easily decivilized" ("Home and Away" 47). The specter of decline—of a tendency toward irrational behavior and substance abuse as outlined by the Victorian medical establishment—is embodied in Almayer's frenzied destruction of his livelihood and dismissal of self-betterment. The gradual and inevitable disintegration of the self first explored in *Almayer's Folly* becomes a recurrent theme in Conrad's work that consistently erodes the notion of European superiority over tropical peoples.

Insanity and mental collapse are also present in *Lord Jim* (1900), which, like *Heart of Darkness*, is narrated by Marlow. The novel recounts Marlow's relationship with the title character, Jim, who is censured for abandoning his ship, the *Patna*, when it struck an obstacle at sea and nearly sank. As Jim recounts to Marlow the events that led up to the accident, he declares, "I suppose you think I was going mad … and well you may, if you remember I had lost my cap. The sun crept all the way from east to west over my bare head, but that day I could not come to any harm, I suppose. The sun could not make me mad." Marlow tells us that as Jim speaks these words, "his right arm put aside the idea of madness." Jim states that the sun could not kill him and continues: "I didn't get brain fever, I did not drop dead either" (58). Jim's unprompted denials of having "brain fever" or having been made delirious by the sun imply that those assumptions would be natural and expected of Marlow. Jim, like Kurtz, eventually flees the company of white men and lives among colonized people—in Jim's case, the Malay. This renunciation of Western society is frequently called "going native," and it is always associated with madness in Conrad's fiction.

Following the shipwreck in *Lord Jim*, one member of the crew commits suicide and another is confined as mentally unsound; the ship's engineer repeatedly tells Marlow that there are "pink toads" under his bed and that the *Patna* had been "full of reptiles" (25). The attending doctor attributes his madness to his long residence in the tropics: "The curious part is there's some sort of method in his raving. I am trying to find out. Most unusual—that thread of logic in such a delirium. . . . He ought to be dead, don't you know, after such a festive experiment. Oh! he is a tough object. Four-and-twenty years of the tropics too" (26). Véronique Pauly argues that the delirium of the engineer parallels the madness that leads Jim to his dereliction of duty and that this "logic" of insanity leads to the "undercurrent of madness and terror flowing in Marlow's narrative" (174–75). Pauly's interpretation is well founded and consistent with the role of lunacy in Conrad's oeuvre, but it does not take into account the historical bases of Jim's madness. As I have shown, the notion that the prolonged exposure to the tropics (and particularly to the sun) contributes to the patient's abnormal behavior was common at the turn of the century. Conrad's fiction is unique, however, in positing that "logic" exists in the delirium of those who go mad in the tropics.[24] In several works, madness in the tropics leads to a particular insight into the human condition that Conrad refuses to specify. He repeats this motif in a typically allusive form in his tropical fiction set in Africa, suggesting it in the insanity of Kurtz and, to a lesser degree, in the breakdown of Kurtz's forerunner Kayerts, who appears in "An Outpost of Progress" (1897).

Indeed, madness pervades Conrad's African fiction. In many ways, "An Outpost of Progress," which Conrad called his "best story" ("Congo Diary" 82), is a clear precursor to *Heart of Darkness*, particularly because the European protagonists go mad in a remote African trading station. The colonial officers Kayerts and Carlier travel to "the center of Africa" to run a trading post for the "Great Civilizing Company" some three hundred miles from the nearest European settlement ("Outpost" 36). Like the doctor in *Heart of Darkness*, the "stager" who drops them off foreshadows their mental unraveling by declaring "they will form themselves there" (32). At first, Kayerts and Carlier enjoy their freedom to be idle and lazy, but they are troubled by the cross marking the grave of their predecessor, who died of fever. The African assigned to assist them, a "civilized nigger" named Makola, is racistly depicted as a duplicitous worshipper of evil spirits who keeps the books and translates for the British (40). He secretly arranges the sale of Africans employed by the company to black slave traders from the coast for six ivory tusks. When Kayerts and Carlier realize that they have been ignorantly complicit in enslaving their employees, they claim to be morally outraged, but eventually decide to keep the ivory and cover up the crime. Following this reprehensible behavior, the two men begin to degenerate mentally and morally: "The memory of people like them, of men that thought and felt as they used to think and feel, receded into distances made indistinct by the glare of unclouded sunshine. And out of the great silence of the surrounding wilderness, its very hopelessness and savagery seemed to approach them nearer, to draw them in gently, to look upon them, to envelop them with a solicitude irresistible, familiar, and disgusting" (43). The climate, isolation from white people, and distance from the European metropole are, Conrad implies, significant factors in the men's moral deprivations; the same intimation is made in *Heart of Darkness*. Yet while in Conrad's view the surroundings are certainly a provocation, the true seeds of madness are found within the Europeans themselves. That the causes of psychological distress are internal reflects the fears of degeneration common in Conrad's time that I have outlined. The omniscient narrator of the story attributes the mental roots of the protagonists' inexcusable actions "to the sentiment of being alone of one's kind, to the clear perception of the loneliness of one's thoughts, of one's sensations—to the negation of the habitual, " which has been augmented by "the affirmation of the unusual, which is dangerous; a suggestion of things vague, uncontrollable, and repulsive, whose discomposing intrusion excites the imagination and tries the civilized nerves of the foolish and the wise alike" (33). This pronouncement suggests that only the strictures of European society ward off immorality, criminality, and lunacy.

After eight months alone in each other's company, the two men argue when supplies run low, and Kayerts shoots the unarmed Carlier in the eye. Conrad narrates Kayerts's complete turn to madness with precision: "He seemed to have broken loose from himself altogether. His old thoughts, convictions, likes and dislikes, things he respected and things he abhorred, appeared in their true light at last! Appeared contemptible and childish, false and ridiculous. He reveled in his new wisdom while he sat by the man he had killed. He argued with himself about all the things under heaven with that kind of wrong-headed lucidity which may be observed in some lunatics" (48). The morning following the murder, Kayerts hangs himself on the cross marking the grave of the previous stationmaster as a steamer approaches—the boat, in fact, that would have relieved him and Carlier of their post. Conrad intimates that Kayerts is driven to suicide by the knowledge that he would be returned to civilization and that he would be condemned for his actions. In the light of his revelation that "one death could not possibly make any difference," Kayerts is unwilling to suffer that fate and thus kills himself (48). The notion that madness and moral depravity afford the insane insights that debunk conventional thought is a dominant theme in both "An Outpost of Progress" and *Heart of Darkness*. These insights distinguish the presence of madness in the works of Conrad from those of Kipling because they allow Conrad to question the inherent rationale for such "outposts of progress," given that colonial officers behave in irrational ways. The very clear explanation of a madman's thought process in "Outpost" is made much more complex and obscure in Conrad's later work. Indeed, while the theme of "Outpost" is very similar to that of *Heart of Darkness*, its style is quite different. Conrad's trademark biting irony is present, but the narrator's descriptions of the station and its surroundings are cold and explicit rather than impressionistic and allusive. In *Heart of Darkness*, Marlow tries to make sense of Kurtz's madness; his mediating voice leads to the modernist tone that is absent in "Outpost." The second major difference between the works is the great disparity between Kurtz and Kayerts. While Kayerts is "perfectly insignificant and incapable" (32), Kurtz is presented as an intelligent, artistic, accomplished official who degenerates mentally. Marlow's attempt to narrate Kurtz's madness is more circumspect because he seeks to gain the wisdom and the insight that Kurtz achieved in the moments of lucidity before his death.

Kayerts's suicide in "An Outpost of Progress" is mirrored by the suicide of the Swedish colonist who hangs himself in the early pages of *Heart of Darkness*. Many textual examples from the narrative illustrate Conrad's interest in mental degeneration. For instance, the captain of another steamer Marlow encounters on his way to Kurtz's station attributes the suicide of a fellow European to the tropics: "'The other day I took up a man who hanged himself on the road. He was a Swede, too.' 'Hanged himself! Why, in God's name?' I cried. He kept on looking out watchfully. 'Who knows? The sun too much for him, or the country, perhaps'" (116). The ambiguous cause of this suicide is representative of Conrad's relationship to medical discourse in his narrative: the purposefully vague and uncertain causes of mental illness resonate with the contemporary association between the climate and insanity, neatly united in the Dutch *tropenkollered*.

While it is clear that some element in the environment—the sun, vegetation, water, or even people—has driven a European to his death, the precise medical trigger remains unspecified, leaving Marlow uneasy about the mental effects of time spent in the African tropics. This is not the only incident of erratic behavior on the part of the "pilgrims" in the wilderness (126); Marlow notes the irrationality of the Frenchmen who fire blindly into the vegetation in an attempt to obliterate the natives: "There was a touch of insanity in the proceeding, a sense of lugubrious drollery in the sight" (115). Again, Conrad refrains from applying any medical explanation for their behavior to heighten the air of mystery and menace that envelops the wilderness.

The mix of contemporary medical theory and allusive language used to portray Marlow's fear of madness is most obvious in his interview with a doctor shortly before he embarks on his Congo voyage. The doctor engages in a popular medical practice of the time by asking to measure Marlow's skull. Phrenology, based on a now discredited theory once popularized by Lombroso, among others, sought to classify individuals racially and mentally based on the size and shape of their skulls. According to Robert Jacobs, Conrad was familiar with Lombroso's theory, which posited a "definitive relationship between primitive physical structure and primitive social behavior" (78). Marlow's exchange with the doctor in *Heart of Darkness* foreshadows the psychological changes that take place in Europeans who venture into Africa: "'I always ask leave, in the interests of science, to measure the crania of those going out there,' [the doctor] said. 'And when they come back, too?' I asked. 'Oh, I never see them,' he remarked: 'and, moreover, the changes take place inside, you know'" (112). The doctor's speech is at once prognostic and evasive. His first response to Marlow's question could be interpreted to indicate high mortality rates among colonists, and his second intimates an invisible mental illness untreatable and unquantifiable by medicine. He uses no medical terms to explain the changes that take place in the minds of his patients, and yet his vague statement clearly connects the tropical sojourn with abnormal psychological developments. The primary danger is not that of bodily infection but rather of a mental one. The physician further reveals the central role madness will play throughout the narrative: "He gave me a searching glance, and made another note. 'Ever any madness in your family?' he asked, in a matter-of-fact tone. I felt very annoyed. 'Is that question in the interests of science, too?' 'It would be,' he said, without taking notice of my irritation, 'interesting for science to watch the mental changes of individuals, on the spot, but . . .' 'Are you an alienist?' I interrupted. 'Every doctor should be—a little' answered that original imperturbably" (112). Like the physician's diagnosis of madness in *Lord Jim*, this doctor's role as an alienist—an early term for "psychiatrist," stemming from the "mental alienation" experienced by the mad—underscores the danger posed to mental health by a voyage in the tropics. As Fabian and Woodruff demonstrate, degeneration was often thought to be exacerbated by mental exhaustion on the part of the patient (Fabian 60; Woodruff, "Tropical Subjects" 773), which helps to explain the doctor's parting recommendation: "Avoid irritation more than the sun. . . . In the tropics one must above all keep calm." The doctor holds up "a warning forefinger" as he bids Marlow farewell with "*Du calme, du calme. Adieu*" (112).

The doctor's visit leaves Marlow feeling unsure as to whether madness is caused explicitly by the tropics, or whether the kernel of madness lies within himself, as implied by the question regarding madness in Marlow's family and the recommendation to avoid irritation. Conrad purposefully maintains this ambiguity regarding the cause of mental illness as the narrative progresses, making both Marlow and the reader uneasy. Later, on an overland trek during which he is exposed to the sun and to many sources of irritation, Marlow wryly recalls the physician's words: "I remembered the old doctor,—'It would be interesting for science to watch the mental changes of individuals, on the spot.' I felt I was becoming scientifically interesting" (122). The nascent madness Marlow detects within himself prefigures its full development in the object of his journey, Mr.

Kurtz, another "emissary of light" who succumbs to madness provoked by his time spent in the wilderness (113). Marlow overhears the manager of the Eldorado Exploring Expedition mention Kurtz as an impediment to his plans in the area, but another man notes that "the climate may do away with this difficulty" (134). Even Kurtz, an exemplar of the colonial effort, is endangered by the African environment. What is it about the climate and the vegetation that Conrad, like so many of his contemporaries, feared would cause madness? Why did he need "to benefit from the European climate for as long as possible" (Letter)? The answer can be found in Conrad's depiction of the wilderness.

In *Heart of Darkness*, the tropical forest is portrayed as a place of timelessness and referred to as the "primeval earth" (176). For Marlow, it is a prehistoric realm untouched by the currents of time because there are no visible signs of human creations such as streets, buildings, or monuments to human progress:

> Going up that river was like traveling back to the earliest beginnings of the world, when vegetation rioted on the earth and the big trees were kings. An empty stream, a great silence, an impenetrable forest.... The broadening waters flowed through a mob of wooded islands; you lost your way on that river as you would in a desert, and butted all day long against shoals, trying to find the channel, till you thought yourself bewitched and cut off forever from everything you had known once—somewhere—far away—in another existence perhaps. There were moments when one's past came back to one, as it will sometimes when you have not a moment to spare to yourself; but it came in the shape of an unrestful and noisy dream, remembered with wonder amongst the overwhelming realities of this strange world of plants, and water, and silence.... It was the stillness of an implacable force brooding over an inscrutable intention. (136–37)

Despite Conrad's modernist, impressionistic style, the union of the depiction of the environment and the protagonist's emotions is a literary motif common to Romanticism. Marlow's fear of being physically lost mirrors his experience of metaphorically losing his way. Conrad envisions the trip upriver as a journey through universal time and personal experience; Marlow calls Kurtz's station "the farthest point of navigation and the culminating point of my experience. It seemed somehow to throw a kind of light on everything about me—and into my thoughts" (107). While Marlow hints at the personal revelation he will achieve at the aptly named Inner Station, the wilderness itself remains empty, silent, and impenetrable: "There it is before you—smiling, frowning, inviting, grand, mean, insipid, or savage, and always mute with an air of whispering, Come and find out" (114). Faced with the emptiness and impenetrability of the forest, Marlow projects on it his own fears, desires, and memories. Thus, his "past comes back" to him in the form of an "unrestful and noisy dream" (137). The tropical environment is a void the protagonist's imagination is free to fill with his own fantasies, fears, and darkest secrets, which include a tendency toward irrational behavior.[25] The vegetation itself serves as a distancing mechanism that separates Marlow's civilized persona from his savage desires. Veiled behind the curtain of plant life, his inner secrets are suddenly made foreign, monolithic, and incomprehensible to him. These fears and desires are reflected back at him in distorted and uncanny forms when he peers into the forest. Indeed, the shock of sublimated self-recognition destabilizes Marlow's sense of self and makes him question his past, his sanity, his very humanity. Marlow marvels at the dimensions of his repressed desires and instincts, which are termed "monstrous passions" (173): "All this [forest and river] was great, expectant, mute. . . . I wondered whether the stillness on the face of the immensity looking at us two were meant as an appeal or as a menace. What were we who had strayed in here? Could we handle that dumb thing, or would it handle us? I felt how big, how confoundedly big, was that thing that couldn't talk, and perhaps was deaf as well" (129). The "dumb thing" that presents itself to Marlow as "an appeal and as a menace" overtakes several characters in the tropics, including Kurtz and the suicidal Swede. Their tendency toward irrational self-destruction is carefully isolated from Marlow's psyche and then silenced by being displaced onto the plant life of the Congo. The incomprehensibility of the jungle extends to the native population that, as discussed earlier in this chapter, was frequently portrayed as inherently insane in psychological assessments made by colonial doctors. The insanity Marlow feels within himself, as well as the specters of mental illness embodied in Kurtz and the Swede, are projected onto the Africans, who are explicitly compared to lunatics:

> The steamer toiled along slowly on the edge of a black and incomprehensible frenzy. The prehistoric man was cursing us, praying to us, welcoming us—who could tell? We were cut off from the comprehension of our surroundings; we glided past like phantoms, wondering and secretly appalled, as sane men would be before an enthusiastic outbreak in a madhouse. We could not understand, because we were too far and could not remember, because we were traveling in the night of the first ages, of those ages that are gone, leaving hardly a sign—and no memories. (139)

The issue of insanity resurfaces here in the form of a deliberate and significant metaphor: the subdued Europeans are confronted by "enthusiastic" madmen. Marlow resists the recognition of his own madness displaced onto the "natives" because he has subconsciously relegated it, and the Africans, to the prehistory of civilization (115). In "Victorian Anthropology," A. James Johnson demonstrates that in his depiction of Africans, Conrad "appropriates the non-European present and inserts it into the European past" (121). Like the foliage, Africans are incomprehensible because Marlow distances them from Europeans culturally, geographically, and temporally. Conrad's elision of the natural environment and the Congolese population demonstrate his participation in the scientific racism of the era. Chinua Achebe was the first to decry Conrad's overt racism in this collapsing of Africans and the vegetation (784–86). As Jean and John Comaroff note: "The vocabulary of natural science was to formalize an existing European association of dark continents with black bodies and dim minds. Comparative anatomical scales and schemes presented the African as the human obverse of the European, the 'link' between man and animal" (35). This supposedly scientific conclusion enables Marlow to associate African humans with African vegetation and thereby distance himself—to be "secretly appalled" by his own fantasies as projected on the Congolese. This projection is incontrovertibly demeaning and bestializing. I disagree with McClure's conclusion in his otherwise excellent book *Kipling and Conrad: The Colonial Fiction*—namely, with McClure's statements that Marlow's descriptions of the Africans are made with "a minimum of prejudice" (135) and that they are treated with "sympathy and respect" (137). Marlow does prevent the European "pilgrims" from mercilessly gunning down many Congolese on the river banks by blowing the boat's whistle, but that does not exonerate him from conflating them with the mute, threatening vegetation, or from his depiction of the helmsman as a dog dressed in men's clothing (140). While Conrad is ahead of his time in attributing madness and savagery to Europeans, he nevertheless denigrates the Africans by presenting them as exemplars of the depths to which a white European can sink.

Some scholars attempt to absolve Conrad from charges of racism by attributing the depictions of Africans to Marlow rather than Conrad (for example, see Hampson 22), but the omniscient narrator in "An Outpost of Progress" also attributes mental unraveling to both African peoples and their surroundings: "The contact with pure unmitigated savagery, with primitive nature and primitive man brings sudden and profound trouble into the heart" (33). This passage from the earlier story is echoed by Kurtz's fate in *Heart of Darkness*. The similarities make it clear that Conrad himself seeks to forward the idea that white men are as brutal as those they colonize when they are stripped of the division between sane and insane afforded them by hierarchical systems of language and Western civilization. For example, as the steamer in *Heart of Darkness* continues through the "night of first ages" (139), the distinction between natives and Europeans becomes blurred. Bereft of a social apparatus that distinguishes colonizer from colonized, Marlow feels an unsettling identification with the Africans and therefore with his own suddenly uncanny desires that he has transferred onto them:

> No, they were not inhuman. Well, you know, that was the worst of it—this suspicion of their not being inhuman. It would come slowly to one. They howled, they leaped, and spun, and made horrid faces; but what thrilled you was just the thought of their humanity—like yours—the thought of your remote kinship with this wild and passionate uproar. Ugly. Yes, it was ugly enough; but if you were man enough you would

admit to yourself that there was in you just the faintest trace of a response to the terrible frankness of that noise, a dim suspicion of there being a meaning in it which you—you so remote from the night of first ages—could comprehend. (139)[26]

Marlow's struggle to dominate this temptation to associate himself with "enthusiastic" madmen rather than the "sane" Europeans derives its urgency from the growing specter of Kurtz's madness: "An appeal to me in the fiendish row—is there? Very well; I hear; I admit, but I have a voice too, and for good or evil mine is the speech that cannot be silenced" (139–40). It is significant that Marlow couches his resistance to "going native" in terms of speech and silence because in doing so he asserts the dominance of imperial discourse over the mute vegetation. In the process, he silences the African voices in the novel. Achebe pointedly accuses Conrad of prohibiting African self-expression in the narrative: "It is clearly not part of Conrad's purpose to confer language on the 'rudimentary souls' of Africa. They only 'exchanged short grunting phrases' even among themselves but mostly they were too busy with their frenzy." Achebe continues by declaring that "these instances . . . constitute some of his best assaults" (786). On an allegorical level, Marlow refuses to let the incomprehensible African milieu silence his own discourse of rationality, whereas it eventually silences Kurtz, the prime exemplar of madness in *Heart of Darkness*.

The Congolese on the banks of the river were not, of course, in a madhouse. Rather, they are incomprehensible to Marlow because he is ignorant of their language, as he admits: "We could not understand" (139). Yet by reducing African speech to mad ravings, Marlow asserts his superiority over the Congolese who watch the riverboat pass by, and he is therefore able to discount their opinions and justify the British legacy of slavery and colonialism. As Susan Sontag has stated, declaring that someone is mad enables the speaker to negate the validity of the madman's opinion and even his fundamental rights: "The perception that some people are crazy is part of the history of thought, and madness requires a historical definition. Madness means not making sense—means saying what doesn't have to be taken seriously. . . . A mad person is someone whose voice society doesn't want to listen to, whose behavior is intolerable, who ought to be suppressed" (liv). Conrad's presentation of the mute wilderness and the unintelligible Africans thus reflects the mental subjugation of the colonial subject and environment by European imperialism that Fanon condemned in *Black Skins, White Masks*.

Similarly, Kurtz's progression from eloquent European to silent madman demonstrates the impact of medical discourse about mental illness on Conrad's work. His madness is portrayed as an incommunicable experience that distances the mad from the sane by silencing them. This silence gives rise to Conrad's modernist narrative style, which privileges his famously impressionistic, nonsequential description over direct speech and the linear progression of time. I argue that

Conrad's modernism derives from Marlow's struggle to narrate the experience of madness, which has been triggered by Kurtz's foray into the wilderness. The colonial project thus serves as a tragic impetus for Conrad's aesthetic and literary innovations. In the novel, Kurtz represents the highest accomplishment of Western civilization. Conrad is careful to note that "all Europe contributed to the making of Kurtz" (154); the chief of the Inner Station has clearly benefited from the fruits of European culture: he is a painter, a writer, perhaps a musician. One of his adversaries describes him as "a prodigy ... an emissary of pity, and science, and progress, and devil knows what else" (127). Yet aside from this brief résumé of accomplishments, Marlow knows little about Kurtz except his renowned powers of elocution. Kurtz's salient feature is his voice, which links him to Marlow's portrayal of civilization in that Marlow believes that Kurtz's imperial voice, like his own, is "the voice that cannot be silenced" (140). Long before their actual encounter, Marlow sets up a dichotomy between the mute wilderness and the eloquent Kurtz:

> I became aware that that was exactly what I had been looking forward to—a talk with Kurtz. I made the strange discovery that I had never imagined him as doing, you know, but as discoursing. The man presented himself as a voice.... The point was in his being a gifted creature, and that of all his gifts the one that stood out preeminently, that carried with it a real sense of presence, was his ability to talk, his words—the gift of expression, the bewildering, the illuminating, the most exalted and the most contemptible, the pulsating stream of light, or the deceitful flow from the heart of an impenetrable darkness. (151–52)

Kurtz, the reader learns, holds sway over both Europeans and Africans because of his commanding powers of speech. His "pulsating stream of light" is used to forward the colonial project, while the "deceitful flow from the heart of an impenetrable darkness" foreshadows his ability to manipulate the native population in addition to the European community. The "deceitful flow" also indicates that Kurtz is able to communicate with the Congolese. To Marlow, his linguistic acclimatization is the ultimate betrayal of British values: in speaking the language of Africans, Kurtz has definitively "gone native."

Speech plays a central role in *Heart of Darkness* because it represents the ability to create a dominant narrative—to dictate history, to establish authority over others, and to direct their actions with the power of a voice. Kurtz is expected to go far both because he has been profitable in extracting ivory and because his voice connotes authority and leadership. A man calling himself Kurtz's cousin describes his power of eloquence to Marlow after the narrator's return to Europe: "But heavens! How that man could talk! He electrified large meetings.... He would have been a splendid leader of an extreme party" (181). Kurtz's power as a colonist is thus directly linked to his power of speech. His entire personality is constructed in direct opposition to the mute wilderness: "He was very little more than a voice" (153). The deepest paradox of the narrative lies in the fact that although Marlow attributes great importance to Kurtz's voice, the reader never hears this voice at its full strength. Instead, the reader receives only whispers, dying words, and reported speech. Like Marlow, the reader is "cut to the quick at the idea of having lost the inestimable privilege of listening to the gifted Kurtz" (152-3). As Marlow's steamer approaches Kurtz's Inner Station, the epicenter of his madness, Conrad gradually and purposefully reverses the dyads of Kurtz=voice and jungle=mute that he maintained in the first portion of the story. Kurtz, the pinnacle of European society, has been brought low—made degenerate—by the time he has spent in the tropics. He has engaged in "unspeakable rites" (155) generally considered to be a euphemism for cannibalism, the crowning rite of savagery that loomed large in European fears regarding Africans, even though it was rarely documented. In this way, Kurtz slowly becomes conflated not with eloquence and the colonial endeavor, but rather with the jungle, the madhouse, and the silence made evident in his inability to narrate his tropical experience to Marlow. The reader rarely hears Kurtz's voice because, on a metaphorical level, his madness has silenced his imperialist discourse; on a psychological level, he has ceded his self-control and eloquence to irrationality and silence.

How does Conrad silence Kurtz, while still making him the central figure in the story precisely because of the power of his voice? First, within the text, Marlow and other characters report his speech indirectly, often revealing only snippets of conversation and hearsay. Second, in several instances, Conrad himself excised Kurtz's direct speech from the manuscript, prior to the publication of *Heart of Darkness* in serial form. Both techniques—one intratextual, the other extratextual—serve to heighten the aura of silence that surrounds Kurtz's persona and isolate him from Marlow, the frame narrator, and ultimately the reader. They also constitute the defining characteristics of Conrad's modernism. The reader learns of Kurtz through a chain of distancing narrators. Indeed, all the information gathered about Kurtz is obtained in an oblique fashion: the frame narrator repeats Marlow's account of overhearing partial descriptions of Kurtz's actions and other people's opinions about him, specifically through the manager of a colonial enterprise, the ship captains, and the young harlequin figure. Marlow first hears about Kurtz through an account from the manager of the Eldorado Exploring Expedition. Marlow overhears him say that Kurtz had come close to returning to Central Station, but had inexplicably returned upriver alone. Marlow remarks: "I seemed to see Kurtz for the first time. It was a distinct glimpse: the dug-out, four paddling savages, and the lone white man turning his back suddenly on the headquarters, on relief, on thoughts of home—perhaps; setting his face towards the depths of the wilderness, towards his empty and desolate station. I did not know the motive.... His name, you understand, had not been pronounced once" (135). This report is the first inkling that Kurtz has abandoned the colonial project, turning his back on the Western world. The reader learns of this "distinct glimpse" of Kurtz fourth-hand, as the description of Kurtz passes from the expedition leader to Marlow, then to the frame narrator, and finally to the reader. For most of the story, Marlow's knowledge of Kurtz is mediated by other Europeans in the wilderness.

This first instance in which the mode of narration itself distances Marlow from Kurtz's actions and nascent madness is repeated and magnified throughout the text. For example, the young Russian harlequin figure who serves intermittently as Kurtz's companion and nurse is amazed by his elocutionary powers, but is himself unable to repeat any of Kurtz's actual speech, which frustrates Marlow. Marlow quotes the Russian's attempt to convey his experience—"We talked of everything. . . . I forgot there was such a thing as sleep. . . . He made me see things—things"—an effort that leaves the young man speechless again: "He threw his arms up" (161–62).

Again, the chain of narrators distances Kurtz not only from Marlow but also from the reader. Despite Kurtz's erratic behavior, the harlequin figure denies that Kurtz could be mad because of his speaking ability, thereby making explicit the inverse relationship between speech and insanity. When Marlow says of Kurtz, "He's mad," the Russian reacts strongly: "He protested indignantly. Mr. Kurtz couldn't be mad. If I had heard him talk, only two days ago, I wouldn't dare hint such at a thing" (163). In the present of the narrative, however, Kurtz has not yet spoken, and thus has not proved himself to be sane. Despite the emphasis placed on Kurtz's speech, he does not speak to Marlow except to whisper "I am glad" in reaction to Marlow's arrival. Kurtz's reticence indicates that he has merged with the "silence" of the impenetrable forest (137).

Even when Marlow is in the presence of Kurtz, Conrad carefully mutes the great speaker. The first time Marlow sees him, Kurtz is being carried on a stretcher. Although Marlow can see him talking and gesticulating, Kurtz's speech remains unheard by Marlow because of the distance, both literal and figurative, between them. Kurtz is further linked to savagery because he is accompanied by natives paying him tribute. They seem to speak for him, letting out a shrill, indecipherable cry. Not only is Kurtz silenced, his physical presence is also effaced. He is described as "an apparition," "an animated image of death," and a "shadow" (165) who speaks to the natives—in their own language, to convince them to let him go. Kurtz's presence and voice thus form the core around which Marlow constructs his tale, and yet those two very elements are remarkable precisely because of their absence. The center of the tale is therefore hollow—an impressive and carefully constructed vacuum.

The indirect transmission of Kurtz's speech is not the only distancing mechanism Conrad employs to increase the narrative gulf between his mad subject and his intra- and extratextual observers. Two elements within the text perform functions similar to the silencing of Kurtz's speech: Marlow's use of binoculars, and his encounter with Kurtz at the late-night ceremony near the station headquarters. Conrad creates this chasm between Kurtz and the other characters in the story with almost no intervening speech from Kurtz himself. In fact, in the few instances in which the station chief does speak, what he conveys is paradoxically the very incommunicability of his experience and of the self-knowledge he has gained in the forest.

The first instance of psychological distancing takes place when Marlow reaches Kurtz's Inner Station and feels an emotional as well as physical proximity to the station chief and his mental condition. He tries to peer into Kurtz's world both literally and metaphorically by gazing into his hut with his binoculars. Marlow observes Kurtz's station house which, because of the lenses, is "brought within reach of my hand, as it were" (164). He feels himself close to Kurtz, tempted to indulge in illicit desires: the consumption of human flesh, the abandonment of the colonial project, the turning away from rational society. The binoculars perform the essential function of allowing Marlow to come artificially close to Kurtz's madness while simultaneously maintaining his distance. It is here that Marlow encounters the most gruesome confirmation of Kurtz's madness, in the form of the shrunken heads of his enemies on stakes around the hut. Marlow first interprets these signs as a warning to other Africans—as Kurtz's means of establishing dominance, much as was done in early modern Europe to make evident a king's displeasure. But then Marlow realizes with horror that all the heads are facing inward, serving as emblems—a celebration—of brutality in and of itself. Marlow's understanding of Kurtz's insanity is made possible by this glimpse into Kurtz's abode and psyche. The sudden proximity of the concrete result of irrational savagery causes Marlow to drop the glasses from his face, thereby reestablishing his psychological distance from Kurtz. The sighting of the heads creates a divide between Marlow and the object of his voyage: by defining Kurtz as insane and separating himself from him, Marlow can maintain his sanity.

There is an additional situation in which Marlow gauges his mental distance from Kurtz's madness. The chasm between Marlow and Kurtz—between sanity and insanity—shrinks when Marlow goes in search of Kurtz after he has escaped from his bed. Out in the wilderness, devoid of any vestige of Western civilization, Marlow feels the attraction of converting to Kurtz's position. He is tempted to "go native" because he associates the drumbeat of the natives with the beating of his heart, and is "pleased at its calm regularity" (172). And yet Marlow struggles to maintain his psychological distance when he confronts Kurtz in a field near the ceremony taking place. Marlow urges him to return, telling him, "'You will be lost … utterly lost.' … I tried to break the spell—the heavy, mute spell of the wilderness—that seemed to draw him to its pitiless breast by the awakening of forgotten and brutal instincts, by the memory of gratified and monstrous passions" (173; ellipses in the original). According to Marlow, "the heavy, mute spell of the wilderness" has silenced Kurtz because it has broken down the barrier between social decorum—often referred to as "restraint"—and Kurtz's "monstrous passions." In literary terms, the wilderness is anthropomorphic: it actively transforms Kurtz. In medical terms, he suffers from what Manson called "degenerative changes" (xii). "The heavy, mute spell of the wilderness" is therefore a vision of the climate constructed and bequeathed by European scientists and doctors of the era. When Marlow summarizes the perceived ability of the tropics to change men into its own form, Kurtz's body takes on the characteristics of the natural environment: "The wilderness had patted him on the head, and, behold, it was like a ball, an ivory ball; it had caressed him, and—lo!—he had withered; it had taken him, loved him, embraced him, got into his veins, consumed his flesh, and sealed his soul to its own by the inconceivable ceremonies of some devilish imitation. He was its spoiled and pampered favourite" (153). This description of Kurtz's transformation from colonial officer to savage madman illustrates both the doctor's vague diagnosis that "the changes take place inside" and the role the wilderness plays in the onset of madness. The effect of the tropics on Kurtz's psyche is described as if it were a virus that had "got into his veins" and "consumed his flesh," thus using an explicitly medical metaphor to describe the effect of the wilderness on a European. Kurtz has been silenced, withered by his own madness. Of all Kurtz's symptoms of madness, his silence is the most important because it forms part of a larger trend of the treatment of madness in Western civilization—namely, the effacement of the subjectivity of the mad by the dominant discourse of rationality, as evidenced by the rise of psychiatry. The elimination of Kurtz's speech and the consequent erasure of his point of view have ramifications in the very way in which Conrad tells his tale. Thus, although Conrad deliberately silences his protagonist, his madness nonetheless permeates the very narrative structure of the work.

The subjugation of the madman by Western society has been studied in depth by Michel Foucault, and its impact on literature by Shoshana Felman. Madness, defined loosely by Felman as "nonsense, alienating strangeness, a transgressive excess, an illusion, a delusion, a disease," has long been sought out and silenced by the sane in the Western world because it presents a challenge to the cultural dominion of rational thought (Felman, *Writing* 2).[27] Indeed, it is only by identifying and partitioning madness that society can define itself, as Foucault notes in his *History of Madness:* "The Reason-Unreason relation constitutes for Western culture one of the dimensions of its originality" (xxix). Foucault sets up a dichotomy between the classical era, in which madness was an "undifferentiated experience" (xxvii) inseparable from sanity, and an originative "caesura that establishes the distance between reason and non-reason … the grip in which reason holds non-reason to extract its truth as madness, fault, or sickness" (xxviii).[28] In 1963, Jacques Derrida criticized Foucault for engaging in the very behavior he criticized: that of silencing the mad through his writing. Derrida argued that true madness could only be expressed through literature.[29]

Foucault views the prescientific period as one in which reason and nonreason are indistinguishable and fluid. This notion, nostalgically idealized by Foucault, finds a darker and more ominous counterpart in Conrad's portrayal of Africans, who live in what Conrad calls the "night of first ages" (*Heart* 139). Conrad emphasizes the utter lack of communication between the scientifically minded Europeans on the steamer and the indigenous population, whom he, like Hegel, portrays as occupying a time outside of history. As I noted in the Introduction, this relegation of Africans to a supposedly less advanced moment in human history provided a philosophical basis for racism and enabled the justification of colonialism and slavery. Foucault's description of the chasm between the mad and the sane in the age of reason is similar to Conrad's schism between Africans and Europeans with one important exception: while Foucault has been criticized for romanticizing the plight of the mad by presenting mental illness as deviant behavior that does little more than irritate bourgeois society, for Conrad madness is a more sinister and gruesome degeneracy that is fascinating precisely because it presents a grave challenge to the established order.[30]

Foucault further links the silencing of the mad to the rise of psychiatry, which is present in burgeoning form in *Heart of Darkness*. Shoshana Felman follows the argument laid out by Foucault to give a succinct theory of the history of madness in the modern world:

> Psychiatry derives, according to Foucault, from the age of reason, the age that casts madness outside civilization by physically confining it, by locking it up within the walls of mental institutions, later to be transformed into the psychiatric clinic, endowed with the authority of an objectifying knowledge. The constitution of this knowledge subjects the mad to the clinician's power and to the clinician's scientific definitions. The mentally disturbed are thereby robbed of subjectivity: they are observed and talked about, but their own discourse is invalidated, their own experience is annulled and voided. Madness becomes the symptom of a culture, but the symptom is incorporated in a silenced body (and a silenced soul) whose suffering cannot say itself. (*Writing* 3)

Conrad makes Kurtz's madness a symptom of a diseased, corrupt Western culture that shows itself to be no better than those it colonized. Accordingly, it is Kurtz's body and speech that are silenced by the text, as I have shown. My reading of Kurtz's madness is a significant departure from the customary interpretation of the "silenced body" as that of a female protagonist silenced by a patriarchal medical establishment. While much late twentieth-century scholarship, led by Elaine Showalter's, has focused on insanity as a "female malady," I concur with scholars such as John Griffith and Valerie Pedlar, the latter stating that "the representation of insanity in men is too various ... to be confined within the rhetoric of feminism" (22). In *Heart of Darkness*, medical discourse silences those who behave in an aberrant fashion, including white men. Simply put, those who depart from traditional colonial practices are construed as deviant. The hegemony of scientific discourse is evidenced in *Heart of Darkness* by the importance of the doctor: as described earlier in this chapter, he states that every physician should be a bit of an "alienist," he measures Marlow's head, and he seeks to analyze Marlow by gathering information about his past. In effect, the doctor subjects Marlow to the power of science by reducing him to a specimen devoid of personal agency. Marlow's conversation with the doctor is peppered with instances in which the doctor disregards Marlow's concerns and assertions that he is not a typical Englishman; in short, he invalidates Marlow's experience in favor of medical opinion and scientific certainty.

The best example of this "theft of subjectivity" of the mad, however, is to be found in the question of language within *Heart of Darkness*. This is clear both in Kurtz's lack of speech that has been studied here, and also in the editing process through which Conrad himself silenced the protagonist of his tale. Kurtz literally becomes Felman's "silenced body," unable express his own suffering or his own insights. The interaction between Marlow and Kurtz exemplifies the gulf that has grown between the mad and the sane since the medicalization of mental illness and the rise of psychiatry. Foucault stresses the lack of intelligibility between the sane and the mad:

> There is no common language: or rather, it no longer exists; the constitution of madness as a mental illness, at the end of the eighteenth century, bears witness to a rupture in a dialogue, gives the separation as already enacted, and expels from the memory all those imperfect words, of no fixed syntax, spoken falteringly in which the exchange between madness and reason was carried out. The language of psychiatry, which is a monologue by reason *about* madness, has been established only on the basis of such a silence. (*History of Madness* xxviii)

Similarly, the dialogue with Kurtz that Marlow has been looking forward to is rendered impossible by the dominant "monologue by reason about madness" spurred by the rise of psychiatry. An examination Conrad's artistic process reveals his carefully vague construction of Kurtz. Conrad's revisions to his manuscript frequently strove to obscure meaning rather than clarify it. Conrad removed some information about Kurtz from his first draft to render him silent and maintain reason's dominance over madness.

There are two surviving drafts of *Heart of Darkness* that were created prior to its publication in serial form; both are incomplete. The first is the manuscript, originally entitled "The Heart of Darkness," that Conrad completed in early February 1899.[31] The second is the typescript made from the manuscript by Conrad's wife, Jessie.[32] While the extant typescript reveals much about Conrad's editing style, it is missing Marlow's interactions with and descriptions of Kurtz, and is therefore less valuable to this study than the manuscript. The overall effect of Conrad's edits to the typescript is one of tightening up the narrative pace, as mentioned by Marion Michael and Wilkes Berry in their thorough essay on the document. This tightening is accomplished by the excision of descriptive passages and sentences, which ultimately enhances the impressionistic and vague aura of the story.

Conrad's handwritten edits to the manuscript indicate his careful obfuscation of meaning in Kurtz's speech and the passages that describe him. While most of the text excised by Conrad appears later in the narrative in a similar form, there are a few instances in which he alters the meaning of Kurtz's words or removes information about him altogether. For example, in the manuscript, Kurtz cries out at the passing vegetation, "Oh! But I will make you serve my ends!," but in the serial publication, the declaration was changed to the much more ambiguous "Oh, but I will wring your heart yet!"[33] In both cases, the "you" evoked by Kurtz is ambiguous; it could refer to the Africans with whom he has been living, the solitary female described by Marlow, or the wilderness itself. Whatever the referent, the alteration to the text removes Kurtz's expressed intention to manipulate his surroundings (the "you") and replaces it with his desire to annihilate or wring the heart of his adversary. While the first version complements the portrayal of Kurtz as a colonial officer determined to make the African environment submit to his will, the second is more in line with his desperate, scrawled instruction, "Exterminate the brutes!," which is found at the end of the treatise Marlow surrenders to company officials after Kurtz's death (Conrad, *Heart* 155). In a similar instance, the serial reports Kurtz as having murmured, "Live rightly, die, die . . ." shortly before expiring, while the manuscript renders this vague phrase more concretely by having Kurtz mutter the word "nobly."[34] Kurtz's determination to "die nobly," which could be construed as a sane desire to give meaning to one's life, is effaced and replaced with an obfuscation left open to interpretation by both Marlow and the reader. It is impossible to tell if these two changes were suggested by editors or Conrad himself, but in either case the overall impact of these alterations is to make Kurtz's meaning inscrutable, furthering the narrative distance Conrad has created between the sane Marlow and the mad Kurtz.

The most important erasure of Kurtz was undoubtedly committed by Conrad himself, in the manuscript. He deletes an entire passage on page 280 in which Marlow states that he burned a journal that Kurtz had kept during his time in the wilderness, keeping only a few letters written by a woman, and a photograph, presumably of Kurtz's Intended. Instead, in the published version of the novel, Marlow says only, "Thus I was left at last with a slim packet of letters and the girl's portrait" (181). By eliminating the diary altogether, Conrad denies Kurtz the exposition of his inner life and reduces his written creations to a collection of letters and a pro-colonial treatise. The notion that Kurtz had kept a diary would have intimated that he had retained an inner life—that he had continued to write and think in a manner suited to the logical progression of time, as most diaries are written in chronological order. In later tropical adventure novels, such as *The Lost World*, *The Lost Steps*, and *The Vortex*, diaries play key roles in establishing the protagonists' points of view. In removing the only evidence of Kurtz's inner monologue, rather than allowing the reader to witness Marlow doing so, Conrad makes it seem that Kurtz really did not have any logical thoughts that could be expressed in writing. It leaves no textual evidence for Marlow to interpret in the same way he attempts to decipher the Russian notes the harlequin figure leaves behind in his copy of *An Inquiry into Some Points of Seamanship*. In deleting any mention of the diary, Conrad strengthens Marlow's perception of Kurtz as a man with no discourse, thereby silencing Kurtz's madness and reaffirming the dominance of the sane over the expression of the insane. It also gives greater impact to Marlow's statement that "all that had been Kurtz's had passed out of my hands: his soul, his body, his station, his plans, his ivory, his career. There remained only his memory and his Intended" (181). The cumulative effect of the manuscript alterations amplifies the narrative distancing Conrad maintains throughout the work, ultimately making Kurtz's actions and words indecipherable to Marlow and the frame narrator, and thereby effacing Kurtz's mad subjectivity.

In *Heart of Darkness*, madness, like lawlessness, is contained in civilization but runs rampant in the wilderness because it is not regulated by judges, doctors, or any other figure of authority. Bereft of civilization and isolated from other Europeans, Kurtz has regressed to Foucault's undifferentiated state between sanity and madness. If Kurtz had been in Europe, his degeneracy could have been contained or even prevented—he was, after all, a guiding light of the imperial movement—but in the wilderness it runs unchecked and is exacerbated by the lack of societal regulation. Marlow highlights this difference when addressing the frame narrator:

> You can't understand. How could you?—with solid pavement under your feet ... stepping delicately between the butcher and the police-man, in the holy terror of scandal and gallows and lunatic asylums—how can you imagine what particular region of the first ages a man's untrammeled feet may take him into by way of solitude—utter solitude without a policeman—by the way of silence—utter silence, where no warning voice of a kind neighbor can be heard whispering of public opinion? (154)

Within the confines of civilization—embodied in the threat of the gallows, gossip, and, most important, the lunatic asylum—madness can be distinguished and contained. Yet in the "utter silence" or absence of such authority, degeneration comes swiftly to colonial residents. Foucault similarly stresses the importance of the rise of the asylum because it is a form of "social segregation ... that guaranteed bourgeois morality a *de facto* universality, enabling it to impose itself as a system of law over all forms of alienation" (*History of Madness* 495). While in Europe the mad are strictly separated from the sane and bourgeois conformity is upheld, in Africa no such delineations are possible. Given the lack of an institution or mechanism by which Kurtz's madness can be silenced, Conrad's very prose moves in to fill that void. His editing of the manuscript and his prose style create an imprisoning structure—a madhouse—in which Kurtz's discourse can be physically restricted and muted. Kurtz is effectively silenced, yet his madness remains as a specter, forming the vacant center of a work that like Kurtz himself is described as "hollow at the core" (165).

Although Marlow is horrified by Kurtz's insanity, he also recognizes that the Inner Station chief has gained access to a deeper truth of self-knowledge. Indeed, Kurtz's speech—excised by Conrad but still present in the manuscript—hints at the revelations concomitant with madness but inaccessible to sane men. The uncivilized desires displaced onto the tropics have collapsed onto Kurtz, driving him mad but also imbuing him with newfound introspection: Marlow specu-lates that the wilderness "had whispered to him things about himself which he did not know, things of which he had no conception till he took counsel with this great solitude—and the whisper had proved irresistibly fascinating" (164). Conrad carefully maintains the delicate balance between the internal and exter-nal causes of mental illness. While the source of madness—those "things about himself which he did not know"—is internal, its onset is provoked by climate and distance from civilization. The tropical forest signifies the furthest distance from the metropolis; the voyage into the wilderness serves as the catalyst for the release of otherwise forbidden instincts; irrationality flourishes; and a commu-nion with "forgotten and brutal instincts" (173) is achieved. Indeed, solitude and isolation are key factors in degeneration: "[Kurtz's] soul was mad. Being alone in the wilderness, it had looked within itself, and, by heavens! I tell you, it had gone mad" (174). It is this struggle within each individual between the natural tendency toward irrationality and the dicta of "civilized" behavior that makes Marlow feel as if he has entered "some lightless region of subtle horrors, where pure, uncomplicated savagery was a positive relief, being something that had a right to exist—obviously—in the sunshine" (165). This sense of unease arises from the coexistence of irrationality and sanity in every human being. Foucault also sees madness as the vehicle through which "primitive savagery" (what Con-rad similarly calls "uncomplicated savagery") and a negation of the notion of progress can challenge the dominant discourse of rationality: "Does [madness] not utter to those who can hear them, like Nietzsche and Artaud, the scarcely audible words of classical unreason, where all was nothingness and night, but now amplified into screams and fury? Giving them for the first time expression, a *droit de cite* [right of abode], and a grasp on Western culture, a point from which all contestation becomes possible, as well as the contestation of all things? By restoring them to their primitive savagery?" (*History of Madness* 532). This notion of the resurgence of "primitive savagery" is extolled by Foucault as a desirable act of rebellion. In Conrad, however, the so-called primitive is given darker overtones because of the theory of degeneration and its influence on the late Victorian cultural consciousness. As Griffith notes: "At the centre of the study of Kurtz's degeneration, and of the theme of degeneracy generally in Victorian culture, lay the idea that man carries with him residual primitivism which may break out at any time" (228). This "residual primitivism" is unlocked by the hot, fetid climate, according to the logic of degeneration in the tropics. It has overtaken Kurtz, rendering him speechless, indistinguishable from the wilderness, and struck down by fever and irrationality. On the rare occasions when Kurtz does speak, Marlow cannot translate their significance into any meaningful statement for the reader; Kurtz remains a silent mystery.

Just before death, Kurtz attains a "supreme moment of complete knowledge." According to Marlow, "He cried in a whisper at some image, at some vision,—he cried out twice, a cry that was no more than a breath—'The horror! The horror!'" (177–78). These are perhaps the most famous and most heavily glossed words in Conrad's oeuvre. In light of what I have argued, the words "the horror" enigmatically allude to the incommunicable self-knowledge Kurtz has gained in his madness. What is lost through Kurtz's silence and the chain of distancing narrators is his own account of the process of "going native"—of returning to the beginning of time, when madness and sanity were undifferentiated. The central theme—Kurtz's transformation from sane to mad—is unspeakable, and *Heart of Darkness* remains an impression of madness rather than a clear description of it. This disjuncture between language and madness is the most important trope in the work, as it affects both the form and content of the story. Peter Brooks has noted that Kurtz's last words

> appear as minimal language, language on the verge of reversion to savagery, on the verge of a fall from language. That Kurtz's experience in the heart of darkness should represent and be represented by a fall from language does not surprise us: this belongs to the very logic of the heart of darkness, which is consistently characterized as unspeakable....What stands at the heart of darkness—at the journey's end and at the core of this tale—is unsayable, extralinguistic. (250–51)

Heart of Darkness is often read as a modernist work because it "engages the very motive of narrative in its tale" (Brooks 238) and because it highlights the inability to communicate one individual's experience to any other. Conrad's fragmentary imagery, lack of a chronological progression of narrative events, and allusive language (in sentences such as "it was the stillness of an implacable force brooding over an inscrutable intention" [137]) all contribute to the intentional opacity of the work. Conrad's literary style is thus a product of both his genius and his struggle to narrate the unnarratable. Through an examination of the presentation of madness in Conrad, it becomes clear that medically inspired theories of madness are responsible for the modernist struggle for narration in *Heart of Darkness*.

In sum, what Brooks and other analysts of Conrad's modernism have missed is the connection between this unnarratability and Kurtz's madness. In fact, there is a definite, causal link between the climate, madness, and the modernist impossibility of narration that makes up the heart of darkness in Conrad's work. Conrad's impressionistic writing style has been hailed as modernist, yet I argue that form and content are connected here. Conrad writes in his most circumspect fashion—a marker of literary modernism—about the contact that Marlow has with Kurtz directly. For Marlow, Kurtz comes to represent the outcome of time spent in Africa—mental and physical sickness, and degeneration—and yet, as he regresses, Kurtz gains an incommunicable secret of self-knowledge that others cannot attain. The influence of medical practices on Conrad's writing style—specifically the isolating and silencing of irrational speech by the theft of subjectivity of the mad—explains why Kurtz is described through circumlocutions, and why his speech is almost always reported indirectly. Thus, the modernism of *Heart of Darkness* is predicated on its setting in the tropics; without the infectious, unrestrained atmosphere in which irrationality flourishes, Kurtz's mad speech would not need to be excised and silenced, and the narrative technique now described as modernist would not have been necessary.

Kurtz is not the only European who finds himself unable to express his transformation in the forest. Like Kurtz before him, Marlow feels the difficulty of narrating the story of his own encounter with the madman:

> [Kurtz] was just a word for me. I did not see the man in the name any more than you do. Do you see him? Do you see the story? Do you see anything? It seems to me I am trying to tell you a dream—making a vain attempt, because no relation of a dream can convey the dream-sensation, that commingling of absurdity, surprise, and bewilderment in a tremor of struggling revolt, that notion of being captured by the incredible which is of course the very essence of dreams. . . . No, it is impossible; it is impossible to convey the life-sensation of any given epoch of one's existence,—that which makes its truth, its meaning—its subtle and penetrating essence. It is impossible. We live, as we dream, alone. (129)

The narrative structure of the work thus takes on the form of concentric circles around a core of unnarratability: Kurtz cannot communicate his knowledge gained in madness to Marlow, Marlow cannot communicate what he knows to the frame narrator, and Conrad cannot express what he sees as the essence of the wilderness to the reader. This inability to communicate is profoundly isolating: "We live, as we dream, alone." Despite Marlow's attempt, the jungle remains a monolithic, unnarratable space—an indecipherable experience for the European protagonist. In this sense, *Heart of Darkness* is the narrative of a failure, as are all the novels examined in this book.

While the protagonists of the tropical narratives studied here all claim to be driven to madness and disease by the wilderness, it becomes clear that it is not the tropics alone that provoke sickness and irrational behavior, but rather that this tendency toward the uncivilized, the homicidal, and the insane stems from the depths of human nature, and is only unleashed by the physical environment. In short, because of its definitive location outside the confines of civilization, the jungle becomes an amalgamation of European fears and fantasies of the tropical climate and its inhabitants. It is a palimpsest on which European writers can inscribe and to which they can attribute the destructive, irrational instincts of human nature. The portrait of the tropics as a realm in which degeneration and insanity flourish both demonstrates the impact of popular medical discourse on Conrad and directly contributes to the development of his modernist style.

The impact of *Heart of Darkness* on later narratives set in the tropics is difficult to exaggerate. The depiction of the tropical climate as a source of death, disease, and madness resonates throughout novels written in a variety of languages. As I will show in Chapter 2, André Malraux explicitly mentions *Heart of Darkness* as an inspiration for his river voyage in Cambodia. Conrad's legacy is particularly noticeable in a work by another Anglophone modernist writer: Virginia Woolf. While the writings of Woolf and Conrad do not initially appear to share stylistic or thematic elements, Woolf's portrait of European madness and disease in the tropics reveals Conrad's impact on later tropical narratives.

Woolf's first novel, *The Voyage Out* (1915), is set in Brazil, a fashionably exotic vacation locale for upper-class British citizens at the turn of the twentieth century. Its characters go about assiduously re-creating the England they have left behind: in the colonial hotel from which they rarely stray, the guests partake in teatime, fancy dress balls, and games of whist. The novel's twenty-four-year-old heroine, the ingenue Rachel Vinrace, leaves the unnamed outpost only once during her stay of several months. Accompanied by her suitor, Terence Hewett, and a party of other hotel guests, Rachel ventures up the river adjacent to the hotel and into the Brazilian wilderness. The group agrees to embark on the five-day voyage upriver to a small village only after much discussion of the lack of bathing facilities and the need for "nice canned vegetables, fur cloaks, and insect powder" (328). While *The Voyage Out* is not a quest narrative like the other novels examined in this book, it nevertheless illustrates the complex interaction between Western protagonists and foreign climates. Woolf employs several tropes European writers often used to portray the wilderness in the early twentieth century. As in Conrad, the wilderness is primordial, removed from societal constraints, and sickening to Westerners. Woolf describes the unnamed river traveled by the protagonists in a manner similar to Conrad's "night of first ages":

> Since the time of Elizabeth very few people had seen the river, and nothing had been done to change its appearance from what it was to the eyes of the Elizabethan voyagers. The time of Elizabeth was only distant from the present time by a moment of space compared with the ages which had passed since the water had run between those banks, and the green thickets swarmed there, and the small trees had grown to huge

wrinkled trees in solitude. Changing only with the change of the sun and the clouds, the waving green mass had stood there for century after century, and the water had run between its banks ceaselessly, sometimes washing away earth and sometimes the branches of trees, while in other parts of the world one town had risen on the ruins of another town, and the men in the towns had become more and more articulate and unlike each other. (335)

The narrator's perspective in this passage—namely, the explicit use of Elizabethan England as a critical vantage point—reveals exactly why the wilderness remains inscrutable to European characters in works set in the tropics. In the novel, the physical environment displays no evidence of human activity and thus cannot be placed within the European conception of history. As Woolf and Conrad demonstrate, when viewed against the backdrop of linear concepts of the passage of time and the notion of well-documented progress, the tropical landscape's constancy of appearance and lack of a written historical record transform the forest into an immutable, untenable, unknowable place in which the Western apprehension of the world can find no purchase.

The undomesticated forest plays a significant role as a catalyst for action in Woolf's novel: it is the site where the otherwise prim English men and women are freed from societal constraint and may freely express themselves, in this case by proclaiming their love. While British customs are scrupulously observed in the colonial hotel, certain liberties are permitted away from the lodgings. As a result, several couples become engaged during short jaunts out of doors. Terence proposes to Rachel in the woods, one of the few places in which walking together unaccompanied by a chaperone is deemed socially acceptable. As is the case in many novels set in the tropics, the protagonists' emotions are reflected in the environment that surrounds them. Just after Rachel and Terence haltingly communicate their love for each other, she associates her feelings with the river: "'Terrible—terrible,' she murmured after another pause, but in saying this she was thinking as much of the persistent churning of the water as of her own feeling. On and on it went in the distance, the senseless and cruel churning of the water" (344). The environment thus becomes a screen on which Rachel's inner life is projected. The parallel between a protagonist's emotions and surroundings is clearly a holdover from nineteenth-century naturalism, but here it becomes not merely a trope but also a driving force of many tropical novels: the protagonist's psyche gradually becomes indistinguishable from his or her wildly fertile surroundings. Indeed, they threaten to overpower the dictates of social decorum. Like Conrad, Woolf creates a novelistic jungle in which the untamed, fetid, pathological wilderness infuses the protagonists' minds with similar qualities.

Rachel is not the only character whose mental state is affected by her environs. The young Oxford scholar St. John Hirst links the wilderness to the possibility of insanity, as seen in the epigraph to this chapter: "I should go mad if I lived here—

raving mad" (348). The notion that one's environment can provoke mental disease is not an original invention of Woolf's. Rather, it was initiated by the spread of European colonialism and reached its apex around the time of *Heart of Darkness*.

Only the influence of centuries of medical opinion regarding the dangers of warm climates for Europeans explains why Woolf, usually so sardonically critical of British anxieties in general, portrays the tropics as a mysterious breeding ground for physical and mental disease that is particularly dangerous for her heroine. In an ironic twist, the locus of Rachel's happiness also becomes the cause of her death. Shortly after her engagement to Terence, she is stricken with fever and dies within one week of her first symptom. It is widely believed that Rachel contracted her illness while away from the hotel. Woolf relays hotel guest Arthur Venning's smug admonishment: "'It was a foolish thing to do—to go up that river.' He shook his head. 'They should have known better. You can't expect Englishwomen to stand roughing it as the natives do who've been acclimatized'" (456). This amateur diagnosis of the protagonist's death echoes to perfection the prevailing expert medical opinions of the day, as indicated by Manson's declaration that "the natives of tropical countries are not injuriously affected … by the climates they live in" (xii). The expatriate society's assumptions about the environment, the indigenous population, and the English constitution are shaped by the medical literature of the day, and reflected in Rachel's lamentable, preventable illness.

Woolf's novel thus dramatizes the Western myths of tropical nature that originate in medical writings, reach their zenith in Conrad's work, and become commonplace in the other novels discussed in this book—that of the wilderness as a monolithic, incomprehensible, diseased space apparently untouched by written human history. The tropical forest is no longer merely a proliferation of vegetation devoid of man-made architecture. Instead, in these novels, it is a vessel for the unknown, the base, the repressed, and the illogical elements of humanity. It ceases to be a physical place and is transformed instead into a literary creation. In this way, the tropical wilderness becomes the jungle.

Chapter 2

Pathological Philosophies of Decay
in *The Way of the Kings*

WRITTEN BEFORE HE TURNED THIRTY, AND BEFORE HE BECAME A FRENCH CUL-tural icon, André Malraux's second novel, *The Way of the Kings* (*La voie royale*), stands in stark contrast to his overtly political novels. This philosophical work, published in 1930, is as much an exploration of the physical and mental decline of its protagonists as it is an exploration of the Cambodian jungle by the young archaeologist Claude Vannec and the aging adventurer Perken. As with other novels set in remote tropical areas, medical terms in *The Way of the Kings* play an important role in both the depiction of the environment and the plight of the main characters. In this case in particular, Malraux portrays the rainforest as the epicenter of disease and decay, and tropical illness becomes a metaphor for the inevitability of human mortality. The author employs medical terminology as a vehicle for his philosophical exploration of his protagonists' confrontation with death. Within the atmosphere of decay that pervades the novel, madness represents the logical culmination of Claude and Perken's struggles against their own mortality.

The Way of the Kings, like other twentieth-century tropical narratives, tells a story of a failure: Claude and Perken intend to remove valuable carved stones from a forgotten and overgrown Cambodian temple and live off the proceeds of the sale of the items. For both men, this quest also symbolizes a rejection of traditional European society and a defiance of death against considerable odds. Instead of achieving their goal, the two are beset by both mental and physical ill-ness caused by tropical diseases. The specter of decay, the dominant motif of the novel, haunts both protagonists in various forms: fever, malaria, delirium, mad-ness, impotence, venereal disease, blindness, and finally, an infected wound that kills Perken. The very specific and varied use of medical conditions makes up the building blocks of Malraux's literary examination of man's fruitless struggle with death. The health dangers endemic to the tropical wilderness come to represent the obstacles every human faces in his or her ill-fated attempt to control destiny. Medical discourse consequently forms the backbone of both the portrayal of the forest and the inevitability of decline that, according to Malraux, defines human existence.

The novel mirrors the general trajectory of other tropical quest tales: a young protagonist decides to venture into the wilderness in search of both the material and spiritual wealth that he finds lacking in modern society. In this case, the archaeologist Claude Vannec embarks on a search for the Royal Way, a chain of ruined temples near Angkor Wat in Indochina, as the French colonial empire in Southeast Asia was known following the Sino-French war in 1884–1885.[1] While this portion of the story is loosely based on Malraux's own experience (he was convicted of looting the ancient Khmer temple of Banteay Srei), the novel soon departs from real life as Claude is joined by Perken, a European adventurer who has managed to carve out his own kingdom from among the native peoples not yet under French colonial rule. On entering the country, the two immediately encounter both human and natural impediments to their quest, ranging from uncooperative colonial officials to the debilitating effects of lethargy induced by heat, insects, and fever. Claude is particularly aware of the physical danger presented by the infectious diseases native to the tropical forest, while Perken is fixated on his own inevitable decline and impotence.

Despite these obstacles, the two men manage to free three valuable bas-reliefs from a forgotten temple before their guides and drivers abandon them, forcing them into the territory of the bellicose Moï people. They hope to gain safe passage through their connection with Grabot, a Parisian acquaintance of Perken who has deserted the army. Grabot is presumed to have "gone native" and to be ruling some of the indigenous population in the area.[2] The similarities between this portion of the novel and Conrad's *Heart of Darkness* are obvious. Kurtz and Grabot share many qualities: both are rumored to have control over the native residents and are instead found to be ailing; both are surprisingly reticent about their experience in the wilderness; and Grabot, like Kurtz, is the empty center around which the narrative revolves. Malraux, like most writers of twentieth-century novels set in tropical European colonies, owes a clear debt to Conrad.

In her memoirs, Clara Malraux specifically mentions that she and her husband had both read *Heart of Darkness* before embarking on their trip to Southeast Asia; she even states that they had envisioned the upcoming voyage as their own version of the work.[3] Additionally, the narrative had been published serially in French in the *Nouvelle révue française* between December 1924 and February 1925, just after Malraux's return from Indochina and prior to the composition of his novel (Cornick 7). Yet important departures from *Heart of Darkness* throw Malraux's particular concern with mental decay and disease into relief. While Kurtz is ill, he nevertheless maintains control over the Africans around him;

Grabot, in contrast, has been enslaved and blinded by the Moï. He embodies the decay and powerlessness of body and mind that both Perken and Claude have come to fear for themselves.

Following a confrontation with the Moï, the three Europeans escape without their profits, and Perken is fatally wounded by war spikes embedded in the ground. Without the medical resources to amputate his leg, Perken is condemned to a slow and painful death by infection, fever, and inflammation of the wound. Perken abhors this manner of ending his life more than the reality of death itself. He often extols the virtues of suicide rather than growing old, concluding: "Decay is the real death" (31). His demise is one of the many instances in which Malraux uses medical terms as metaphors for his protagonists' confrontations with Thanatos. The tropics, with their myriad dangers and unknown maladies, serve as the ideal arena in which man struggles against his destiny. In an interior monologue, Claude explicitly links his adventure in the wilderness to his desire to combat the "cancer" of his bourgeois existence:

> But to accept, while you were still alive, the futility of your own existence, like a cancer, to live with the clamminess of death on your hand.... What was this need for the unknown, this temporary destruction of the relations between prisoner and master, which those who didn't know it called adventure, if not a way of defending himself against death? The defence of a blind man, aiming to conquer death in order to raise the stakes.... To possess more than himself, to escape from the futile lives of the men he saw around him every day. (33)

Within the forest, the only obstacle between each protagonist and his ability to possess more than himself (*posséder plus que lui-même*; *La voie* 48) is the gradual and debilitating illness that affects him. Indeed, mental and physical ailments replace the societal constraints that the protagonists have left behind. Although Claude and Perken have escaped a bourgeois existence by risking their lives in the wilderness, they are nonetheless still enslaved to their fates. In this way, the social restrictions against which both men rebel are overshadowed by the larger limitations of human mortality embodied in illness. As the novel progresses, the symptoms of illness increase, causing each protagonist to fail in his stated quest. Bodily decline is paralleled by the complementary loss of mental control—the loss of the ability to think rationally, which is what had set the protagonists apart from the forest inhabitants. For each man, then, the sickness is both a symptom and a cause of his eventual defeat by his own mortality.

In addition to the general atmosphere of ill health, there are several examples in the novel of physical ailment being linked to personal failure: Claude's delirium brought on by a fever that makes it impossible for him to escape the region with his looted bas-reliefs; colonial official Albert Ramèges's liver abscess and his inability to break free from his colonial duties; Grabot's blindness and impotence,

and his enslavement by the Moï; and Perken's death from infection and his failure
to establish his own kingdom. All these conditions illustrate Malraux's careful
use of medical symptoms to explore madness, personal failure, and death.

Claude and Perken's fears of disease and injuries are in part a reflection of
the author's anxiety over his own physical and mental health. Malraux may have
been particularly sensitive to medical diagnoses: he was known for his rapid and
often disjointed speech, as well as twitches, and according to several accounts he
suffered from a mild form of Tourette's syndrome.[4] A fictionalized description
of his maternal grandmother in *The Way of the Kings* mentions that "she was
indifferently consumptive" (15).[5] This indication that his grandmother Mathilde
suffered from tuberculosis has not been confirmed by biographers (it is only
known that she died in 1890), but her actual cause of death is less important
than Malraux's mention of it in the novel. The similarities between tuberculosis
(a wasting disease often known as consumption) and the slow, wasting diseases
of the tropics (malaria, other fevers, and infections) make it clear that decay in all
its medical forms was of great import to Malraux. The presence of mental illness
also appears in the form of suicide, which is often portrayed in Malraux's fiction
as a noble act of defiance in the face of inexorable human decline. It was not
unknown in the author's family: his father gassed himself shortly after the publication of *The Way of the Kings*, and according to his biographer Olivier Todd,
Malraux "would often allow people to believe, and perhaps believed himself"
that his grandfather Alphonse Malraux's supposedly accidental death was actually a suicide (*Life* 483n5).

Aside from his personal history, Malraux's concern with madness and death
was also fueled by the general anxiety the French public felt about the deleterious
effects of the tropics on European colonizers. A study of Malraux's portrayal of
several mental and physical ailments common to residents of warm climates—
including malaria, fever-induced delirium, a liver abscess, venereal disease,
impotence, skin disorders, blindness, and a gangrenous infection—reveals his
careful, deliberate use of medical language to present the tropics as a locus of
human decay and degeneration for both indigenous and colonial residents.

Much of Malraux's stylized description of tropical diseases is clearly gleaned
from the popular medical opinion of the time. The best source of information
regarding the national consensus about health in the French colonies can be
found in documents from the Exposition Coloniale Internationale, held from
May to November 1931 in Paris. Several publications from the exposition provide
a portrait of French interest in its colonies that is almost precisely contemporaneous with the publication of *The Way of the Kings*. The fair was promoted to its
millions of spectators as a demonstration of the benefits of colonialism for *la plus
grande France*.[6] The potential eradication of tropical diseases, which affected both
indigenous and colonial residents, was chief among these advantages.

The official guide to the show states that, before the arrival of the French
in Indochina, "justice was venal, the state of war endemic, populations deci-

mated by famine and sickness, commerce limited to insignificant exchanges, the administration xenophobic and stuck in its ways, the fate of the workers lamentable....Our protection, you should well know, has delivered millions of men and women from the nightmare of slavery and death. Today the way of life of these people is more similar to ours than you would believe" (Exposition 19–20). The notion that the French could save the Indochinese from themselves extended to curing the physical ailments that afflicted the region's inhabitants; as a consequence, the success of medical treatment in the colonies was of great political importance. For example, within a massive replica of Angkor Wat, various booths were set up to glorify France for saving Cambodia's culture and improving its well-being. One booth praised the colonial officers who had "protected the Cambodian race from its own weaknesses, from sickness and pernicious outside influences, by means of schools, roads, hospitals, and dispensaries" (Exposition 57). To illustrate this lofty endeavor, the Inspection Board of Medical and Sanitary Services of Indochina published a series of pamphlets about its work in the region, displaying them all in the Indochina pavilion at the Exposition. These slim volumes, covering malaria, beriberi, cholera, and many other tropical maladies, detail the ways in which the French colonial government had improved the health of those living in the territory and the public health challenges it still faced. The pamphlets provide an invaluable snapshot of medical theories at the time Malraux's novel was published, and I will use them to highlight the prevalence of popular medical terminology and conditions in his work.

The most dominant affliction in the region was and continues to be malaria. In the 1920s, malaria was nearly twice as common as any other disease among those treated in Indochinese hospitals, with twenty thousand cases on record in 1929 alone. The second most common ailment was syphilis, with only half as many patients. The other significant diseases, in descending order of importance, were bronchitis, tuberculosis, cholera, smallpox, beriberi, dysentery, and leprosy.[7] The prevalence of malaria in the tropics is reflected in two of Malraux's literary works: *The Conquerors* (1928; translated into English in 1976) and *The Way of the Kings* (1930). A brief look at the earlier novel will set the stage for an in-depth analysis of Malraux's later work.

Set in China, a country to which Malraux had not yet traveled, *The Conquerors* is a political novel in which the hero, Garine, foments revolution among Cantonese rebels before ill health forces him to flee. Malraux is carefully ambiguous regarding Garine's actual affliction; only his death is certain. The author repeatedly refers to his protagonist's general feeling of climate-induced enervation in allusive terms, mentioning only malaria and dysentery by name. The cumulative effect is a general atmosphere of festering malaise. Because of its overtly political content, *The Conquerors* is much more typical of Malraux's work than the philosophical *The Way of the Kings*.

What marks them as works of the same author is the similar struggles of the protagonists to overcome tropical disease and its resulting fatigue and mental disorientation in order to take action, be it in pursuit of a revolution or the pillage of temples. It is important to note that the tropics are all a single fetid jungle for Malraux; his descriptions of rural China and Indochina are virtually identical. For example, each novel opens with a scene onboard a ship in an atmosphere of torpor in which the imagery of sweaty hands is used to convey discomfort with the climate. In *The Conquerors*, the suffocating stasis of the ferry aggravates the narrator: "We make our way along the low banks of the river through dense, steamy air, our hands dripping sweat" (25). While in *The Way of the Kings* the descriptions of the wilderness are more elaborate and lyrical than those of the largely urban setting of *The Conquerors*, the same sense of heat and torpor are evident in the description of a similar ship scene in *The Way of the Kings*: "In spite of the night, the air stuck to Claude's hand like a clammy hand as soon as he fell silent" (24). Malraux's collapsing of the climatic differences between China and Indochina is significant because it enables him to create a fictional environment in which the air is imbued with its own capacity to sicken the protagonists.

The similarities between the two novels extend beyond the climate to encompass the main characters, who are often adventurers. In *The Conquerors*, a special envoy from France to China tells the narrator that Garine belongs to the category of *adventurers*: "They're men who've never been able to conform in ordinary society, who've asked a great deal of life, who wanted to give some meaning to their own lives" (*Conquerors* 11). In the later novel, both Claude and Perken feel driven to *donner un sens à leur vie* (give meaning to life; *Les conquérants* 33). For example, as he prepares for his journey into the jungle, Claude overtly rejects the trappings and responsibilities of a bourgeois existence: "He had no desire to sell cars, stocks and shares, or speeches, like those of his friends whose slicked-down hair signified their distinction, nor to build bridges, like those whose badly cut hair signified their know-how. Why did such people work? To gain esteem. He hated the esteem they were seeking. For a man without children and without a god, submission to the order of man was the most profound submission to death" (*Kings* 31–32). Indeed, for all of Malraux's protagonists, escaping the "submission to the order of man" is accomplished by fleeing from French society and attempting to gain control over residents of a warmer region. Garine's direction of the Cantonese revolutionaries embodies his rejection of the status quo and his thirst for power; the same motivating factors are evident in Perken's desire to carve out a kingdom for himself among the Stiengs north of Angkor Wat and in Claude's determination to become rich in the forest.

Most important, the protagonists of both novels suffer from gradual, debilitating illnesses that impede their success and that are untreatable in the tropics. While Perken is located too far from a colonial hospital for the life-saving amputation of his leg to be performed, Garine's companions note that his decision to stay in the country guarantees his death: "In any case, in Canton the quacks say he should return to Europe, and that if he stays here for some time he'll leave his bones behind. Everyone is more or less sick in Canton, apparently" (*Les conquérants* 67).[8] The idea that departure from the tropical climate was the only sure way to relieve symptoms of malaria and dysentery was particularly common early in the twentieth century, despite the efforts of doctors to cure colonial patients on site. Malraux shows a familiarity with medical discourse of the era both in this respect and in the form of medical texts, which the protagonist of *The Conquerors* reads in an effort to stay healthy. When the narrator of the novel enters Garine's office, he notices Garine's concern for his health:

> There are a few books on the desk. The Fathers' Sino-Latin dictionary. Two medical books in English: *Dysentery, Malaria*. When Garine comes back, I ask him if it's true that he's not taking care of himself.
>
> "But of course I take care of myself! Of course! I don't always take care of myself too carefully, because I have other things to do, but none of that's very important—to get well I'd have to go back to Europe; I know that. I'll stay there as long as I can. But you don't expect me to leave now!" (77–78)

Garine's recognition of the healing climate of Europe and the dangers of the tropics plays on the centuries of assumptions that influenced many European writers. As mentioned in Chapter 1, Conrad had noted before embarking on his trip to Africa that "it would be prudent to benefit from the European climate for as long as possible" (Letter). While Conrad wrote out of genuine self-interest and concern for his own physical well-being, Malraux clearly makes use of popular medical opinion for literary purposes: both Garine and Perken are paradoxically made into philosophically stronger, more valiant figures through their struggles with illness and their refusal to sacrifice their goals for the sake of medical treatment.

Malraux also displays his interest in the health risks facing residents of the tropics when Nicolaieff, a companion of Garine, says to the narrator: "Tropical diseases, you know, you don't fool around with them, young fellow. When you've got one, you take care of yourself. If not, you pay for it. And maybe it's just as well.... Human, all too human, as Borodine says. That's where disease takes you if you don't stop to treat it" (161).[9] Again, Garine's illness and his determination to remain in country despite it, viewed as romantic and foolish by the Russian Nicolaieff, throws his bravery and strength of character into relief for the narrator. Garine himself ironically recognizes his dire straits and the historical weight behind his condition: "Be pretty damn foolish to die here like some colonial type" (173). This sort of black humor and the recognition that malaria and dysentery need not be death sentences given the advances in tropical medicine reveal a fundamental difference between the historical moments in which Conrad and Malraux were writing. While in the late 1800s Europeans in Africa had died at exceedingly high rates and Conrad himself had returned stricken with dysentery, knowledge about tropical diseases had progressed sufficiently by the second decade of the twentieth century to make death no longer a foregone conclusion.[10]

Given the portrayal of malaria as a dangerous yet treatable condition by the medical community, the decisions by both Perken and Garine to forgo medical treatment in pursuit of their goals gain added significance: Malraux seeks to depict their refusal of treatment as rejections both of their own mortality and of Western civilization as represented by the medical community.

In the generally lawless colonial atmosphere of both novels, doctors become representatives of the French social and legal world that Perken and Garine have repudiated. In both works, doctors are presented as weak characters, and often referred to as *toubibs* (quacks). While Garine's refusal of treatment guarantees his death, it also represents his stance against the "submission to the order of man" that he so abhors (*Conquerors* 32). He shows himself to be a willing martyr to his revolutionary beliefs. For Garine, medical treatment comes to represent the French society that he has left behind, and his rejection of it indicates the liberation he seeks in China. In *The Way of the Kings*, medical treatment comes too late to save Perken's life. The provincial doctors who treat him—one a British opium addict and the other a young Cambodian physician—have neither the resources nor the ability to cure him. His death is a further indication that illness has defeated civilization as embodied in the doctors. The secondary young protagonist in each novel—the narrator in *The Conquerors* and Claude in *The Way of the Kings*—is left with a clear lesson: the ability of a man to give sense to life by rejecting bourgeois society also requires him to acknowledge that this liberation will cost him his life.

Both *The Conquerors* and *The Way of the Kings* conclude with the protagonist facing certain death, preceded by a long decline from an ailment contracted in the tropics. While Garine is the only character in Malraux's earlier novel to be affected by his stay in the tropics, *The Way of the Kings* is rife with characters who are mentally and physically altered by their environment. The setting of this later novel in the dense rainforest of Indochina instead of in an urban Chinese atmosphere accounts for part of this difference, but it is also clear that Malraux's interest in sickness and its treatment—a constant in his work—peaks in *The Way of the Kings*. As in his earlier novel, Malraux mentions several medical conditions by name, but he also refers to medical ailments in vague and stylized terms, thereby creating an ambiance of infectious and mysterious malaise. This allusive rather than direct mention of scientific discourse contributes to Malraux's lyrical style, which—as many critics have acknowledged—represents a departure from his normally staccato prose in other writings (for example, see Ellis 31).

Mental disease and tropical illness are often incorporated into the descriptions of Claude, Perken, and their surroundings as key constituents of the cloying tropical climate. Yet even in these seemingly stylistic descriptions of illness, Malraux manages to include medical information that reveals his knowledge of the subject. For example, after the protagonists have passed several days in the forest, the narrator evokes a general atmosphere of distortion and disease that nonetheless makes reference to a specific medical cause: "The jungle and the heat, though, were stronger than their anxiety: like a man sinking into an illness, Claude was sinking into this ferment, in which the shapes swelled and grew and decayed outside the world where men mattered, dividing him from himself with the force of darkness. And everywhere, insects" (59). The subtle references to dreaming, sickness, hallucination, and insects all indicate that Claude may be suffering from malaria. A brief look at the impact of malaria on French Indochina at the time Malraux was writing will illuminate his use of medical metaphors for literary purposes.

The threat of malaria presented a serious hindrance to the colonial endeavor in French Indochina. The medical authors published in conjunction with the Exposition Coloniale Internationale of 1931 recognized and addressed the problem in works such as *Sur la lutte contre le paludisme dans les collectivités ouvrières* (*Est Cochinchine et Sud-Annam*) (On the struggle against malaria in the workers' collectives [East Cochin-China and South Annam]) by Dr. Henry G. S. Morin, director of malaria services at the Pasteur Institute of Indochina. As E. Delamarre, the inspector general of work in Indochina, notes in his foreword to Morin's text, "Malaria is, in Indochina, as in the majority of tropical countries, the most dangerous, the most subtle, and the most tenacious enemy that has afflicted human beings devoted to the occupation and exploitation of virgin territories" (7). Indeed, Morin notes that in a region where malaria is endemic, it can reduce the working population by 40 percent in two months if no preventative measures are taken (10). The tone of the text, the specific recommendations for personal prevention of the disease, and its date of publication shed light on the climate of medical thought surrounding the historical moment in which Malraux was himself traveling through Indochina and writing about the region.

In his publication, Dr. Morin includes a detailed analysis of the method of transmission of the disease, the types of mosquitoes that carry it, and the means of preventing its spread. He shows that in other malaria-infected areas, such as Panama and British possessions in Malaysia, the disease was effectively resisted when a combination of quinine treatment and mosquito eradication was pursued. The level of detail in his analysis shows the brisk pace of scientific advancement in the early twentieth century with respect to malaria. It was, after all, only in 1898 that the British doctor Ronald Ross had proved that malaria was transmitted by the Anopheles mosquito. Thus, at the time of his Congo voyage, Conrad had known that the use of quinine could aid in the treatment of malaria, but he would have been aware neither of other preventative measures nor of precisely how the disease was contracted. Malraux, however, clearly benefited from the increase in medical knowledge with respect both to his health and to his literary creation. He and Clara both took quinine and slept with mosquito netting, and as a result emerged from their time in Southeast Asia uninfected.[11] More important, the medical experts' descriptions of malaria and its symptoms contributed to Malraux's writing style by depicting malaria as an anthropomorphically insidious and cunning form of mental as well as physical debilitation. In fact, there is a significant parallel between the tone adopted by the colonial officers (such as Dr. Morin) writing about malaria and the way in which Malraux describes the jungle and his protagonists' growing feverishness. This is not to say that Malraux had read many of the medical treatises on malaria at the time of his trip or the composition of *The Way of the Kings*, but rather that the author, like many French travelers in the region, would have possessed a popular knowledge of the disease—a popular knowledge constructed in large part by the scientists and doctors of the day.

Malaria was often described as having a sinister and sly personality because of its dormant phase, during which an individual could unwittingly become infected, and to the cyclical nature of its symptoms, which included various spells of fever and chills, delirium, and lethargy. For example, in the preface to Morin's work, Inspector General Delamarre refers to the disease as *sournoise* (cunning), in addition to calling it subtle and tenacious (7). This type of personification of illness is prevalent in both medical and fictional works of the time, and thus makes malaria not only a medical menace but a cultural repository for fear of the tropics as well. Malraux both participates in and benefits from the anthropomorphic presentation of illness by using it to maximize the aura of stagnation and danger in his novel.

Malraux shows his familiarity with the medical opinions about and descriptions of malaria in several ways. He portrays the indigenous population of Indochina as a community decimated and enervated by the disease, much as Dr. Morin laments the loss of a viable workforce for the same reason. For instance, Perken describes to Claude the bleak atmosphere in the remote interior of the country: "The natives in the last village are so riddled with malaria it's made them senile and incapable of doing anything. Their eyelids are so blue, it's as if someone had been hitting them for a week" (*Way* 22).[12] The mention of the blue eyelids and mental decay of the malaria sufferers shows Malraux's knowledge of the disease, learned firsthand from his travels.

The specter of *gâtisme* (senile decay), however, is the most significant descriptor of the disease for the author's purposes (37). Malraux uses the notion of mental and physical senility inherent in malaria to serve as a metaphor for the figure of death, which is inescapable for every human being. This is particularly the case for Perken, as I will explore later. Malaria and all other tropical diseases are stand-ins for death and decay—two of Malraux's frequent topics—and Claude and Perken's struggles against these diseases are emblematic of their attempts to give meaning to their lives before succumbing to the inevitable. Thus, malaria is frequently associated with lethargy, physical disintegration, and the deplorable health of the tropics' inhabitants (both indigenous and European), who are powerless to stop the advance of the disease: "Two more nights and two more days, and they came to a last village shivering with malaria, lost in the universal disintegration of things beneath the unseen sun" (66). The sun, providing heat but no light because of the thick foliage, contributes to the atmosphere of fetid rot that Malraux creates in the novel. Indeed, every aspect of the environment, from the invisible sun to the plant and insect life to the malaria-riddled natives, adds to the paradoxical portrayal of the forest as a place of simultaneous extreme fecundity and inescapable decay. The author creates an implicit contrast between the magnificent works of Khmer art that Claude hopes to pillage from ruined temples and the pitiful state of health of the region's inhabitants, all of whom are described as having medical defects, including fevers and the scaly skin condition eczema. Malraux makes it clear that the fertile and aggressive foliage threatens to overtake not only the remnants of Asian art but also all human volition, as Claude and Perken, like the natives, are stricken with disease.

Malaria is only one indication of the pernicious effects the tropics have on Europeans. In addition to the very specific references to malaria, Malraux invokes general fevers and delirium that impede Claude in his search for the stones. The greatest threat presented by the fevers is the inability of the mind to control the body, as rational thought cedes ground to animal impulses. Thus, as he and Perken attempt to free the stones, Claude is tempted to give up: "He was overcome by fatigue, exhaustion, the disgust of a worn out creature. If only he could lie down . . . After so much effort, the jungle was again as powerful as a prison. He felt dependent, his will—his flesh itself—surrendered, as if with each pulse, his blood was running out . . . He imagined himself sitting here, hugging his arms to his chest as if in a fever, hunched over, losing all consciousness, obeying the summons of the jungle and the heat with a feeling of liberation" (75; ellipses in the original).

In this way, the fear of mental fatigue is even more disturbing that any physical debility. As with the references to malaria, Malraux's specific medical knowledge of the symptoms of tropical fevers form part of the lyrical literary imagery he uses to express the physical and mental impact of the environment on his protagonists. By combining the image of the forest as a prison with Claude's desire to give in to the lethargy caused by fever, Malraux clearly indicates that the fusion of these two elements make up the central obstacle to his protagonist. Sickness caused by the wilderness makes it difficult for Claude to remove the stones he has sought, and it serves as a symbol of his inability to overcome his human weakness and inevitable mortality. As the novel progresses, madness invades the protagonists' weak minds. Malraux deftly translates the physical illness caused by the forest into a sense of mental and psychological lethargy as well:

> The unity of the jungle was asserting itself now. For the past six days
> Claude had given up trying to separate the creatures from the shapes,
> the life that moved from the life that oozed. An unknown power linked
> the fungus and the trees, made all these fleeting things swarm on
> this marshlike soil, in these steaming, primeval woods. What human
> action had any meaning here? Whose will retained any force? Every-
> thing spread, grew soft, made an effort to adapt to this world which was

> revolting and attractive at the same time, like the look on an idiot's face,
> a world that attacked the nerves with the same despicable power as those
> spiders hanging from the branches, from which he had found it so dif-
> ficult to turn away his eyes. (60)

The wilderness, then, is repeatedly characterized as the antithesis of rational
thought; it is a softening of the mind as well as of the body. The description of
the forest as a space in which everything grows spongy and indistinguishable
parallels the incipient mental and physical release that tempts the protagonists.
For Claude, the forest is like "the look on an idiot's face," horrible and attractive
at the same time. The use of spiders to evoke a "despicable power" that attacks
Claude's nerves demonstrates one of the ways in which Malraux constructs his
own literary wilderness through the imagery of insects, illness, and decay. The
author uses spiders, mosquitoes, and other inhabitants of the forest to portray
the entire area as rotting, oozing, and threatening. Indeed, insects—the essential transmitters of many infectious tropical diseases—play a central role in the
novel. Claude, like Malraux himself, is disgusted by all the insects that appear in
the work. For Claude, as for many explorers, they are a fundamental part of the
danger of the tropics. In *The Way of the Kings*, any mention of fever or discomfort
is often accompanied by the presence of insects, most often mosquitoes, as in
the description of "the last villages, with their malaria-riddled natives, columns
of mosquitoes whirling above their heads in the evening, as dense as rays of sun-
light" (83). This sense of disgust extends from mosquitoes to other insects and to
all other aspects of tropical life.

Claude is very attentive both to his own sensations, which he often links
to heat-induced delirium in the warm climate, and to the appearance of others,
from which he makes his own amateur diagnoses. By taking medical diagnosis into his own hands, Claude symbolically replaces the doctor, a figure of the
French authority that he seeks to escape by entering the forest. In the absence of
a medical professional, Claude appropriates medical terminology and becomes
an authority figure in his own right. In these instances, philosophy merges with
medicine: each individual's physical maladies lead to a recognition of shared
mortality and an opportunity for greater psychological connection. For example,
Claude immediately encounters opposition to his plan to follow the Royal Way
on meeting Albert Ramèges, director of the French Institute. The two men speak
at cross purposes and Ramèges appears reluctant to give Claude the assistance
he seeks. While struggling to make the director see things from his point of
view, Claude muses: "He's pale, most likely a liver abscess: he'd understand me
so much more easily if he realized that what really interests me is man's determination to defend himself against his own death through this turbulent sense of
eternity, if I linked what I am saying to his abscess! But never mind" (36). This
rapid attribution of the director's pale complexion to a serious physical condition reveals several facets of Malraux's relationship to medicine and his use of

it in the novel. First of all, Claude's non sequitur is explicable only if a concern for personal health and its relation to a personal philosophy are at the forefront of Claude's mind (and clearly Malraux's as well) throughout the novel. Second, Malraux shows his extensive knowledge of popular medical opinion of the time, which held that liver abscesses were more common in the tropics than in France, and were caused by excessive eating and drinking in hot weather (Gaide 254). Lastly, the notion that the director's illness has been brought on in part by the climate makes Claude sympathetic toward him, since he feels that he too is defending himself against death "through this turbulent sense of eternity." According to Claude, Ramèges's liver abscess is the cause of his unwillingness to break free of the official position, just as Claude's fever threatens to prevent him from removing the bas-reliefs. Thus, Malraux intimates, Claude feels sure that if he can appeal to the official in terms of their shared and inevitable mortality, he can convince Ramèges to support him in his quest and thereby defy his own death. In attributing Ramèges's resistance to a medical condition brought on by the tropics, Malraux avails himself of the general idea that colonists gradually lost health, mental balance, and moral fiber while in a warm climate.[13] Claude, then, is thwarted in the completion of his plan by both his own illness and that of Ramèges, both of which have philosophical ramifications that are even more important than their physical impact. Malraux deftly manipulates his knowledge of medical maladies for maximum literary effect, imbuing physical symptoms with existential implications.

All the medical conditions portrayed in the novel underscore the encroachment of death on human life, in the face of which the protagonists struggle to give their lives meaning. Perken is more concerned with the inexorable decline of old age than he is with death itself: "Growing old, that's it, growing old. Especially when you are separate from other people. Decay. The thing that weighs heavy on me is—how can I put it?—my condition as a man: the fact that I'm growing old, that this horrible thing called time is growing inside me, inexorably, like a cancer" (98). As with other physical problems in the novel, aging is discussed in medical terms, in this case as an untreatable cancer. Malraux uses a whole host of medical metaphors to express his protagonists' distress at their inevitable decline: cancer, tumors, fevers, infections. Significantly, all the medical conditions employed as metaphors are incurable and therefore take on an aura of inescapable destiny, thus creating a parallel between illness and fate, human nature and death. Many of the metaphors Perken uses to describe his own aging process involve venereal disease, which indicates both Perken's obsession with exotic eroticism and Malraux's knowledge of the prevalence of sexually transmitted diseases in the French colonies.

Several sexual forms of decay are explored in *The Way of the Kings*: syphilis, gonorrhea, and impotence all contribute to the novel's atmosphere of purulent decomposition. Perken often mentions syphilis as a consequence of carnal indulgence in the tropics and a symbol of powerless decline. By the end of the novel, both Perken and Grabot are impotent, Perken from his advancing age and possibly syphilis (which could manifest itself in madness), and Grabot because he has been castrated by his captors. Prior to his castration, Grabot had also suffered from gonorrhea and even used it to sadistically blind himself. Perken's desire for indigenous women and the frequent use of venereal disease to evoke decay reflect the colonial medical community's portrayal of indigenous residents as unclean carriers of sexual infection.

European colonies were frequently viewed as places stricken with venereal disease because of the overwhelmingly male colonial population's visits to local brothels, such as Claude and Perken's visit to one such establishment in Djibouti. The scarcity of European women in the colonies can be attributed to the common opinion that the climate led to sterility and disease for white women (Stoler, *Carnal* 46–7). Malraux exhibits his awareness of the supposed effect of the climate on European women when Perken notes the changes in his former wife, Sarah, after time spent in the tropics: "You know the way white women look in their mirrors and realize they're always going to have that flushed complexion they acquired in the Tropics" (51). Given the general absence of white women, the resulting contact between European men and Indochinese women was thought to merge the exotic with the erotic, as evidenced by Perken's comment: "I'm only now starting to understand their erotic cults" (54). Sexual relations with natives, however, were also thought to lead to mental, physical, and moral decline.

The connection between warm climates and venereal diseases was established long before France colonized Southeast Asia. For example, referring to syphilis in his 1748 treatise, *The Spirit of the Laws*, Montesquieu writes:

> Two centuries ago, a disease unknown to our fathers traveled from
> the New World to this one and came to attack human nature at the
> very source of life and pleasures. Most of the important families of
> southern Europe were afflicted by a disease that became so common
> that it was no longer shameful and was merely deadly. It was the thirst
> for gold that perpetuated this disease; men continued their voyages to
> America and brought back new seeds of it each time they returned.
> For reasons of piety one wanted to let this be the punishment of the
> crime, but the disaster had entered marriages and had already cor
> rupted childhood itself. (241)

The notion that inferior residents of tropical places could contaminate European bodies and pollute the future health of the nation was, like syphilis, brought back from North and South America by European colonizers. As Montesquieu makes clear, syphilis was viewed as a divine punishment for the thirst for material wealth; Malraux perhaps unwittingly echoes this sentiment in his depiction of Perken. *The Way of the Kings* thus extends the association of colonized regions with diseases capable of debilitating the best of Europe and the implication that

Europe has brought syphilis on itself. Montesquieu also uncannily anticipates the late nineteenth century European fear of the ravages of syphilis being passed on to the children of the afflicted. His ideas in this respect are a forerunner of the degeneration theory based on Lamarckian genetics that would be popular in South America during the late nineteenth and early twentieth centuries, which I will discuss in Chapter 3.

Malraux's presentation of Perken's disease makes it clear that turn-of-the-century theories of racial degeneration through miscegenation and moral depravity caused by contact with indigenous residents had not yet been extinguished in French Indochina.[14] According to this logic, Perken precipitates his own mental and corporeal decline by seeking sex with local women. In his treatise on colonial medicine, Dr. Morin states that individuals weakened by venereal disease were especially susceptible to other infections as well: "Venereal infections should not be neglected, as they constitute a considerable source of weakness. The first preventative measure consists of including a sufficient number of [French] women in the workforce" (25–26). From this statement, it is clear that Morin sought to integrate European women into the colonial workforce because he hoped that their presence would reduce the frequency of Frenchmen's visits to local houses of prostitution. Sexual disease, therefore, was another menace the tropics presented to the European adventurer.

The physical threat that venereal disease represented for the French colonist is magnified in the novel by the way Malraux employs syphilis as a philosophical as well as medical barrier to the protagonists' goals. Perken, for instance, views it as another challenge through which he must prove his bravery and risk his life: "Should I be afraid of making love because of the pox? I don't say: I don't care. I say: I accept it." (50). Syphilis is described in the novel as a wasting disease in order to compare it to Perken's destiny. Speaking of Sarah, Perken declares: "All the hopes she'd had as a young woman began to eat away at her life like a bout of syphilis caught in adolescence—and the contagion spread to my life, too....You have no idea what it's like, to know your destiny is limited and inevitable, you're like a convict being read the prison rules: the certainty that you will be this and not something else, that what you haven't had, you'll never have" (51; ellipsis in original). If syphilis represents decay and the closing off of possibilities for the future, Perken defies the danger by engaging (or attempting to engage) in activities that risk contagion. This mirrors Claude and Perken's other behaviors that flaunt medical prescription, such as not using mosquito netting or taking quinine, as well as their decision to enter hostile territory and disobey the French colonial authorities. Medical discourse and disease therefore offer Malraux the lexicon and imagery with which he portrays his protagonists' rejection of their destinies. Their intention to shun Western civilization and escape the inevitable confrontation with death is a type of madness in itself. The protagonists' refusal of medical precautions and treatment reflect this flight from rational thought.

Perken's desire to defy his own inevitable sexual decline through his increased interest in sex with local women explains his definition of eroticism as "the need to reach your own breaking point" (5).[15] As his physical capacity for sex wanes, Perken states that "there comes a time when the idea of sex, the idea of youth, comes back to haunt you, stronger than ever" (5). Malraux makes it clear that Perken's sexual desire has increased in inverse proportion to his effectiveness in establishing dominance over the indigenous population. Claude observes Perken's monologue about indigenous women: "'No, they aren't bodies, these women: they are … yes, possibilities. And I want …' He made a gesture which Claude could barely make out in the darkness, like a hand crushing something. 'Just as I wanted to dominate men.'" Perken concludes, "Now all my old dreams are in my loins" (54–55). The transference of Perken's dreams of lucrative pillage to sexual exploits occurs when it becomes clear that no medical intervention can save his life or enable him to regain control of his lost territory. Perken summons young prostitutes to his bedside, thereby shifting his failed dominance over the land to an attempted domination of the indigenous women. Yet Perken's erotic desire to dominate the women from the local brothels is as futile as his aspiration to dominate the native communities not yet under French rule: he fails in both attempts. Perken is thus overcome by the decay that he so fears. Bereft of the power to control both men and women, he soon succumbs to the fever caused by his injury, an episode I will examine shortly.

Sexual decay is also embodied in the figure of Grabot. While at first Claude and Perken view him as a source of European strength in the forest because they believe he has established his own kingdom, Grabot turns out to be a manifestation of many forms of decay: gonorrhea, blindness, castration. These physical deformations represent his enslavement by the very people Claude and Perken thought he was ruling; rather than dominating the environment and its inhabitants, he has submitted to them. The similarities between Grabot and Kurtz show the debt *The Way of the Kings* owes to *Heart of Darkness*. Both tales include a dramatic reversal of expectation: Marlow and Perken expect to find Kurtz and Grabot fully in command of the indigenous people around them, but instead discover both renegades dependent on the locals for survival. The appearance of the men horrifies their pursuers because they epitomize the savagery they were intended to master and eradicate. Both men are discovered to have "gone native," but Grabot represents an even greater figure of degeneration than Kurtz because he has been enslaved, blinded, and castrated by the native people, whereas Kurtz, though ill, still retains some autonomy.

To Perken and Claude, Grabot had been the representation of the ultimate adventurer because he had shown he was willing to risk everything to obtain his objectives. For example, Grabot had allowed himself to be bitten by a black scorpion simply to rid himself of fear. Perken explains, "The first time he saw one, he felt a violent revulsion, so he went and got himself stung on purpose. To reject the world unconditionally means you're going to have to suffer terribly in order to prove your strength to yourself. In all that, there's an immense primitive pride, but life and quite a lot of suffering have finally given it a shape" (88). Grabot's willingness to inflict physical pain on himself to conquer fear is emblematic of Malraux's often-expressed need to confront death in order to defy it. The "primitive pride" that Grabot derives from this experience is precisely that which Claude flees his bourgeois life to obtain. Malraux thus maintains an opposition between the "primitive pride" that the wilderness appears to offer all who enter it and the constraints of traditional French society, in which Claude feels his only option to be a life of industrial drudgery.

Another instance in which Grabot serves as a rather perverse role model for Perken and Claude comes from an incident that occurred while Grabot was in the army: using pus from his gonorrhea, Grabot intentionally blinded himself in one eye to spite a major with whom he was engaged in a feud. Perken recounts Grabot's initial visit to the major, a doctor in the infirmary. The doctor initially refused to accept that Grabot was ill, so Grabot returns a second time. Perken tells Claude what then transpires:

> The doctor reacts: "You again?" "Spots." "Where?" He [Grabot] opens his hand and shows him six *boutons*. He's sentenced to a month in prison. He immediately writes to the general, tells him he has an eye disease. As soon as he gets into prison—I forgot to tell you he had gonorrhea—he takes some pus from the gonorrhea, knowing perfectly well what he's doing, and sticks it in his eye. The major gets punished, but Grabot loses the eye, of course. He's one-eyed. (56)[16]

This passage plays on the double meaning of *boutons*: the word signifies both "button" and "spot," the latter often caused by skin rashes and infectious diseases. Malraux avails himself of this medical wordplay and a venereal disease common to the tropics to demonstrate that Grabot is willing to deform his body in order to bend his antagonist to his will. Grabot shares this readiness to undergo suffering to achieve his objective with both Garine and Perken; despite their ill health, both pursue their respective goals, Garine to lead revolution in China and Perken to defend his territory from the encroachment of French forces. Malraux depicts the determination of all three characters to persevere in their aims in spite of their physical maladies as a gesture of defiance of their own mortality and a symbol of their refusal to conform to the social mores embodied in their doctors' recommendations. The medical terminology and conditions mentioned in *The Way of the Kings* thus reflect not only Malraux's familiarity with those conditions but also his manipulation of them to address issues of greater literary and philosophical importance.

In a masterly, ironic twist, Grabot's original act of self-determination contributes to his eventual submission to his indigenous captors. When Claude and Perken finally locate him, Grabot is chained to a millstone in a Moï hut. Rather than ruling the Moï, he has been enslaved by them and his remaining eye has been fed to dogs. Claude and Perken are horrified by Grabot's complete abjection. The narrator observes that Claude feels "a holy terror, a horror of the inhuman, such as Claude had known earlier when confronted with the pyre" at the sight of the man from whom he and Perken had hoped to seek protection (108).

Like Kurtz, Grabot barely speaks after being rescued by Claude and Perken. His degeneration is so complete that at first he appears unable to speak French. Claude describes his few spoken words as

> harsh … emerging from an abyss of humiliation, but not bestial: what made them horrible was their simplicity. In the other hut, they had tried in vain to arouse the man's spirit: had it now returned only to reveal the most horrifying degeneration? And those dreams of torture, those tensed fingers, whose eyes were those nails ready to gouge? The hand was shaking at the end of the arm: there was no expression on the face, but the toes were curled. This body could speak—as soon as they had opened the hut with the millstone, that hand held out for food, that back accustomed to the throatlash—and only of what it had suffered. The language of the flesh spoke so elegantly that Claude forgot, for a moment, that they themselves were the ones most likely to be tortured. (114)[17]

The spectacle of Grabot, a man converted from the epitome of the European adventurer into a nearly speechless and dehumanized slave, represents the apex of the novel's trajectory and the pinnacle of the forest's power over the men who venture into it. It also represents the culmination of Malraux's use of physical symptoms to portray inherent human weakness.

Throughout the novel, the author uses the protagonists' bodies to express their fragile mortality and their powerlessness to control their own destinies. Grabot's physical appearance and scant verbal ability represent the zenith of this dynamic. Almost entirely deprived of speech by "the most horrifying degeneration," Grabot's body speaks for him: his hand craves only the sustenance necessary to keep him alive, and the scars on his back reveal his subjection to his captors. His "language of the flesh" is more powerful than any utterance. His very physical presence belies Perken and Claude's ability to master their surroundings and defy mortality. Grabot's lack of speech, like Kurtz's, indicate his mental effacement, his degeneration, and the possibility that Claude too could end up mute, mad, enslaved, and castrated. The mental faculties of both Perken and Claude begin to unravel, and Claude is filled with the desire to shoot first himself and then Grabot simply "to eliminate that face, that hatred, that presence—to chase away that evidence of his own condition as a man, like a murderer chopping off his own telltale finger" (116). Perken and Claude are thus confronted with the downfall of their idol and the proof that they, too, will decline and be overtaken by their physical, mortal bodies and the loss of their rationality.

For Perken, the realization that Grabot has been castrated is even more devastating than his deprivation of sight. Both Perken and Grabot are known for their erotic exploits, and the loss of this ultimate representation of manhood resonates with Perken because he also fears the loss of the ability to use his sexual organ: "It was clear now that there was a world of atrocities beyond those gouged eyes, that castration he had just discovered" (122). This final humiliation completes Grabot's transformation: the man who was once willing to endure physical suffering in order to inflict his will on others is now left unable to dominate either men or women. Grabot's castration and lack of sexual power become the central menace presented by the tropics for Perken, which is reflected in his impotence. His lack of virility is an invisible castration that haunts him as much as the loss of his territory to the French government.

Despite Perken's obsession with castration, Grabot's most significant deformation is his blindness. Malraux avails himself of the long-standing literary trope surrounding a lack of vision: from *Oedipus Rex* to *King Lear*, the loss of physical sight has been associated with the development of inner clarity. Grabot embodies humanity reduced to its most elemental form, since he has realized that he is a slave both to his captors and to his inescapable mortality. In addition to its conventional literary significance, blindness—a dominant motif in all of Malraux's work—takes on a unique meaning. Brian Thompson has written that throughout the author's novels, "blindness comes to represent, to make present, one aspect or another of man's condition as Malraux sees it—his vulnerability, his dependence on forces outside himself, his solitude, and the impossibility of fully communicating with others" (165). In *The Way of the Kings*, blindness is used as a manifestation of decay—most notably in the figure of Grabot, but also in a number of descriptions of other individuals, and even in the depiction of Indochina itself as a territory in decline.

In the novel, blindness always serves as an indicator of submission, from Grabot's total enslavement to the larger metaphor of Indochina as a territory blinded and possessed by others. In one instance, Malraux explicitly compares Cambodia to a blind man. Looking at the forest, which he calls "malarial life," Claude muses:

> The fetidness reminded him of a blind man he had seen in Phnom Penh, chanting the Ramayana in the middle of a pitiful circle, to the accompaniment of a rough guitar. There was a connection between that old man, who no longer roused anyone with his heroic poem but a circle of beggars and servant girls, and this decaying Cambodia: a tamed earth, a domesticated earth, where the hymns were as much in ruin as the temples, a dead earth among the dead.... Ahead of him the enemy, the earthbound jungle, like a clenched fist. (41)

The fetid foliage itself appears to be responsible for the ruin of ancient temples and the mendicant state of the blind musician, just as it is responsible for the malaria that plagues its residents. The forest strips everything that enters it down to its most elemental form: art decomposes, music is reduced to "a rough guitar," and humans lose their most valuable sense and their free will. Indeed, many figures are transformed into blind slaves by their time in the wilderness. As with the blind musician, Grabot is compared to Asia in terms of decomposition: "He, too, was decaying beneath the weight of Asia, like the temples. . . . A man who had dared to destroy one of his own eyes, and had tried to enter a region like this one alone, without any safeguards" (115). Likewise, the narrator describes how, nearly lost in the wilderness, Claude feels his sight and his self-determination slipping away from him: "He moved forward like a blind man. No matter how hard he tried, his eyes were almost useless here, and he had to rely on his sense of smell. The gusts of hot air that assaulted his nostrils were full of the smell of humus, which jarred his nerves: how was it possible to see the spikes when the path was covered with rotting leaves? He felt as dependent as a slave with his legs tied" (94). Claude's sensations of blindness and powerlessness anticipate the horror he will feel at his discovery of Grabot. They also indicate a regression to a more elemental mode of being. Malraux is careful to mention that despite his deformity, Grabot is "not bestial" but merely degenerated. Through his "language of the flesh," Grabot shows that he no longer broods over his own mortality, but rather that he exists only in the most fundamental human state: bereft even of language, he seeks only sustenance and shelter. Like Gloucester in *Lear*, Grabot reaches the depths of human debasement in blindness. Yet unlike Gloucester and Lear, Grabot cannot describe his suffering. The character's inability to give voice to his condition is a hallmark of the European tropical adventure narratives examined in this book. As I will make clear in subsequent chapters, the Latin American novels set in the wilderness seek to fill this void by narrating each protagonist's metamorphosis in the wilderness.

Grabot's degeneration signals the transformative power of the tropical environment in the novel. Like Kurtz in *Heart of Darkness*, he has regressed to a prehistorical state in which language has no place. The few words that he does speak refer only to his hopelessness and lack of will to change the present situation: "What bloody difference does it make?" (113). Malraux makes it clear that in the absence of French social and legal constraints, Grabot has retreated to a state of physical and mental subsistence. His enslavement implies that any white man can be dehumanized outside the confines of Western civilization. The once attractive sense of primitive pride for which Grabot was notorious has quickly devolved into an abject state and taken him back through human development. Malraux thus avails himself of the theories regarding the degenerative effect of the jungle on Frenchmen to heighten the philosophical ramifications of Grabot's enslavement.

After Claude and Perken encounter Grabot in the mill hut, the three men take refuge in another hut nearby. The Moï surround them, and Claude and Perken feel that their lives are in jeopardy. Terrified by the certainty that they will be subject to the same fate as Grabot, Perken feels his destiny closing around him and begins to go mad. He is overcome by "the insurmountable humiliation of man hunted down by his own destiny. . . . The struggle against decay exploded inside him, like a sexual fury, exacerbated by Grabot, who was still going round in circles in the hut as if around the corpse of his own courage" (120). Tormented by the prospect of physical pain and the loss of human dignity that he sees in Grabot, Perken enters into the ultimate decline, that of the disintegration of his mental faculties. His horror at the likelihood of his own enslavement and psychological degradation explodes in both physical and mental sensations. As if rebelling against his impotence, Perken feels a sudden sexual fury, inspired by a nearby gravestone adorned with two figures clutching their red, swollen genitals. His sudden sexual desire is as ineffectual as his desire to evade death. Mentally, his encroaching irrationality overtakes his thoughts; he feels himself entering "a bewitching madness, as if he were suddenly inspired" (121). Malraux links Perken's madness to the same root cause as the physical ailments that afflict the protagonists, the forest: "Madness, like the endless jungle beyond the edge of the clearing" (122). Like Kurtz before him, Perken has been mentally and physically ravaged by the forest.

The idea of a gradual mental unraveling of a European in the tropics did not originate with Malraux; indeed, the loss of sanity is a frequent motif in twentieth-century tropical narratives. While Malraux's use of the motif was undoubtedly shaped by Conrad, his depiction of Perken's insanity nonetheless takes on several unique characteristics. While Marlow can only describe Kurtz's descent into madness secondhand, Malraux depicts Perken's experience via a third-person omniscient narrator. This narrator explains that when Perken is faced with slavery and torture, "his passion for the freedom he was about to lose overcame him to the point of delirium" (123). In his delirium, Perken feels himself "flung sexually onto this dying freedom, lifted up by a fanatical will possessing itself before this imminent destruction," and "plunging into death itself" (124). Unable to face the anticipation of slavery, Perken seeks out his own death by advancing on his enemies. Madness in *The Way of the Kings* is different from insanity in the other novels analyzed in this book in that Perken is driven mad by his own fear of physical and mental domination by inhabitants of the forest, such as that which has befallen Grabot. In *Heart of Darkness*, on the other hand, madness is caused by a process of actually "going native"—of undergoing racial degeneration to the point that the protagonist, according to Conrad, becomes like the indigenous people. In the most famous example of degeneration in *Heart of Darkness*, Marlow is shocked by the thought that Kurtz engaged in cannibalism. In *The Way of the Kings*, however, even when Claude suspects that Perken has gone crazy and may commit suicide, he does not envision him joining the Moï and partaking in their mode of living but only becoming subject to them. This difference is encapsulated in the fact that while Kurtz rules the Africans around him, the Moï have enslaved Grabot. Kurtz is mad because he is degenerate; Perken goes mad because he is forced to confront his own mortality. In his depiction of Perken's demise, Malraux clearly takes advantage of contemporary medical associations between tropical illnesses (such as malaria and yellow fever) and madness in order to portray Perken's madness as both philosophical and medical in nature.

During the first third of the twentieth-century, theories about insanity cases in the tropics were in a state of flux. The general consensus still held that "the climate" rather than any specific microbial or neurological cause was responsible for madness among European colonials. In 1927, for example, Alexandre Le Dantec, a professor of medicine at the University of Bordeaux, remained convinced of the "slow effect of heat on the nervous system." Dr. Le Dantec recounts the history of a French officer "who went mad the first time when he went to Saigon. Sent back to France, he recovered his health. Sent to Guyana, another spell of madness, sent back to France, where he recovered and was declared 'unfit for service in hot climates'" (ASNOM).[18] During the same era, the increased study of the effects of malaria led colonial doctors such as a Dr. Comméléran to investigate the disease as a cause of mental illness, having observed alternating bouts of mental irritability and lethargy in malarial patients.[19] Malaria and syphilis were also thought to exacerbate tropical neurasthenia, which could lead to insanity.[20] Freudian theories regarding insanity had not yet had a major impact on colonial medicine.

Many different elements of Perken's psychosis are consistent with the contemporary medical thought regarding "colonial psychosis." According to Dr. Charles Joyeux, "Tropical psychosis can be observed particularly in isolated outposts in which there are few Europeans.... People say that the tropical sun contributes to the malady.... This psychosis sometimes ended in a tragic fashion, in murders and suicides" (252). These views echo those voiced by the Anglophone physicians discussed in Chapter 1. Malraux's frequent evocations of the tropical sun, the total isolation of Perken and Claude, and the former's suicidal tendencies reveal the author's familiarity with the popular medical opinion of the day and are used to give Perken's mental unraveling a scientific validity.

The atmosphere of fetid malaise that Malraux has carefully constructed through the use of medical metaphors now drives Perken toward the ultimate insanity: the desire for self-annihilation. Unable to bear the realization that he can no more control his own fate than Grabot could his, Perken believes that the only way to dominate the circumstances of his own demise is to seek it out actively. His madness is thus a manifestation of his desire to control his destiny. Ironically, his decline into a "bewitching madness" (121) is not so much the culmination of his submission to what he perceives as the malevolent force of the wilderness as a reaction against it. It is similar to Grabot's determination to be stung by a scorpion in order to banish his fear of it. Malraux foreshadows Perken's decision to confront his death in several conversations with Claude about the value of suicide in the face of insurmountable obstacles, in which Perken says: "It's when you decline that you have to kill yourself" (88). Perken concludes that the forest is the best place to take his own life: "In the jungle, you could at least kill yourself in peace" (120). Rather than turning his gun on himself, Perken decides to confront the Moï in order to choose his method of ending his life. The consideration of suicide as a final attempt to gain control is common among Malraux's protagonists in several of his novels, including *Man's Fate* (*La condition humaine*, 1933) and *The Conquerors*. In each case, the protagonist fails to kill himself. Real life, unfortunately, was different for Malraux: as previously mentioned, his father, Fernand-Georges, gassed himself in 1930, after losing money in the Parisian stock market.

Seeking his own annihilation, Perken leaves the hut and begins walking toward the Moï who are lying in wait in the dusk; Claude conjectures that Perken is now "mad" (130). As Perken advances, he falls on some of the war spikes the Moï had planted in the ground, injuring his knee. The pain simultaneously brings him out of his madness and robs him of the chance to die by a method of his own choosing. Perken is brought back to his right mind by the damage inflicted on his body. His vacillations between madness and sanity represent a major shift from the way madness is presented in *Heart of Darkness*. Whereas Marlow describes Kurtz as a man driven mad and made degenerate by the jungle and his contact with the native inhabitants, Perken's temporary fit of madness bears more resemblance to a bout of malaria than to Conrad's presentation of degeneration. Thus, medical discourse merges with Malraux's literary aesthetic to portray Perken's confrontation with his own mortality as both medically and philosophically motivated.

Although his physical injury marks the return of his mental faculties, it also heralds the onset of Perken's demise. The damage to his knee leaves him feeling feverish and ill. It is significant that the wound is caused by weapons planted in the earth because the injury represents the culmination of the telluric forces at work in the novel. Claude and Perken have both been haunted by the notion that the forest itself seeks to harm them, and the infection caused by the spikes brings these fears to fruition. The wound and the resulting pain make Perken aware that he has lost his chance to control his fate; as the fever overtakes him, he is filled with anger: "With the fever, hatred of man overwhelmed him, hatred of life, hatred of all these forces which were again dominating him, gradually dispelling his terrible memories, like the memory of ecstasy" (131). By linking fever and ecstasy, Malraux makes it clear that altered states can combine both pleasure and pain, hatred and relief. Like his sexual relations with indigenous women, Perken's madness represents a fleeting liberation from the knowledge that man is powerless in the face of his own physical weakness. With the return of sanity, the adventurer feels that he has been conquered anew by his mortality.

Claude and Perken eventually escape without their bas-reliefs after making a deal with the indigenous people to trade Grabot for jars of alcohol. This conclusion to the third part of the novel therefore represents a double failure: both men are deprived of the ability to determine the course of their existence, Claude through the loss of his profit, and Perken by his failure to meet death on his own terms. The two men make their way toward the remote region in which the latter once lived. The final part of the novel details Perken's slow, agonizing death from his infected wound as he watches militia forces move into the territory he formerly controlled.

Yet again, Malraux makes use of medical motifs and the presence of two ineffectual doctors to demonstrate the powerlessness of Western medicine in the face of human mortality. The pair of adventurers arrives at a Siamese village in search of medical treatment for Perken's wound. The first doctor who attends to them is a British physician who appears to be afflicted with the same lethargy that Claude and Perken have felt in the tropics. Claude interrupts the doctor during lunch, but the physician refuses to attend to the sick man until he has finished his meal (136). After examining of Perken's swollen knee and its black, puckered wound, the doctor remains listless: "He shrugged his shoulders again and seemed to be thinking, then he looked at Perken again, resentfully. 'Couldn't you have settled for a quiet life?'" (137). The doctor's remark reflects the general consensus even among the medical community that time spent in the tropics was bound to lead to an illness of this sort, and that the only way to avoid becoming sick was to avoid the region. For example, in 1931, the magazine *L'écho* of Paris expressed the dominant opinion: "Leaving the city—exposing yourself to the African or Indochinese bush—means you must be punishing yourself for something. No one can understand why an intelligent, active youth would have the imprudence to leave the calm, happy position of a functionary to go live in the tropics, to acquire some pernicious fever, and associate with colored people" (qtd. in ASNOM). Perken bristles at the doctor's affront, accuses him of being addicted to opium, and informs him that he is the famous Perken. The doctor's attitude calls into question the validity of Claude and Perken's quest, thereby setting up a diametric opposition between medical science and the adventurers' determination to give meaning to their lives in the wilderness. The doctor is therefore a manifestation of the Western civilization that Claude and Perken have left behind; his exhortation to them to simply settle for a quiet life expresses the same attitude toward a bourgeois existence that the protagonists seek to escape.

The doctor's diagnosis is the death sentence that Perken has been awaiting: "All right, Mr. Perken, listen carefully. You have suppurated arthritis in the knee. Within two weeks, you're going to die like an animal. And there's nothing we can do about it, do you understand? Absolutely nothing" (138). Perken's injury represents another instance in which Malraux's knowledge of medical conditions contributes greatly to his literary aesthetic. A "suppuration" (festering inflammation of the knee) evokes the same sort of swollen, distorted imagery with which Malraux has described the foliage. The pus from Perken's festering wound merges with "the life that moved and the life that oozed" (60). His foot decays from gangrene as if from the "gangrene of the jungle" itself (78). The body, then, comes to mimic its surroundings, signaling that Perken is decomposing like everything else in the jungle. The infection will poison his blood; Perken's true enemy is his own body, rather than any exterior menace. Malraux uses medical terminology to reveal that the human organism will rot away despite the individual's efforts to defy mortality or give his life meaning.

The British doctor's name, which the protagonists learn after he has departed, is "Blackhouse." His very name conveys a sense of hopelessness, futility, and death. His reliance on opium is a crutch—a further manifestation of his moral weakness, according to Perken: "Any white doctor on his rounds in this region is bound to be a character: addicted to either opium or sex" (139). On a metaphoric level, the doctor's addiction indicates the ineffectual nature of Western medicine in combating the tropical illnesses that threaten European colonists in Indochina. The suggestion of opium addiction and sexual indulgence refers to the two most common forces that incapacitated colonial officers in Indochina. The French-trained Siamese doctor from whom Claude seeks a second opinion tells him that if an amputation were possible Perken could be saved, but that in the jungle no such equipment is available.[21] Thus, although Malraux maximizes his knowledge of medical conditions to portray the tropics as the epicenter of decay in the novel, he nevertheless portrays medical professionals as virtually powerless in the face of the diseases they struggle to counteract. They are representatives of the society Perken has rejected, and are completely ineffective in combating the forest's power of decay. Perken is left to confront his fate with no more medical assistance than a few vials of opium, which he refuses to take because they are indications of weakness for him. Out of a sense of loyalty and shared destiny, Claude vows to accompany him through his final days.

Insects are a symbol of the insidious power of the wilderness in the novel. As Perken gradually succumbs to the fever caused by his wound, they surround him as the flies do Orestes in Sartre's *The Flies* (1943): "Perken was sinking into a stupor. Very close to his ears, mosquitoes buzzed softly. The pain of the bites was transparent, covering the pain of his wound like filigree. It, too, rose and fell, inflaming the fever, forcing Perken into a nightmarish struggle not to touch himself.... Everything he had thought about life was decomposing beneath the fever like a body in the earth" (163). Malraux uses mosquitoes, known carriers of infectious diseases such as malaria, to heighten the portrayal of Perken's powerlessness in the face of his own demise. Insects of all sorts, from the spiders that dangle before Claude's eyes to the bugs that cover the bas-reliefs, represent the "microscopic life" that the protagonists abhor because they cannot control it (66). Anticipating Sartre's later work, insects—particularly mosquitoes—signify destiny. Ellis has noted that in all of Malraux's writings, insects are associated with "all manifestations of human impotence, of failure, and of the absurd" (31). Perken's failure to prevent the mosquitoes from biting him is a metaphor for his inability to stave off death, and he expires soon thereafter. Malraux's medical knowledge about the role of mosquitoes in the spread of tropical diseases thus merges with his aesthetic goals in employing insect life as a demonstration of destiny.

Perken's certain death inspires him to continue his quest to prevent the militia from entering "his" territory. The ongoing construction of a railroad by the French guarantees his loss of control over the land as surely as his infection assures his death. The encroachment of the militia on the region Perken had hoped to control parallels the advance of his fever. He is determined to fight them both, and yet "he was relieved to rediscover the militiamen and death: linked to one another, both advancing towards their goal like the great columns of smoke" (153). His subjection to his fate is the final example in a series of instances in which physical suffering is both a symptom and a cause of an individual's tragic inability to fulfill his goals before death.

The Way of the Kings is populated with characters whose medical impairments prevent them from accomplishing their objectives. Among them, three stand out: Grabot, Ramèges, and Perken. In his blindness, Grabot is the ultimate symbol of a man who suffers physically because he has been subdued by another social group. In his attempt to leave behind wealth in Paris and his participation in the social world in general, he has become trapped in another world in which he is the slave; his subjection manifests itself in his blindness and castration. Likewise, Claude sees Ramèges as a diseased individual who tows the official line and obstructs Claude in the pursuit of his goal; Ramèges's liver abscess is both the cause and the symptom of his unwillingness to break free from the official position. Perken himself eventually succumbs to domination by others as well: it is no coincidence that his death occurs within earshot of the French colonial forces as they build a railroad through the territory he sought to control. His physical well-being and his ultimate goal fail at the same time. The infection that ravages his body is a metaphor for the rule of law embodied by the French colonial forces; its unstoppable progression crushes Perken's earthly aspirations.

All these failed attempts at self-determination make *The Way of the Kings* an existential tragedy. Both Claude and Perken repeatedly state that their desire to enter the tropical forest stems from their rejection of French society and, more important, from their determination to make their actions meaningful. Claude in particular rejects the notion of the afterlife and affirms the existential maxim that life is given meaning only through action, not through ideas: "What to do with the corpses of ideas which dominated the conduct of men who thought their existence was useful to some kind of salvation, what to do with the words—those other corpses—of those who wanted to live their lives according to a model? There was no purpose in life, but that in itself had become a condition of action" (32). For him, adventure represents this action; it signifies an engagement with the world rather than flight from it. Claude's desire to act as a rebellion against human mortality links *The Way of the Kings* to the rest of Malraux's corpus of texts. All his heroes—particularly those of *The Conquerors* and *Man's Fate*—take similar action, struggling against their own mortality in their desire to foment political revolution. With its countless illnesses, however, it is the forest rather than fascism or any other political force that presents the greatest obstacle to the protagonists of *The Way of the Kings* in their attempt to give existential meaning to their lives.

Disease of all kinds is linked to both physical and philosophical struggles with mortality in *The Way of the Kings*. The varied maladies from which the protagonists suffer dramatize their fight for physical existence and psychological validation within the rainforest. Medical conditions are therefore an essential component of the dominant motif of the novel because they provide the language with which Malraux constructs his protagonists' confrontations with mortality. The tropics' enervating qualities present the biggest danger: both Claude and Perken are often tempted to give in to the lethargy caused by fever, the madness fueled by delirium, the hopeless subservience imposed by blindness, or the slow death delivered by untreatable infection. Since decay is, according to Perken, "the true death" (31), various forms of suicide—such as putting a gun to one's head, voluntarily walking into certain ambush by the Moï, or refusing life-saving medical treatment—emerge as valid yet failed acts of heroism in the novel. *The Way of the Kings*, like the other tales I analyze in this book, is a narrative of failure. The existential validation the protagonists seek in the wilderness is belied by the irrefutable truth of universal human decay. Malraux skillfully uses medical motifs as an indispensable literary tool in his evocation of a fetid jungle that becomes the site of man's unsuccessful attempts to give meaning to life in the face of death.

Chapter 3

Writing in *The Vortex*: Madness, Medicine, and the Lost Notebooks of Arturo Cova

José Eustasio Rivera's *La vorágine*, known in English as *The Vortex*, is a narrative of a failed adventure, but it is not a failed narration, as John Brushwood characterized it in 1975 (43).[1] Like many tropical adventure tales, *The Vortex* is narrated in the first person, by Arturo Cova, an upper-class Colombian poet. As the novel opens, Cova flees Bogotá with his underage lover, Alicia, whom he has recently impregnated. The couple hides out with Cova's friends in the rural Colombian plains to avoid their families, who would undoubtedly force them to marry. Life on the frontier is lawless, and Alicia is soon kidnapped by a local strongman named Narciso Barrera. Cova pursues them into the depths of the wilderness. The novel we read is supposedly Cova's diary, written in the wilderness. Cova, the sophisticated urban poet, slowly loses his mind as he travels deeper into the heart of the jungle and simultaneously into the depths of his own psyche. The voyage into the forest is thus both a literal and a metaphorical journey. As Cova gets farther away from civilization, he becomes less civilized himself. He begins to behave in irrational and self-destructive ways, such as threatening to kill the members of his expedition party and himself. He is eventually reunited with Alicia, but by this time they are completely lost in the jungle. Their son is born prematurely in the wilderness. Cova's journal entries become increasingly erratic as they recount his mental unraveling. The novel ends abruptly when Cova leaves the diary behind in the hope that someone will find it and rescue them. The last line of the novel, delivered by a frame narrator who has indeed found and published the diary, is one of the most famous lines in Latin American literature: "¡Los devoró la selva!" (*La vorágine* 385) or "The jungle devoured them!" (*Vortex* 320).

The novel, published in 1924, is often maligned for containing too much straightforward character exposition and a ragged, indeterminate conclusion. Yet both of these criticisms point to the novel's constitutive element: the madness of the narrating protagonist, Cova. In fact, the unbroken first-person narrative passages that early scholars of the work disparaged are the source of Rivera's greatest originality. In them, the madman speaks freely, unchecked by a distancing third-person narrator. This seemingly technical detail transforms the way in which the tale is told. The first-person narration allows for direct exposition of Cova's mental unraveling, which in turn unravels the novel's narrative coil, leaving behind a tale whose form is as tattered as the protagonist's psyche and as unruly as the wilderness that surrounds him. In addition, the first-person narration gives Cova's madness an intimate quality at which *Heart of Darkness* only hints. While Conrad's reader can only infer Kurtz's madness through Marlow's intentionally obscure mode of storytelling, in Rivera's novel the reader is thrown directly into Cova's psyche. The reader is thus forced into the raw "vortex" of Cova's insanity without the benefit of the distancing mechanism provided by Marlow's framed narration in *Heart of Darkness*.

Insanity is the central theme of *The Vortex*, yet scholars have thus far neglected evidence that Cova's madness reflects Rivera's own preoccupation with mental health.[2] The impact of his personal fear of insanity goes far beyond biographical detail. Medical vocabulary is used as a descriptive tool in the novel. It forms the backbone of the representation of the tropics and its inhabitants, infusing them all with an aura of sickness and decay. The privileged position given to illness makes the novel reminiscent of decadent literature of the late nineteenth century in which sickness plays an important role, such as José Asunción Silva's *De sobremesa* (1896; awkwardly rendered in English as *After-Dinner Conversation: The Diary of a Decadent*) and Jorge Isaacs's *María* (1867). In *The Vortex*, however, the locus of the malady is the wilderness rather than the city or the drawing room. Rivera's portrayal of madness reveals his thorough familiarity with early twentieth-century medical opinion: the author suffered from convulsive fits and depression that required frequent attention from doctors. For Rivera, medical terminology was also a major component of a new type of writing that sought to present Latin American literature as both modern and autochthonous. To this end, Rivera availed himself of medical and social theories imported from Europe and reformulated by Latin American doctors and health officials. These theories shape both the form and content of *The Vortex* and make Cova's madness the structural and artistic bedrock of the novel.

Rivera's obsession with mental health was political as well as personal. Cova's self-diagnosed madness and his uncertain fate are emblematic of the author's concerns about the well-being of Colombia as a young nation. They also reflect the contemporary debate over degeneration of the "Colombian race" among the country's elite during the first decades of the twentieth century. At that time, European scientific theories cast doubt on the future development of Latin American nations because of their racial miscegenation. This concept was debated within Colombia, with political and medical texts calling for a period of national regeneration in the face of this supposed racial degeneration as well as political and military failures. The sickness of the protagonist's body and mind in the novel thus represents the sickness of Colombia's body politic. In this way, *The Vortex* offers a strong counterpoint to the vision of nation building that is presented in other telluric Latin American novels such as Ricardo Güiraldes's *Don Segundo Sombra* (1926) and Rómulo Gallegos's *Doña Bárbara* (1929). Those texts emphasize the dominion of man over nature and the consequent forging of national identity based on the triumph of a white, well-educated Latin American protagonist over his environs. *The Vortex*, in contrast, recounts the mental and physical destruction of such a man on his own soil.

Yet Cova's madness is not an entirely negative condition: it grants him access to the lyrical poetic power necessary to evoke the tropical forest around him. His altered state of mind is a prerequisite for artistic creation in the form of the diary he leaves behind, and on an allegorical level, the diary represents a new mode of autochthonous literature. As a result, the unsettling fate of Cova and his family has important resonances within the cultural, political, and literary contexts of the time that go far beyond the usual critical interpretation of the novel as a protest against abuses by the rubber oligarchy. Cova's madness and the deliberately uncertain conclusion of the novel are indicative of two ideas that are held in tension throughout the work: the protagonist's demise serves as a metaphor for the sickness of Colombia as a nation, and yet this very sickness is the source of its great literary innovation.

Authors of *novelas de la tierra* (the Spanish American regional novel of the 1920s) often addressed contemporary political situations and consciously strove to present a new form of modern Latin American literature strongly rooted in the region itself. As a result, nonliterary discourses such as those of the legal and scientific disciplines permeate telluric novels in order to demonstrate Latin America's engagement with modernity.[3] As Doris Sommer has shown, these novels intended to bolster the ideals of national unification and modernization by associating the forging of the nation and its literature with domestic tales of marriage and procreation.[4] In this sense, Rivera's novel offers a disturbing counternarrative to books such as *Doña Bárbara*. *The Vortex* presents a vision of a nation whose future, embodied in Cova and his son, is imperiled by mental and physical illness brought on by telluric forces. Indeed, medical discourse plays an important and largely unexplored role in the literary construction of the nation.[5] As Nancy Leys Stepan has written of Rivera's historical moment, Latin America "was involved in nationalist self-making, in which the setting of boundaries between self and other and the creation of identities were increasingly carried out by and through scientific and medical discourses" (*Hour* 7). While biography and literary creation should not be conflated in a facile manner, Rivera's own life and work do manifest the impact of recent scientific advances on Colombian cultural discourse, especially in *The Vortex*.

The prevalence of medical discourse in the novel simultaneously demonstrates Rivera's familiarity with contemporary medical theory and highlights the perceived danger of the unrestrained wilderness (a metaphor for barbarity) to the future of Colombia as a nation. Various health problems depicted in the novel emphasize the weakness of Colombians in contrast to the land: the illnesses that afflict many characters, such as malaria and other fevers endemic to the tropical rainforest; the poor health and short lifespan of residents of the forest caused by abysmal working conditions; and most important, the carefully developed insanity of the novel's protagonist, which is fueled by the climate. All these elements portray Colombia as a nation without control over its land and in political chaos. At the heart of this dire mix of medical and political debility lie the fears of racial degeneration (*degeneración de la raza*) that were being debated in Bogotá in the 1910s and 1920s. These debates demonstrate the metaphoric link between personal health and national strength. Rivera's own medical ailments, legitimate and acute as they may have been, are symptomatic of those of the Colombian elite and are reflected in his novel.

This chapter examines four facets of madness at play in the novel: Rivera's concern with his own health and the medical treatment he received before succumbing to a cerebral infection; the way in which the vocabulary of medicine and mental illness is used to depict the forest and Cova's insanity; the protagonist's madness as a reflection of the fears of national racial degeneration that plagued Colombia at the time *The Vortex* was conceived and written; and the process by which sickness transforms Cova into a writer uniquely capable of evoking the lyric possibilities of his surroundings. All these factors make *The Vortex* a radically modern novel because the narrator's unstable mind affects the form of the work itself. By presenting the wilderness as the source of overpowering literary inspiration, *The Vortex* breaks a path for all later novelas de la selva.

José Eustasio Rivera's medical history was characterized by periods of good health marred by episodes of melancholic withdrawal and a series of cerebral ailments. One of these ailments eventually culminated in his death in a New York hospital in 1928 at the age of forty. Elucidating the specific medical conditions with which Rivera was diagnosed poses a challenge to twenty-first-century scholars because so few medical documents survive and, to a greater degree, because his biographers and acquaintances were reluctant to broach the sensitive and highly personal topic of Rivera's health. I am not interested in making a posthumous diagnosis of Rivera's illness; rather, I am interested in the diseases from which Rivera *thought* he may have been suffering. My approach to the novel is therefore neither diagnostic nor psychoanalytic but historical, in that it examines Rivera's life and Colombian medical theories to reveal the ways Rivera employs the latter to dramatize madness in his novel. When these factors are taken into account, it becomes clear that madness and medicine function as principal motifs in the novel; each is heavily laden with literary and political signification.

There are several indications that Rivera believed he may have been suffering from syphilis and a nervous disorder, both of which were thought to cause madness, delirium, and psychotic behavior. Rivera's various biographers offer a surprisingly wide range of medical conditions from which Rivera may have suffered. While the best of them, Eduardo Neale Silva, is extremely cautious in making a postmortem diagnosis, stating delicately if vaguely that "something was happening to Rivera" (153), others are quick to state that Rivera was plagued by fears of syphilis, neurasthenia, suicide, and malaria.[6] The reticence among Rivera's family, friends, and biographers with regard to his health was surely due to their reluctance to damage the image of the Bard of the Tropics (*cantor del trópico*), as Rivera was known, with a diagnosis unbecoming a national poet. Their disinclination to make explicit his particular illness may have been exacerbated by the taboos against discussing mental and sexual problems around the turn of the century and even well into the mid-twentieth century. The task of illuminating the dark corners of Rivera's medical history becomes that of reading between the lines of his biography in conjunction with a close examination of the medical climate in Colombia at the time. An exploration of Rivera's own fears about his health within the historical context of Colombia in the 1920s sheds light on the ways in which the centrality of the protagonist's madness affects the composition of *The Vortex*. In what follows, I will examine Rivera's reported afflictions against the backdrop of medical discourse to show how they determine the construction of madness and the forest in the novel.

Rivera, born in 1888, was a native of Neiva, in the province of Huila. While his home was described as "modest and honorable" (Neale Silva 15), many of his family members had served in various high-level posts within the Colombian government and military.[7] This political and military past set Rivera apart from other boys of his age, and may have helped him gain admittance to the *escuela normal* (normal school) in Bogotá, which he attended beginning in 1906. It was during his time in the capital that Rivera suffered from his first bouts of ill heath. In 1909, Rivera began the fifth year of study (he had been placed in the second year on his arrival at the school) but was forced to suspend it because of a "tenacious headache and general despondency" (Neale Silva 82–83). While he would later complete his studies and receive a law degree in 1917, these two complaints would afflict him in increasing orders of magnitude for the rest of his life. The second period of ill health occurred during his trip to the plains in 1918, when he was incapacitated in the village of Orocué in Casanare. Rivera was unwell several times while in the country:

> On certain occasions he was overcome by powerful headaches that obliged him to spend hours—sometimes days—mute and motionless, seated under a tree on the patio, his eyes closed, as if he were dreaming. And if someone knocked at the door, he would slip inside. During these periods of despondency, his spirits were clouded by black visions and

he lost his habitual stoicism.... One supposes that this same illness had afflicted him in 1909 when he gave up his studies. Something was happening to Rivera. His illness went through cycles of greater and lesser gravity. Once, on a hunting expedition near Orocué, a similar attack left him limp and senseless. (Neale Silva 153)

While this description of clouded spirits (*espíritu nublado*) clearly indicates what we now call depression, Rivera was treated for what seemed to be "a nervous disorder," an amorphous diagnosis that could cover everything from epilepsy to neurasthenia (Rosselli 246). According to Rosselli, common treatments for epilepsy and other nervous disorders during the second half of the nineteenth century in Colombia included the prohibition of any type of stimulant, including tea, coffee, and spirits; the weekly use of a laxative; the wearing of flannel; leaving the head uncovered; and frequent warm baths (175–76). At several times during his periods of ill health, Rivera was indeed encouraged to avoid coffee and alcohol, and to avoid exerting himself lest he irritate his nerves (Neale Silva 194).

Several months after the trip to the plains, Rivera moved to Sogamoso, the site of a tribunal that was to judge some legal matters in which he had been involved. Again, the poet was overcome with the same afflictions. He was visited by "the illustrious doctor Don Julio Sandoval," and Rivera spent two months convalescing from his illness in the home of Soledad Murillo (Neale Silva 155). Gabriel Camargo Pérez, a native of Sogamoso, determined that "José Eustasio Rivera suffered from a little bit of neurasthenia and nothing else. In his vest pocket, he kept a small revolver bullet that he always showed to Soledad, saying, 'This will be the one. Life is despicable. I have no illusions about life'" (qtd. in Neale Silva 156).[8] Such depressive and suicidal thoughts would plague Rivera throughout much of his life, and undoubtedly influenced his creation of Arturo Cova as a psychologically delicate poet. In his novel, Rivera describes Cova as "neurasthenic"—a slightly unusual adjective for an upper-class Colombian male at the time, as neurasthenia was thought to afflict primarily women. *Neurasthenia* was originally popularized by the eminent American doctor George M. Beard in *A Practical Treatise on Nervous Exhaustion* (*Neurasthenia*), which was published in1883.[9] The theory gained renown in Colombia only following the French translation of the work in 1895 and its subsequent diffusion by Jean-Martin Charcot and his disciples. The first appearance of *neurasthenia* in Colombia is attributed to Dr. Julio Rodríguez Piñeres, who in 1898 summarized his findings on the condition in his doctoral thesis, "Neurastenia (Agotamiento Nervioso)" (Neurasthenia [nervous exhaustion]; Rosselli 260). Its symptoms were largely akin to those of what we now call depression and were attributed to an exacerbation of weak nerves by all sorts of stimuli, such as alcohol, caffeine, and foreign climates. The disease was thought to lead to racial degeneration and, most significantly, madness and occasionally suicide.

Unlike Camargo Pérez, other friends and relatives of Rivera maintained that he suffered from recurrent malarial attacks that he contracted while away from Bogotá. For example, in 1918 while in Orocué he suffered an attack of fevers, reputedly from malaria (Neale Silva 157). In March 1921, Rivera suffered his most serious and most publicized illness while on a hunting trip with Félix Dussán Vargas in Purificación. The painful attack was characterized by convulsive fits:

> In a short time, Rivera was laid out on the floor with his hands clutching his head; this was followed by a convulsive fit that left him writhing. His friends ran to help him without knowing what had happened. Delirious, the poet shook and seemed to be in terrible pain. Emergency measures were taken for sunstroke, but since the victim did not respond, it was decided that the trip should be canceled. The attacks continued, each time more serious, and as it was impossible to keep him still, a straitjacket was improvised in which Rivera was tied hand and foot and taken to Purificación. (Neale Silva 181)

Articles were published about this incident in the March, April, and May 1921 editions of *El tiempo*, one bearing the title "Serious illness of poet Rivera in Purificación." The articles state that Rivera had suffered seizures and was unconscious for several days. He was seen by Dr. José María Lombana Barreneche, an eminent doctor and presidential candidate (and, according to Humberto Rosselli, a proponent of the nascent study of psychiatry in Colombia [260]). According to Neale Silva, "One of [Rivera's] friends explained the case to the doctor, saying that Rivera had been self-medicating with certain new injections, in the belief that they were treating his malaria. It is likely that José Eustasio gave his friends this explanation to avoid revealing anything about his private life" (181–82). Such statements by Rivera's biographer frustrate scholars because they show Neale Silva falling prey to the antiquated notion that his subject's private life is not fodder for biography. In contrast, Rivera's friend Ricardo Charria Tobar is more explicit about his diagnosis and treatment. A self-described intimate of the author and a medical student, Charria Tobar formed part of a medical team that discussed Rivera's condition. Through Charria Tobar, we learn that Rivera was in a state of "manic exaltation, shouting out words that horrified the Sisters of Charity," for which reason he was soon transferred to a nearby hotel in a straitjacket (117). The team received word that the poet had been receiving injections of arsenic, and the group meditated on possible complications: "At that time, we were all obsessed with syphilis, and arsenic treatments, particularly in intravenous form, were so popular that they were often used as a simple restorative measure. Arsenic was also used to treat chronic malaria" (117). The members of the medical team were divided between malaria and sunstroke as the cause of illness, but in any case they recommended via telegram the immediate cessation of the use of arsenic and a dose of quinine instead. While it is unclear if Rivera had been medicating himself with arsenic before his illness in Purificación, it is obvious that he became very concerned about his health from this point forward. Charria Tobar continues, "Rivera, like the rest of his generation, was obsessed with syphilis, for which reason he traveled to Panama, where he underwent rigorous lab and clinical tests in a hospital. All results for syphilis were negative" (119).[10] According to Neale Silva, the doctors later determined that Rivera's fits were not a result of malaria or syphilis but rather a cerebral infection of indeterminate origin (182).

The uncertainty surrounding Rivera's ailment reflects the scarcity of scientific information regarding mental disorders in Colombian medicine during the early twentieth century and this same community's hesitance to discuss sexual and mental problems freely, especially as such problems would counter Rivera's image as an illustrious and vibrant poet. The theories of Freud had not yet had a major impact on Colombian medicine and psychology at this time, so any diagnosis Rivera received would have been based on nineteenth-century medical knowledge.[11] Both complications from syphilis and nervous disorders of the time were thought to give rise to fits of irrationality, such as the manic state mentioned by Charria Tobar. A comment by a friend at the time of Rivera's examination indicates that the poet's preoccupation with his health centered on his lucidity and mental competency rather than his sexual behavior: "An officious and talkative friend assured Rivera that during his illness he had gone mad, and he [Rivera] had been heard to say such-and-such to the doctor. Although the patient did not scare easily, he thought it prudent to have himself examined by specialists in Bogotá as soon as he got back to the capital" (Neale Silva 182). No other evidence remains of Rivera's medical treatment on his return to Bogotá. These incidents and several that followed imply, however, that the author was treated for mental rather than physical illness.

While the nascent science of psychiatry did little more than prescribe injections (often of morphine) and bed rest, it seems that Rivera followed these instructions assiduously, particularly when under stress. For example, several months later, Rivera was accused of disparaging Colombian letters while representing his country on a diplomatic mission to Peru. Such a scandal erupted among the literati of Bogotá that Rivera suffered another attack of nerves. According to Neale Silva: "He felt poorly and took to his bed; it was the same illness as always. He repeated that it was a relapse of the malaria he had contracted months ago on the plains, but he had the good sense to ask that he be treated with the medicines he had with him. 'For two days he was in such bad shape that we feared for his life,' said Don Antonio Gómez Restrepo. 'The poor man had lost his mind and was delirious and convulsing'" (193–94). Again Neale Silva manifests his skepticism about Rivera's true ailment without being specific as to its origin. This is indicative of a disorder or condition that Neale Silva thought unbefitting a well-known author, and one Rivera clearly took pains to conceal by maintaining that he suffered from complications from malaria rather than any innate pathology.

In the spring of the following year, 1922, Rivera began writing *The Vortex* in Sogamoso. Neale Silva is careful to mention the tranquil life and cautious diet (avoiding alcohol and sweets) to which the poet adhered in order to maintain his mental stability. It is clear that his mental health was a primary concern during the composition of the novel itself, and it is thus not surprising that some of the medical terminology with which Rivera was surrounded crept into his literary activity. Of the composition of the novel, Gabriel Camargo Pérez notes that "whenever [Rivera] was writing, he preferred to stop rather than strain his nerves," as if the act of writing scenes of a mental unraveling might be enough to provoke a nervous fit (11). Having written the first part of the novel during the spring and summer, Rivera embarked on a voyage in September 1922 with a group who intended to demarcate the borders between Venezuela and Colombia. The invitation had been extended to him after the lawyer of the expedition dropped out.

This trip would have an enormous impact on the novel both in terms of Rivera's politics and of his focus on the insalubrity of his surroundings. The group went from Bogotá to Baranquilla on the Magdalena River and from there by sea to Puerto España in Trinidad and on to Venezuela. Some of the details of the trip were later disputed by its participants, but it is known that Rivera traveled on the Orinoco River leg of the journey and that in November he renounced his post and abandoned the group because of personal and strategic disagreements with the leader of the expedition, Justino Garavito. Lacking supplies, including food, Rivera and others who had also abandoned the mission sent urgent telegrams to Bogotá and received no response, perhaps inspiring Rivera's depiction of Cova's failed attempts to communicate with Colombian authorities.

Ill health followed Rivera from the plains to the forest, much as it does for the characters in his novel. The engineer of the Venezuelan portion of the group, Escobar Larrazábal, noted in his diary: "December 26. Our friend Rivera is feverish. Little by little malaria invades our camps. We already look like the undead: shriveled, opaque, and dirty skin, glassy yellow eyes, a listless pace, breathlessness and general decay" (qtd. in Neale Silva 241). Neale Silva summarizes additional entries in Larrazábal's diary thus: "The days passed like a long and feverish torture. Heavy heads, fevers and chills, and always the thirst, which seemed to crack the lips and tongue. In the midst of confusing dreams and frightening visions, the poet thought he saw his boss: 'I'm going to blow your brains out,' he told him, while he rattled the revolver against his face, cursing him" (241). In April 1923, Rivera was living in the area of Yavita and suffered two new attacks of malaria (Neale Silva 250). Following the months he spent near the country's frontiers, Rivera returned to Bogotá to denounce the atrocities he had witnessed and heard about. The impact of this trip on Rivera's political and literary work cannot be overestimated. Rivera had come to see the Colombian tropical forest as a site of abuse, sickness, and death, rather than an idealized natural world. His only other book, *The Promised Land* (*Tierra de Promisión*), had been published in 1921, before his travels through the forests of Colombia and Venezuela. A slim volume of sonnets, *The Promised Land* had garnered praise and earned Rivera the moniker Bard of the Tropics. Read against the background of his later work, however, the poetry offers a conventional vision of the wilderness as a place of bucolic tranquillity:

> The jungle of wide domes, with whirling winds in rite
> Of symphony, preludes its matins towering;
> And, like fine violins, as two boughs moaning sing,
> The fronds emit deep sighs, now swaying left and right. (17)[12]

Rivera's experience in the forest would transform his imagery from "whirling winds in rite of symphony" into a nightmarish vortex.

After his return from the interior of the country, there are no reported accounts of health trouble until Rivera's arrival in New York City in 1928, where he intended to oversee the translation of his novel into English. On November 5, he was seen by a Dr. Hurtado for flulike symptoms. Shortly afterward, he was overcome by "cefalagia" (extreme headache) and suffered from convulsive fits. Rivera was taken to Polyclinic Hospital, where he remained comatose until the 28th. He returned to consciousness briefly before developing a high fever and succumbing on December 1, 1928.

These bare facts regarding the author's death have been interpreted in a variety of ways. Rivera's biographer refers to the "black legend" surrounding Rivera's death: it was rumored that he had been poisoned, or that his death was the result of his "life of sexual excess … the orgiastic wasting of his vitality," the latter a clear reference to syphilis and sexual neurasthenia (Neale Silva 445). The death certificate officially stated the cause of death as "Hemiplegia (primarily) and Malaria (secondarily)"—an eerie coincidence, given that Arturo Cova cries out "¡Hemiplejia!" when he believes himself to be dying during one of his psychotic fits (Rivera, *La vorágine* 374). *Hemiplegia* refers to a paralysis of one side of the body, but Neale Silva's later consultations with medical professionals throw this cause of death into doubt.

Regardless of the actual cause of death, which will never be known, the widely differing rumors that circulated at the time indicate the precarious state of medicine when faced with diseases involving both mental and physical symptoms. Because empirical knowledge regarding the inner workings of the brain was lacking, mental problems fell under the broad category of "neurosis," which was as subject to political and cultural interpretation as it was to scientific fact. The rumors about Rivera's health and his own concerns therefore demonstrate the melding of medical and political discourse, the fusion of science and culture. A brief look at popular sociomedical theories of the time will illuminate this trenchant practice of mixing politics and science for nationalistic purposes.

During the nineteenth century many Latin American doctors acquired medical training in Paris. In the twentieth century, however, the United States gradually surpassed Europe as the most popular site of study for aspiring doctors (Stepan 72). In Rivera's lifetime, then, the Latin American medical community interpreted and tailored scientific advancements from Europe to suit its own purposes, especially when it came to issues of race. One of the dominant trends in European medicine during the early decades of the twentieth century that made its way to Latin America via France was the practice of eugenics and its concomitant theory of racial degeneration, which forms an important subtext in *The Vortex*. First suggested by the polymath Francis Galton in his *Hereditary Genius* (1869), eugenic theory posited that the human race could be improved by selective breeding, and conversely, that reproduction by people thought to be genetically "unfit" would lead to a degeneration or decline of the human race. *Degeneration* was made a household word by Bénédict-Augustin Morel and Max Nordau, as discussed in Chapter 1, while eugenics gained popularity at the turn of the century following the reexamination of genetic studies conducted by Gregor Mendel and Jean-Baptiste Lamarck. These studies offered concrete proof of the ways in which genes were passed from one generation to another, and therefore seemed to give credence to eugenic theory. In contrast to Britain and the United States, where theories derived from Mendelian conceptions of genetics were prevalent, in Latin America the Lamarckian branch of eugenics was dominant, maintaining that acquired characteristics could be passed from parents to children (Stepan, *Hour* 64–65). As a result, Latin American eugenicists promoted physical, moral, and mental hygiene in addition to controlled reproduction as a means of improving society. The importance of this detail becomes apparent in my analysis of *The Vortex* because Arturo Cova is clearly concerned about both his own mental health and tendency toward alcoholism, and about the danger of passing those degenerate defects acquired in the wilderness on to his progeny.

What exactly did the eugenics debate in Colombia look like? In her excellent *"The Hour of Eugenics": Race, Gender, and Nation in Latin America*, Nancy Leys Stepan is quick to point out that theories of eugenics and racial degeneration differed from country to country within Latin America, although all of them did subscribe in some fashion to the Lamarckian concepts imported from France. The Latin American medical community undoubtedly had a conflicted relationship with the concepts of eugenics: the engagement of its members with theories of degeneration and selective breeding indicated their commitment to scientific and cultural modernity, but Latin Americans were nevertheless regarded by eugenicists outside the region as "'tropical,' 'backward,' and racially 'degenerate'" because of their mixed racial heritage and the climates in which they lived (Stepan, *Hour* 8). Each Latin American country confronted its backwardness in the eyes of the European scientific community in its own way. While Mexicans celebrated their *mestizaje* (mixed race identity), as José Vasconcelos did eloquently in *La raza cósmica* (*The Cosmic Race*, 1925), Argentines pursued a goal of racial purity through immigration and reproduction, adhering to J. B. Alberdi's popular slogan, "To populate is to govern." Alcides Arguedas, the author of *Pueblo enfermo* (A sick people, 1909), was convinced that Bolivia's impoverished status resulted from the country's high concentration of indigenous inhabitants: "Without the predominance of indigenous blood, from the beginning the nation would have had a more consistent orientation, adopting material and moral perfections, and today it would be at the same level as other places favored by immigration flows from the old continent" (31). In each country, an increase in the number of citizens treated for insanity and alcoholism was thought to indicate the onset of degeneration.

In Colombia, the medical community was divided as to whether a process of racial degeneration afflicted the country. Medical societies debated the pertinence of European theories to Colombia and other South American nations: "In countries like Brazil, Argentina, and Mexico, the prestige of eugenics sparked the interest of Colombian doctors in the topic of race, which was widely debated" (Obregón Torres 87). The most vocal proponent of degeneration was Professor Miguel Jiménez López, whose lecture "Locura en Colombia" (Madness in Colombia, 1916) emphasized the increase in cases of neurosis among the Colombian population as evidenced by a jump in the number of patients examined for "alienation." Rosselli recounts that Jiménez López blamed several factors (283). First, he cited genetic inheritance, noting that "the genetic mixing of Spanish colonizers and aboriginal races is not biologically felicitous. The aboriginal races were deficient since before the Discovery, they were precociously degenerate. The conquistadores had monstrous personalities; they were abnormal specimens, with a sickly emotional capacity and passionate and perverse morals" (qtd. in Rosselli 283–84). Other causes of degeneration were the Colombian educational system, which produced "a fragile and degenerate nervous system"; alcoholism; syphilis; and a litany of social ills that included "national misery, violence in the struggle to survive, a lack of proportion between one's needs and the ability to meet them, nonconformity among the inferior social classes, the importation of decadent customs, sensual foreign literature, and the scandalous work of the press" (qtd. in Rosselli 284). Jiménez López's argument caused such a stir within and without Colombia (the *Bulletin de l'Amerique Latine* published a review) that a series of nine conferences were held in Bogotá to discuss his findings.[13] Other doctors vigorously resisted the assertion that Colombians were genetically unfit, arguing instead that environmental factors were the sole cause of alienation, and could therefore be corrected by behavior modification. In any case, the debate regarding what Jiménez López called the "renovation of our race" raged in Colombia through the 1940s, well after it had fallen from academic favor in Europe after its association with Nazi racial policies (qtd. in Rosselli 284).

Both the fear of degeneration and the concerns regarding the achievement of national greatness through selective reproduction are evident in the afflictions that strike characters in *The Vortex*: tuberculosis, syphilis, alcoholism, and mental illness.[14] Their presence demonstrates Rivera's own familiarity with the scientific debates of the day and their political implications for the ways in which

Colombians perceived their own nationhood. Latin American political and social discourse during the early twentieth century was marked by medical terminology and the rhetoric of the body politic. Discussions of national progress and modernity were couched in terms of society's health, and underdeveloped economies and social vices presented examples of social sickness on a national level, as the very title of Arguedas's *Pueblo enfermo* underscores. Arguedas advocated seeking out the roots of Latin America's "collective way of life, and principally, the primitive, sick, and baseless way of thinking, for it is necessary to explain social phenomena in biological terms. . . . A poorly trained brain is unable to assimilate new information, and the same thing occurs in a collective sense. If all the cells are sick or attacked, it is clear that the whole must suffer the same pathological abnormalities" (237). The ill health of any segment of the population, therefore, indicated a pathological condition for the entire nation and required modern scientific practices to cure it. As other authors of telluric novels such as *Doña Bárbara* would do later, Rivera clearly aligns himself with the secular scientific elites who viewed themselves as bringing modernity to his country. Rivera does so by incorporating medical discourse into his novel and giving evidence of Colombia's weakness in the form of the sickened characters in it. As Stepan notes, the time at which Rivera was writing was marked by changes in the ways educated Colombians viewed themselves:

> The history of eugenics in the region must be seen as part of a generalized endorsement of science, as a sign of cultural modernity, and as a means by which the various countries of Latin America could emerge as powerful actors on the world scene. The period 1880 to 1930 was one of considerable intellectual growth and institutional consolidation in science. . . . In this period the scientific community acquired its national form and traditions. Scientists strove to develop technical skills and create societies that would encourage new, scientific outlooks; they worked to develop national surveys of their natural resources and contracted foreign specialists to aid them in undertaking programs of education and research. (*Hour* 40)

Rivera formed part of this modernizing movement. Educated in Bogotá for both the *bachillerato* and his law degree, Rivera came from a distinguished family and literary circle. He was selected for diplomatic missions in attempts to solidify Colombia's borders with its neighbors, and was therefore involved in literally constructing the limits of the nation. Like Domingo Faustino Sarmiento before him, he sought to reform Colombia's political system and to make the rivers navigable, he was frustrated by rampant corruption, and he even spoke out against his own party in Colombia's government. He was renowned as the Bard of the Tropics and gave speeches on "Colombian-ness." Rivera was thus invested in the relative modernity of Colombia with respect to other nations and sought to reform the country under the banner of national pride. Throughout Latin America, patriotism became linked to eugenics in the 1920s as the aftermath of World War I sparked a desire for national regeneration.[15] As a member of Colombia's government and a frequent visitor to doctors himself, it is thus not surprising that the coded language of eugenics seeped into Rivera's writing, however unconscious of it he was himself.

Given his history of nervous disorders, his documented injection of drugs, and his preoccupation (according to friends and acquaintances) with the possibility of having syphilis, Rivera may have been concerned about *racial poisons*, which Stepan explains was "a term eugenists used to refer to such things as alcohol, nicotine, morphine, venereal diseases, and other drugs and infections. These poisons were called 'racial' because, though the habits and diseases were first acquired or experienced in one individual's lifetime, they were believed to lead to permanent, hereditary degenerations that in the long run could affect entire populations or nations.... Avoidance of sexual 'contamination' was therefore a logical social recommendation derived from eugenic science" (*Hour* 85). While it is impossible to say whether Rivera himself subscribed to these eugenic principles in his personal life, their influence strongly marks *The Vortex*, both in its content and in the vocabulary used to create it. Indeed, there are several ways in which Rivera's use of medical discourse about degeneration makes up an underlying motif of the novel and contributes to both his political and aesthetic endeavors within it. His protagonist engages in many behaviors considered to be racially poisonous, all apparently stimulated by his departure from Bogotá. For example, Cova drinks to excess, a habit that he explicitly states was not common for him. His multiple amorous relations gives rise to fears of sexual contamination, which are evident in his sexual liaisons with Griselda and Zoraida, and his avoidance of indigenous women while away from the city. The most important of all these dangerous behaviors, of course, is Cova's madness. His drunken raging and irrational behavior result in Alicia's kidnapping, putting his unborn child and potential spouse in danger. His racial future, in the form of his son, is thus placed in jeopardy by his own indulgence in what eugenicists would have called "racial poisons."

Many readers, particularly early critics of the novel, fell into the easy trap of conflating Rivera and Cova, and Rivera's experience with Cova's. I do not propose here that Rivera necessarily incorporated his own medical history into the novel in a conscious fashion, nor do I read the narrative of Cova's descent into madness as a thinly veiled autobiography. Rather, as with any novelist, Rivera's own experiences filter into his fiction in both expected and surprising ways. His repeated use of proto-psychiatric vocabulary is representative of his participation in the medical discourse of the day, and forms an essential component of Cova's personality. It is impossible to read *The Vortex* without entering Cova's psyche, and the title of the novel reflects not only the environment that surrounds the protagonist, but also his own internal psychological morass and the resulting chaotic narrative structure that stems from it. After Cova enters the forest, madness becomes the narrative engine of the work and the creative spark for the diary he leaves behind. The prevalence of medical terminology used to describe Cova and other characters in the novel reveals the ways in which the specter of madness shapes all aspects of Rivera's creation: Cova's demise, the novel's narrative style and structure, and the author's fears regarding the future of Colombia as a nation.

Following the publication of *The Vortex* in 1924, Rivera was at pains to emphasize the veracity of the abuses he detailed in the novel. For him, the success of the novel's goal of reformation would depend on its perceived level of verisimilitude, and the medical information he had chosen to include would play a key role in this respect.[16] Rivera was adamant that his novel was a true reflection of life in the Amazon: "I saw all these things. The characters in the book are all living souls and some of them even bear their real names" (qtd. in Neale Silva 305). Given the author's own pronouncements about living through what he wrote about, it is not surprising that in the first edition of the novel he included a picture of himself in the wilderness and labeled it "Arturo Cova." Yet it is important to recognize that the documentary veneer that coats the novel was carefully prepared and constructed by the author, from the postcards he purchased in Manaos and passed off as photos of Clemente Silva, to the pseudo-paratext framing the narrative that claimed that Rivera was no more than the editor and compiler of Cova's diary. While these elements have long been mentioned by Rivera's critics, none have mentioned the relation between medical discourse and Rivera's insistence on the authenticity of much of his work. For readers of the 1920s, medical terminology added a depth of credibility to Rivera's narrative, from his mention of "tablets" for malaria treatment (41) to Cova's determination that he suffered from "catalepsy" (162).

The use of scientific terms also indicates a level of modernity and urbanity for the protagonists: Cova and his father's friend Don Rafo are familiar with the latest terms and theories that have arrived from Europe. The upper-class nature of ailments such as neurasthenia also serve to set Cova apart from the other characters in the novel; as Clemente Silva mentions, they may suffer from the "witchery" of the forest, but certainly not from neurasthenia (229). Rivera also thought that a fictionalization of historical events would spur the Colombian government to remedy the injustices he had witnessed in the Amazon. In this sense, the description of physical and mental suffering in the novel has a political motivation: both Cova and Silva describe atrocities and ill health as endemic to the jungle, which forwarded Rivera's argument that Colombia desperately needed the sophisticated medicine and the rule of law established in urban areas to spread to the ill-defined frontiers of the country.

Indeed, the first appearance of medical vocabulary in the novel lends authenticity to the narrative: Don Rafo carries with him "the best quinine, and pills for fevers" (41). Other scholars have commented on Rivera's technique of placing technical terms in italics and even including a glossary in a revised edition of the novel.[17] This incorporation of specialized vocabulary was designed to make the narrator of the story more credible—to show that he was an expert and would be imparting secrets or unusual knowledge regarding the outer regions of the country to the Colombian reader. Medical terms form part of this rhetorical attempt to establish narrative authority.

Various characters in the novel are also described in medical terms, many of which would have resonated with contemporary readers of *The Vortex* in a way that is lost on the twenty-first-century reader. For example, the corrupt judge who stops Franco and Cova on the plain and attempts to extort money from them is coded in the medical jargon of the era: "The *consumptive* face of the Señor Judge was as *biliously* yellow as his celluloid glasses, and as repulsive as his *tartar*-covered teeth. Ludicrous as an *ape*, he leaned his sunshade on his shoulder to wipe his neck with a towel, cursing the demands of justice that imposed on him so many sacrifices, such as this of traveling poorly mounted through savage regions, in unavoidable dealings with ignorant and ill-born people, risking the dangers of Indians and wild beasts" (105; emphases mine). This passage shows that anyone of an urban upper class with commensurate education who is forced to spend time in the wilderness will be at risk of wasting away. Here, the *señor Juez* has not only become impoverished and corrupt, he has also begun to decay. His face is described as consumptive (*tísico*) and bilious (*bilioso*; *La vorágine* 104), implying that he suffers from tuberculosis. His teeth are covered in plaque, which suggests that his entire body is susceptible to rot. A further indication of his degeneration is the animalistic appearance attributed to his physique: his posture and gestures are simian, as if the course of evolution has been reversed in his case. In keeping with fears regarding degeneration, he has been dehumanized by the "unavoidable dealings with ignorant and ill-born people, risking the dangers" of further contact with the indigenous population and beasts. The language used to describe Cova's irrational behavior is similarly laden with medical significance.

While many medical conditions permeate the novel, such as the scourge of malaria and the judge's tuberculosis, none is more important than the encroaching insanity of Arturo Cova. The language used to portray his madness recalls the aesthetic of *modernismo* and decadent literature in which illness is fetishized and transformed into a vehicle for literary expression.[18] Cova's first introspection into his own mental health contains elements of both scientific terminology and literary imagery:

> My nervous sensibility has caused me to suffer many mental crises, moments when reason seems anxious to divorce itself from my brain. Despite my physical vitality, my diseased brain chronically exhausts me, for even during sleep I'm not free from the fantasies of my imagination. These illusions will reach their greatest intensity during periods of excitement—soon, however, to plunge me into fits of depression. Like

a symphony, I run the gamut of emotions. From choleric rage I pass to
complete docility; from prudence to bursts of rashness. (*Vortex* 67; *La
vorágine* 131)[19]

In this passage, Rivera avails himself of several terms in common use among Latin
American doctors to describe Cova's mental instability. Depicting his temperament as *nerviosa* places Cova within the class of *neurosis*, a category of nervous
defect that at the time included epilepsy, hysteria, and neurasthenia, suggesting
that Cova could suffer from any of those disorders.[20] At the same time, references
to music, depression (then known as melancholy), a *mal de pensar* (translated here
as "diseased brain"), and fantasies of the imagination induced by his nervous
disorder clearly align *el poeta* Cova with *modernista* writers such as his fellow
Colombian José Asunción Silva, who used his own very real psychological pain
to stimulate his literary creation.

The blend of *modernista* and Romantic aesthetics and the autochthonous
theme of Rivera's work are a result of the transition in literary currents that was
occurring in Latin America at the time. Rivera belonged to the so-called *generación del Centenario* (the centenary generation) whose era was marked by a shift
from the individualism of *modernismo* to a concern for the collective in the aftermath of Colombia's civil war.[21] Few *centenaristas* besides Rivera are read today,
and the movement was soon overshadowed by the writers of the *vanguardia*. Carlos J. Alonso even suggests that the conflict between man and the environment in
the novel is a metaphor for Rivera's reaction against the literary vanguard whose
popularity was increasing at the time *The Vortex* was written (154–62). I argue
that the failure and mental unhinging of Rivera's protagonist in the wilderness
are proof not of the author's opinion of poetry but rather of his comprehensive
vision of Colombia's struggle to modernize itself, which was in keeping with the
centenaristas' literary goals. In this general sense, I agree with Alonso that it is
necessary to read this *novela de la tierra* as demonstrative of the Latin American
author's thorny engagement with modernity. As Neale Silva stresses, the *centenarista* movement "had to function in an era of searching and reassessments imposed
by the necessity of modernizing all spheres of life in Colombia. Consequently,
the movement had to face the most current problems, and its spokesmen had to
find solutions in areas that were as yet unfamiliar to them" (168). Rivera's protest
novel undeniably sought to reform Colombia's oversight of its border regions,
lest the pathology of the tropical wilderness contaminate the rest of the country.
The principal mechanism by which Rivera communicates this urgent need is the
modern medical terminology he uses to diagnose and describe Cova's madness.

As Cova leads his small group of companions through the wilderness in
search of Alicia and Barrera, Rivera uses carefully selected medical terms to convey the vulnerability of his protagonist's "nervous sensibility" when faced with
what he perceives as the menace of the forest: "Under its influence man's nerves
become taut and ready to attack, are ready for treachery and ambush" (231). At

first, only Cova is affected, and his familiarity with contemporary medical language and poetic talent enable him to express his incipient madness eloquently:

> My companions would try to cheer me. "Don't tire yourself out," they would say. "One must know what fevers are." Nevertheless, I know that the trouble was something more serious than mere fevers. I tried desperately to convince myself I was normal....After breakfast I stretched myself out on the roots of a mahogany tree, and, face upward to the festoons of flowers, laughed at my ills, attributing all my past fears to neurasthenia. Yet all of a sudden I began to feel that I was dying of catalepsy. My head was spinning, death was upon me, and it was no dream. I tried to protest, I tried to move, I tried to cry aloud, but I was powerless. I felt my nerves crystallizing. My heart was thumping in a glassy case. The balls of my eyes flashed fire as they hardened. (162)

The image of the *caja vítrea* (glassy case) is characteristic of Rivera's descriptions of madness (*La vorágine* 229). It evokes the clinical specificity of a medical tool, demonstrating his scientific modernity. It also indicates a *modernista* sensibility in its focus on art objects similar to Rubén Darío's interest in Eastern decorative items.[22] Two other medical terms stand out here: *neurasthenia*, which I have already examined, and *catalepsy*, a type of nerve paralysis resulting in muscular rigidity, in which the afflicted is unable to move.[23] Around the turn of the century, catalepsia was classified as a type of neurosis, along with other afflictions from which Cova also seems to suffer, which Rosselli has cataloged as "hysterical insanity, epileptic insanity, acute delirious hysteria," and "neurasthenia" (246). The precision of these details may seem curious to a twenty-first-century reader, but to a reader in the early 1920s, it would have indicated a specific type of nervous illness that, according to the medical elite, was plaguing more and more Colombian citizens.

One of the best examples in Rivera's work of the importance of contemporary scientific theories is his treatment of Cova's alcoholism. While on the plains near Casanare, Cova begins indulging in behaviors that Rivera had been specifically instructed to avoid because they were thought to exacerbate a nervous patient's condition. Cova's explanation of his relationship to alcohol reveals common thoughts about the effect of intoxicants on an individual's psyche: "My system rejects alcoholic stimulants, although they bring forgetfulness to pain. The few times I've been drunk, I got so out of idleness or curiosity—to kill tedium or to know the tyrannical power that bestializes drinkers" (67).[24] This statement on the detrimental effect of alcohol is taken directly from the medical literature of the time. The scientific term *organismo* (system)—rather than the more common *cuerpo* (body)—has a distinct medical resonance, and the notion that spirits would "bestialize" an individual stems directly from fears that alcohol was linked to racial degeneration and madness (*La vorágine* 131). At the end of the nineteenth century and the beginning of the twentieth, the Colombian medical establishment sought to eradicate alcoholism because it was thought to cause delirium, mania, and degeneration in a large percentage of the population: "Alcoholism was perceived as the cause of 'racial degeneration' and as a threat to the future of the country" (Obregón Torres 86). Arguedas cited the famous Spanish writer Miguel de Unamuno, who listed alcoholism as a symptom of racial unfitness: "I believe that alcoholism is, in a great number of cases and in general as a social malady, an effect rather than a cause of the imperfect adaptation to civilized life. I believe that in the most degenerate alcoholics, it is not so much the alcohol that produces degeneration, but rather that a latent, even larval degeneration finds in alcohol a way of springing forth" (qtd. in Arguedas 59).[25] Rivera's portrait of Cova as sensitive to alcohol therefore reflects his familiarity with the medical discourse of the time and his concerns regarding degeneration. Cova's subsequent psychotic behavior while drunk would not have been surprising to Rivera's readers at the time of publication, given the anti-alcohol campaign being waged by medical professionals. Rivera's association of alcohol with degenerate behavior is further indicated by a later scene in which an indigenous man—an archetype of the racial degeneration that threatened to overtake Colombia—dances in a ceremony as if suffering from *delirium tremens*, a fit of convulsions caused by excessive drinking (144).

It is thus not surprising that the first manifestation of Cova's madness is a jealous and alcoholic rage in which he threatens both Alicia and Barrera, shouting: "Kill him! Kill him! And then you, me, everyone, everyone! No, I'm not crazy! And don't say I'm drunk either. Mad? No, you lie, not mad! Take from me this fire that burns my brain!" He records in his diary the sensations he was experiencing: "Then in my mad delirium I sat down to laugh. The whirr of the house, spinning around in swift circles, amused me and refreshed my head. 'That's it! I hope it doesn't stop, because I'm crazy!' … As my convulsion passed, I tried to walk, but the ground was speeding under my feet" (74–75). Cova's *delirio vesánico* (*La vorágine* 138), which the translator Earle K. James renders here as "mad delirium," is a specific medical term found in clinical diagnoses of the era. It was intended to distinguish the condition from other sorts of delirium, such as "delirium of persecution" (Rosselli 246). In addition, Cova's "convulsion" implies that this too was a case of *delirium tremens*, which would associate Cova with degenerate indigenous alcoholics, in contrast to the upper-class poet he was when he first embarked on his journey. Indeed, Cova's relationships with the people around him, all of whom come from lower social classes and economic levels, as well as racial heritages different from his, are characterized by both attraction and repulsion, identification and rejection. His contact with indigenous healers and their way of practicing medicine reveal this uncomfortable negotiation between Cova's education and social status and the uncanny recognition of aspects of himself in others.

Cova's first encounter with indigenous medicine comes after he has been shot in the arm by Barrera. The one-eyed healer Mauco prays over him, rather than giving him the sort of medical treatment Cova would be accustomed to in Bogotá:

The idlers quieted down, as though in a church, and old Mauco, after
making some magical signs in the air, mumbled a string of words he
called the "Prayer of the Just Judge." I looked at Clarita with surprise,
unable to believe that the whole business was serious. But she, too, was
a convinced believer in the incantations. "*Gua chico*!" she explained.
"Mauco knows of medicines. He's the one who kills the worms in the
animals' sores, praying at them. He cures persons and animals." (81)

Cova's incredulity at the entire proceeding sets him apart from people such as
Clarita, a "convinced believer" who trusts local medicine more than any theory
imported from Europe. Cova's description of the scene offers an outsider's anthropological perspective, as he neither explicitly rejects nor accepts the treatment,
falling asleep rather than participating fully. In several instances, Cova plays the
ethnologist, asking the chief to "tell me of his traditions, his war chants, his
myths and legends" (141). Yet his findings are in keeping with the racial theories
of the time that insisted indigenous groups prevented Colombia from becoming
a modern nation because, as Cova states, "those primitive, nomadic peoples have
neither gods nor heroes nor country, neither past nor future" (141). In passages
such as these, Rivera clearly demarcates the boundaries between his protagonist and what he believes to be the native, credulous, degenerate population of
Colombia's frontiers, but he also intimates an eerie similarity between Cova and
those whom the protagonist disdains. For example, while living in the wilderness, Cova walks into the residents' camp with two gray ducks, one dead and one
alive. He is informed that according to this particular ethnic group, "the souls
of these savages dwell in different animals, and that the one that harbored the
cacique's resembled the gray duck I had killed" (142). On seeing the dead duck,
the village elder is thrown into "epileptic convulsions" and "would probably die
simply from having set eyes upon the lifeless bird" (142).[26] Cova quickly produces
the live bird, and the elder's health is restored. There is a strong element of the
uncanny here, since Rivera was known for having convulsive fits himself, and
Cova recognizes that his own delirium manifests itself in similar ways. Thus,
Cova's encounter with a "savage" (142) with whom he presumes to have nothing
in common and yet shares a nervous disorder offers a subtle counterpoint to his
insistence that he is far superior to those who surround him. It is also reminiscent
of Marlow's defiant exclamation when faced with the unintelligible cries of Africans in *Heart of Darkness*: "An appeal to me in the fiendish row—is there? Very
well; I hear; I admit, but I have a voice too, and for good or evil mine is the speech
that cannot be silenced" (140). Cova, too, is quick to reestablish the distance
between himself and his indigenous doppelgänger: "The puerile incident sufficed
to accredit me with supernatural powers over the destinies of souls. Thereafter no
Indian dared gaze upon me, but I was present in his thoughts, exerting unknown
influences over his hopes and griefs" (142).[27] Both of these situations are subtle
yet significant indications that Rivera and Conrad are deeply conflicted about

ideas such as degeneration and racial divisions. Even as they seek to maintain hierarchies between themselves and others, both demonstrate the susceptibility of each man, no matter how European in heritage, to degenerate when placed in an insalubrious environment.[28] Prolonged contact with the natives and time spent in the enervating and contaminated forest slowly whittle away at their protagonists' precarious mental health. Cova's depression and mania become so pronounced that he is haunted by a *demonio trágico* (tragic demon; *La vorágine* 216) as well as the "relentless specter" of suicide such that he feels the desire to murder his companions to save them from starvation in the wilderness (*Vortex* 149).

Another factor that was thought to lead to insanity at the time *The Vortex* was written was syphilis, a disease often viewed as the result of sexual relations with "unclean" indigenous women.[29] The resulting "cerebral syphilis" could, according to Lamarckian genetic theory, be passed down from parents to children, resulting in nervous disorders such as infantile syphilis and the consequent degeneration of the race. Rivera's doubts about his own sexual health, as noted earlier, are symptomatic of this concern. The imagery of syphilis is even used to evoke the destructive nature of the forest in *The Vortex*: "The *comején* [termite] gnaws at the trees like quick-spreading syphilis, boring unseen from within, rotting tissue and pulverizing bark, until the weight of branches that are still living brings the giant crashing to the ground" (230). Cova's much-discussed sexual activity in the novel depicts him as at risk for just this sort of ailment, particularly when he comes into contact with nonwhite women.

In addition to his sexual relations with Alicia and Griselda, it is Cova's intimacy with Zoraida Ayram that presents the gravest danger to his sexual and mental health. Zoraida is a Turkish woman who runs a clandestine rubber camp in the wilderness. Everything about Zoraida is presented as contaminated: her foreign name and nationality indicate the possibility of an infelicitous racial mixture, and her camp is filled with an atmosphere of rot and illness. Cova records the squalor: "In dirty hammocks hung over smudge fires as protection against mosquitoes, lolled women with sores—reeking of iodoform, their heads wrapped in handkerchiefs. They did not hear me, they did not move.... Sick people appeared. From all parts came naked brats and pregnant women" (251–52). The original text, which is far more medically precise than the English translation, tells us that the women in the camps are covered with *fístulas hediondas* (foul-smelling fistulas; a fistula is a canal or cavity caused by the deformation of tissue from disease, such as Crohn's disease). Despite this horrifying sight, Cova feels simultaneously attracted to and repulsed by Zoraida, "La Madona" (the Madonna), much as he did with the indigenous healing rituals. After having sex with her in order to guarantee his safety, he feels sickened and sexually weakened by the experience: "Physical and moral calamities have allied themselves against me in these listless days. My decay and skepticism are the result of erotic exhaustion, the sapping of my physical vigor, sucked out by the caresses of Zoraida. Like a candle extinguished when overturned on its own flame, she has burned up my virility with her kisses" (290).[30] While Cova's sexual relationship with Alicia is (re)productive and ultimately racially invigorating because it produces an heir, sex with the foreign Zoraida produces "decay" and resonates with contemporary fears of disease and "sexual neurasthenia," the latter thought to be caused by unproductive expenditures of sperm. Cova's relationship with La Madona reveals anxieties about the notion that the future of Colombia's nationhood depended on the sexual health and practices of white upper-class Colombians like the protagonist and, conversely, that that future could be imperiled by unproductive, racially mixed sexual activity.[31] Sexual interaction with nonwhite Colombians on the frontiers of the nation was thus a dangerous activity both for Cova and for his nation as a whole, as it could lead to sexual disease (including insanity) and degeneration, as well as the failure to produce healthy Colombian citizens.

Indeed, the issue of paternity gains in importance as the novel draws to a close. Word reaches the protagonist that Alicia is in fact pregnant, and Cova's greatest hope for the future mingles with the greatest danger: his son is born in the wilderness at seven months of gestation, and "his first plaint, his first cry, his first wail was leveled at the inhuman jungles" (318). The danger to Cova's premature son is a metaphor for the danger of Colombia's untamed frontiers to the nation as a whole. As Stepan notes, within the rhetoric of degeneration, "children especially were thought of as biological-political resources of the nation, and the state was regarded as having an obligation to regulate their health" (*Hour* 78). Bereft of any help from the state, the refugees are beset by groups of plague-ridden natives who harass them for victuals and drive them farther upriver. Cova refuses to allow them to board his vessel: "Impossible! . . . They'll endanger Alicia's health! They may infect my son!" (318). The novel leaves the fate of the protagonist and his family in doubt, thereby serving as an ominous warning of the consequences of failing to "regenerate" the nation properly.

It is clear that the madness and implied demise of Cova present a dire forecast for the modernization of the Colombian nation as conceived by Rivera. Yet, while Cova may leave no human legacy behind, he does leave a literary one. In this respect, the protagonist's insanity does not indicate a solely negative outcome in the novel, because it enables him to tap into the literary possibilities of the verdant foliage. As Sylvia Molloy insightfully states, Cova's "unhealthy itinerary makes him, finally, a writer" (493). Indeed, Cova's mental unraveling plays an essential role as a catalyst for literary creativity, specifically for the evocation of the Colombian tropics. The relationship between madness and artistic creation has important consequences in the novel itself and more broadly for literature written about the Latin American *tierra* (land) on an allegorical level.

Because of his increasing physical debility and mental unhinging, Cova finds the best expression of his experience in the forest to be not a book of sonnets extolling the beauty of nature, but the scattered and desperate prose document he writes in old ledger books. Cova begins writing his diary while in Zoraida's camp, and he eventually leaves it behind as a textual beacon by which Clemente Silva can rescue them. On a metaphorical level, the diary will serve as a symbol of a new kind of writing about Latin America. The narrative device of the found manuscript is certainly not Rivera's invention, but it gains added significance from its place and nature of composition. Written in the very heart of the wilderness itself, like Kurtz's report scribbled in his hut, the diary is out of place: few can read it, and its power as a protest document is guaranteed only if it is found and read. Its symbolic value, however, goes far beyond the account of one person's journey through the wilderness. It simultaneously and paradoxically becomes an artifact of culture and a synecdoche for the wilderness itself.

Issuing from the forest, the diary does not attempt to describe the environment so much as to recreate it as Cova experienced it. The increasingly incoherent narrative reflects Cova's mental state and allows him to evoke the similarly unruly wilderness that surrounds him. It purports to mimic the natural world using medical and literary terminology, thus serving as a textual stand-in for the forest. The decay of Cova's mind and the rot of the vegetation thus merge seamlessly, giving rise to a new type of autochthonous literature. In this way, the diary also becomes a pioneering cultural document on a historical level: the novel is a new way of writing about Latin America in which medical pathology becomes a vehicle for literary innovation. In this sense, *The Vortex* is a departure from the other *novelas de la tierra* with which it is usually associated.

Rather than taming the Latin American land with legal terms and modern ideas imported from the capital, as Santos Luzardo does in *Doña Bárbara*, Cova is broken down by the earth. He is made degenerate and unstable by the wilderness, which advances a completely different literary and political message from that promoted in Gallegos's novel: the new Latin American literature is to be found not in a tale of triumph of man over the land, but in one of the brute power of the forest over those who enter it.

The *novela de la tierra* is often interpreted as a dramatization of the struggle between the forces of civilization and barbarism, as expressed most famously in Domingo Faustino Sarmiento's *Facundo*. While in *Doña Bárbara* writing is generally an act that divides the civilized from the barbarous, in *The Vortex* writing is a pathological condition that expresses the barbarity of the earth itself. From Silva's attempt to find his son by carving messages into tree trunks to Cova's final missives to the Colombian government, all the various forms of writing in *The Vortex* are narratives of failure that recount their own capitulation to the power of nature. If as a lawyer Santos Luzardo uses language to inscribe ownership on the land, as a poet Cova is able only to narrate his own destruction and that of his companions. In doing so, his prose mirrors the land, creating a literary Latin American jungle rather than a tidy narrative of domestication. While Luzardo's writing is transformational in that it changes the very nature of the land by dividing it, Cova's composition is dictated by the forest and is made possible by his own madness. Rivera's literary evocation of the tropics therefore avails itself not of legal discourse as does Gallegos's work, but rather of medical terminology and a portrait of lunacy.

The shift in Cova's aesthetic expression from dandified poet to disheveled narrator is paralleled by his increasing irrationality, making it clear that insanity is his creative spark. For example, even before he entered the forest, Cova hoped that it would become the source of his literary inspiration, much as it had been for Rivera in *The Promised Land*: "Perhaps the source of all my poetry was in the secrets of the virgin forests, in the caress of gentle breezes, in the unknown language of all things; in singing what the rock sings to the wave that bids it good-bye, what the flaming sky sings to the swamps, the stars to the vastness that holds the silence of God" (*Vortex* 99). What Cova creates rather than neat, ordered poetry (akin to what Rivera had already written) is a ragged and fractured tale that rejects bucolic visions of nature and replaces them with nightmares, hallucinations, and an environment toxic to those that enter it. In one of the most famous passages in the novel, Rivera uses Cova's voice to explicitly dismiss both Romantic and *modernista* poetic aesthetics: "Where is that solitude poets sing of? Where are those butterflies like translucent flowers, the magic birds, those singing streams? Poor fantasies of those who only know domesticated retreats! No cooing nightingales here, no Versaillian gardens or sentimental vistas!" (230–31). While Rivera's text is marked by certain Romantic literary tropes, such as the close association between the emotions of the protagonist and the natural world that surrounds him, the new poetic language that Cova employs to describe the vortex of the wilderness is characterized by modern medical terminology. After rejecting the aesthetic of "cooing nightingales," Cova explains that his forest is full of "dropsical frogs" (a reference to the medical condition then known as dropsy), as well as an "aphrodisiacal parasite" with flowers emanating "a sticky smell intoxicating as a drug," a "*pringamosa* that irritates the skin," and "the purging grape" (231). This new literary jungle that is as "intoxicating as a drug" (231) is constructed using a medical lexicon that had been unavailable to most nineteenth-century Latin American writers. While decadent writers may have fetishized illness and converted it into an aesthetic stance, Rivera's novel emphasizes the untamable, incurable aspects of the tropics. If tuberculosis was the disease of the drawing room, malarial fever, beriberi and delirium are those of the rainforest. The shift in vocabulary used to describe the environment takes place over the course of the novel, from the Romantic invocation of the forest in the opening of Part 2—"Oh jungle, wedded to silence, mother of solitude and mists" (127)—to the brief, staccato diary entries leading to "The jungle devoured them!" (320). As the novel progresses, the frequency of medical terminology and the specter of illness increase in tandem with the story's narrative disarray.

Cova's discovery of his newfound poetic voice and his mental unraveling are inextricably linked. In *The Vortex*, madness is an essential component of writing about the selva. Alonso rightly recognizes that the forest is silent when the main character is mentally balanced and that "the language of nature only becomes intelligible to Cova in an instance of near-death delirium" (137). During his hallucinations, the trees speak to Cova on several occasions, encouraging his erratic behavior. It is only following one of these episodes that Cova unlocks the destructive and literary power of his surroundings. Clemente Silva informs him that he has finally felt "the witchery of the jungle" and Cova admits, "For the first time I saw the inhuman jungle in all its horror, saw the pitiless struggle for existence" (230).[32] Rivera rails against the barbarity of the wilderness embodied in Narciso Barrera just as Sarmiento excoriated the Argentine dictator Juan Manuel de Rosas in *Facundo*. Like Sarmiento, Rivera is nevertheless seduced by cruelty's same destructive and powerful pull, which he describes using a lexicon of illness. It is here that the narration acquires momentum:

> The jungles change men. The most inhuman instincts are developed; cruelty pricks like a thorn, invades souls; covetousness burns like a fever. It's the thirst for wealth that sustains the weakening body, and the smell of rubber produces the "madness of millions." ... But reality travels slower than ambition, and beriberi is a bad friend. On remote trails in the solitude of the jungle, they succumb to fever, embracing the trees from which the latex oozes. Lacking water, they stick their thirsty mouths to the bark, that the liquid rubber may calm their fever; and there they rot like leaves, gnawed as they die by rats and ants—the only millions that ever come to them. (177)

Clemente Silva tells Cova that it is the earth itself that degrades the men who inhabit the forest, as if the mental degeneration implied by Cova's madness could be stopped if order were imposed on the land. He notes that any of the trees that haunt Cova's mind "would seem tame, friendly, even smiling in a park, along a road, on a plain, where nobody would bleed it or persecute it" (229). It is only in the remote parts of the forest, Silva maintains, that each man is assaulted by "the jungle giddiness, and we want to flee, and we get lost" (230).[33] This drive to pacify the land, to gain control over the flora and fauna on the margins of national territory, and to bring racially eugenic blood to Latin America clearly aligns Cova not only with twentieth-century modernizers like Gallegos, but also with the Spaniards who had participated in the "conquest" of the New World.

Indeed, while on his journey, Cova likens himself to the conquistadores: "Over those hostile regions we marched barefooted, like the legendary heroes of the Conquest" (149). This gesture of solidarity reveals the importance of reenacting and rewriting the history of the region in Rivera's novel, and in all twentieth-century tropical adventure novels written in Latin America. In this respect, Cova's found manuscript indicates Rivera's desire to tell the story of his nation in his own words, and the broader desire of many Latin American writers to reinvent the story of their own literary origins.[34] Writing therefore becomes a tool of nation building—a means of defining Colombia by revisiting the task of domesticating it. Just as Rivera literally sought to define the parameters of his country by delineating the boundaries between Colombia and Venezuela while on his diplomatic voyage into the interior, in *The Vortex* he seeks to become the nation's literary founder by creating a narrative that embodies the land itself.

The great irony of this twentieth-century conquest narrative, of course, is that the desire to reclaim the legacy of the "conquest" always proves to be a failure. The sequence of events in Rivera's novel is less like the trajectory of Hernán Cortés and more like that of Álvar Núñez Cabeza de Vaca, whose narrative recounts not a conquest of land and peoples, but rather the ways in which the wilderness alters the protagonist, as opposed to the other way around. Cova's madness and increasingly incoherent diary are symptomatic of the impossibility of retelling the conquest narrative. While he intends to inscribe his mark on the land in the form of his notebook, the earth and its irrationality are instead inscribed on him in the form of his mental and physical distress. Rivera alludes to parallels between those who enter the forest to extract its human and plant resources in the contemporary era, and those who did so in the age of "the epics" in terms of their shared suffering:

> There is something magnificent in the story of these pirates who enslave
> their peons, exploit the environment, and struggle with the jungle. Buf-
> feted by misfortune, they leave the anonymity of cities to plunge into
> the wilderness, seeking a purpose for their sterile life. Delirious from
> malaria, they loose themselves of their conscience, and adapt themselves
> to the environment; and with no weapons but the rifle and the machete,
> they suffer the most atrocious needs, while longing for pleasures and
> plenty. They live exposed to the elements, always ravenous, even naked,
> for here clothes rot on one's body. (231–32)

In this passage, with the exception of his mention of the rifle, Cova could be describing the conquistadores as easily as the foremen who exploit poor rubber workers. The mention of malaria shows how little had changed in the management of the disease during the intervening centuries. Yet while the Spaniards eventually triumphed in their mission to subjugate much of Colombia, Cova's quest and those of countless others end in failure. Rivera's narrative thus gains its claim to being autochthonous Latin American literature because it delves into the dangerous seduction of self-annihilation and the innate human potential for irrational, destructive behavior, showing the darker side of the civilization-barbarism divide in doing so.

In Rivera's pathological tale, the impact of medical discourse is twofold. First, it indicates Rivera's concerns with the ability of Colombia to modernize itself because of the theories of racial degeneration that were common in the scientific community when he was writing *The Vortex*. Second, the seemingly dismal mental health of the novel's protagonist nevertheless serves as a trigger for literary creation. Cova's madness thus transcends its historical roots and becomes an important aesthetic statement by the author. The Latin American novels I will discuss in the following chapters all share Rivera's presentation of the rainforest as a wild and untamed place that serves as an engine for artistic creation. This is not the case in the European texts that have been examined thus far: in Conrad, madness is an incommunicable experience that distances the mad from the sane by silencing them, and in Malraux, madness is a symptom of the proximity of death. In Rivera, however, the madman speaks in the first person without a mediating frame narrator. The mad first-person narrative is thus the defining characteristic of the novel. Whereas the protagonists of Conrad and Malraux's novels are able to shift their fears of degeneration and madness onto others, Cova's first-person narration renders this impossible; indeed, it is Cova himself who must confront his own tendency toward depression and irrationality rather than displacing the possibility of mental illness onto another. Rivera opens a path to a new means of evoking the Latin American tierra, not through traditional literary imagery but rather through the skillful manipulation of medical terminology. *The Vortex* is thus a much more modern novel than has been previously recognized, because Cova's mental instability transforms the very shape of Rivera's narrative. While other *novelas de la tierra* have omniscient narrators that lend them stability on a formal level, Rivera's novel is made into an unsettling vortex by the narrating protagonist's madness. Critics have interpreted Cova's inconsistent and maniacal ramblings as flaws in *The Vortex*, but they are in fact its greatest literary innovation and the source of its modernity.

Chapter 4

"No era para narrado":
Narrating Madness in *Canaima*

THE VENEZUELAN AUTHOR RÓMULO GALLEGOS IS OFTEN VENERATED AS THE Latin American embodiment of the triumph of civilization over barbarism. This secular canonization is based largely on two factors: his great novel of 1929, *Doña Barbara*, and his brief stint as president of his country in 1948. Yet Gallegos's *Canaima*, published in 1935, debunks this facile dichotomy between what he called *la ciudad y el monte* (the city and the wilderness; "La necesidad" 439). In a stark contrast to his previous writings, Gallegos's civilizing rationalism gives way in *Canaima* to the seductive insanity of the wilderness. While in *Doña Barbara* the urbane, learned Santos Luzardo defeats the superstitious, lawless title character, in *Canaima* there is no clear victory of civilization over barbarism. In the latter novel, Gallegos allows himself to revel in his protagonist's devolution from an educated creole into a madman. The protagonist Marcos Vargas, a potential "Messiah" (249) who could lead the country down a positivist path of order and progress, is instead lost to what Gallegos portrays as the vicissitudes of the forest and the attraction of irrationality at the close of *Canaima*.[1]

Canaima is a much more complex and perplexing narrative than *Doña Barbara* precisely because of Marcos's capitulation to madness and to the wilderness. The novel represents a major thematic and aesthetic departure from Gallegos's earlier works, which all upheld the primacy of reason and adherence to Western notions of progress. Gallegos's prose is also affected by this change: in *Canaima*, the moralizing, didactic tone and diction of his earlier works mix with a poetic lyricism that Gallegos uses to evoke the madness of several characters. The result is a novel that explores the dark underbelly of the civilization-barbarism divide, and perhaps inadvertently extols the enigmatic allure of the irrational rather than serving as a cautionary tale or an inspiration for national modernization. *Canaima* takes on epic, allegorical proportions because it demonstrates the clash between rationalism and mysticism in which Gallegos ultimately privileges the spiritual apprehension of truths inaccessible to the intellect over the maxims of positivism. In the novel, this conflict manifests itself in the competing discourses of rationality and irrationality. For example, characters of European descent are known to the indigenous forest inhabitants as *racionales*, a term that proves to be ironic. Early in *Canaima*, Gallegos sets up a dichotomy between Marcos Vargas's rational mode of thought and the intuitive, mystical approach to the world demonstrated by the Guaraúno Ponchopire. At its core, the work narrates the gradual erosion of the former by the latter. Many characters who are supposed to offer the nation Western-style progress, such as domestication of the land and harnessing the power of the great rivers, instead behave in irrational, self-destructive ways. What emerges, then, is a mosaic of madness in which several individuals become unhinged while living in the rainforest. Gallegos's description of their insanity in the tropics changes his prose from didactic realism to lyric exaltation of the maddening wilderness. In this sense, Gallegos's novel bears an affinity to José Enrique Rodó's famous *Ariel* (1900), which exhorted Latin American youth to take pride in their region's spiritual and cultural resources rather than imitating the materialistic concerns of their northern neighbor, the United States.

The clearest expression of Gallegos's uneasy negotiation between the rectitude of progress and the attraction of the irrational forest is the mix of scientific and poetic terminology used to portray madness in the novel. I will focus here on Gallegos's use of both a positivist psychological lexicon and a lyric vocabulary to depict various forms of insanity in *Canaima*. The most in-depth representation of madness, of course, is that of Marcos Vargas, whose decision to live among the indigenous population embodies for Gallegos the irrational turning away from progressive society. Yet *Canaima* presents an entire panorama of personalities who are driven mad in the wilderness. Marcos's apparently magical powers are evoked with mystical, lyrical language quite distinct from the clinical approach Gallegos takes to the madness of characters such as José Francisco Ardavín or Count Giaffaro. The unifying factor in all these cases of lunacy is that they are provoked by "Canaima," an animistic deity found in several cultures that Gallegos depicts as the root of madness and evil in the wilderness.

Earlier critics have accused Gallegos of not giving psychological depth to his characters. Emir Rodríguez Monegal stated that in *Doña Bárbara* "the essential humanity is lost" and that the novel was "superficial" and "touristy" (Rodríguez Monegal 110). José Balza noted Gallegos's "light approach to the symbolic depths" (xvi). Yet beneath the archetypal veneer of such constructions as the *Hombre Macho* (Macho Man), Gallegos is deeply interested in the psychology of his characters.[2] A close reading of the language he employs to evoke the mental states of those who go mad in *Canaima* demonstrates his involvement in the scientific and the literary movements of his time. His focus on psychology puts him on the cutting edge of Latin American science of the early twentieth century; his character descriptions fuse the nascent science of the mind, as psychology was known in its early phases, with philosophical and spiritual explorations. The cohabitation of these diverse philosophies within the novel is evident and aesthetically powerful in the madness of many of the characters, most notably in the protagonist. In *Canaima*, Gallegos uses a scientific and psychological approach rooted in positivism to arrive at a questioning of those very principles. His meticulous exposition of forms of irrational thought leads him to a fascination with—and an almost involuntary appreciation for—the so-called barbarism that he condemned in his political life and writings. In this respect, Gallegos's narrative voice echoes Sarmiento's in *Facundo*, in which the author had railed against the strongman Juan Manuel de Rosas but simultaneously taken advantage of the lyric possibilities of unbridled barbarity in contrast with sedate rationalism. In fact, *Canaima* serves as a microcosm of a broader trend in Latin American literature during the first half of the twentieth century. As I noted in the Introduction, this period saw writers of the Latin American *novela de la tierra* shifting their gazes away from European models of prose and poetry and seeking literary inspiration in the flora and fauna of their home countries. Gallegos, like many authors of the time, struggled with his intellectual and aesthetic orientation, at times extolling European modes of government and art and at others rejecting them.

In *Canaima*, taking on the distancing gaze of the psychologist enables Gallegos the narrator to explore and indeed to enjoy the pleasures of an intuitive spirituality that he saw inherent in the wilderness while still maintaining his ostensibly rational, positivist foundation. Herein lies the central tension of the novel, which makes it much more interesting than the famous *Doña Barbara*. The Gallegos of *Canaima* is subversive with regards to "civilization": he mocks the racionales and European scientific practices; he shows the falsehoods inherent in written documents and instead praises the supposedly indigenous custom of mystical, nonlinear thought and expression; he shows the poetry in madness. The insanity of several characters thus becomes the best example of Gallegos's conflicted relationship with progressive, rational thought. Madness is presented both scientifically and lyrically; it is both cabalistic and clinical. In fact, as in *The Vortex*, the technical bent of the author's descriptive passages contribute to their lyricism. Pathology and poetics merge once more to evoke madness, and through them the author arrives at the boundaries of language. The narrator shows that Marcos Vargas's insanity exceeds the limits of expression when the narrator states that Marcos's experience "could not be told in stories" (232). Gallegos's exact words in Spanish state that Marcos Vargas's experience "no era para narrado" (160), implying that it either could not be narrated or *should* not be narrated. Accordingly, Gallegos's description of Marcos Vargas's transformation in the later chapter "The Storm" ("La tormenta") approaches a lyricism unlike the rest of the author's straightforward narrative. The poetic, allusive language serves as the best tribute to what the author perceives as the mystical transformative capabilities of Latin American nature.

An exploration of Gallegos's intellectual roots in positivism and his later shift away from those principles sheds light on the uneasy coexistence of rationalism and mysticism in *Canaima*. Rómulo Gallegos came of age in an educational climate in which positivism informed debates regarding the future of Latin American nations. Originally elaborated by Auguste Comte (1798–1857) in the nineteenth century, the philosophy of positivism upheld logic and empirical reason, rather than theology or metaphysics, as the true path to knowledge. The young Gallegos came to the positivist movement in Venezuela following his disillusionment with the Catholic Church: as a boy he had been religious and even thought of becoming a priest, but he was introduced to positivism on arriving at the Universidad de Caracas (Liscano 36). By the time the author enrolled in the university, the tenets of positivism had mixed with those of other intellectual currents of the turn of the twentieth century: racial theories of degeneration, anticlericalism, evolution, literary realism, and the dawn of the science of psychology.[3] Positivism became the dominant cultural mantra in Venezuela even after it had passed its zenith in Europe; Gallegos therefore rode the wave of the movement in Venezuela because of his attendance at the university. As Gallegos's friend and biographer Juan Liscano notes: "The graduates from this center of learning would become the first sociologists, historians, and scientists to apply the ideas of positivism and evolution to their respective fields. . . . Science was thus freed from its idealistic subjectivism, and departments of anthropology, ethnology, folklore and botany were created" (36). The sociological strain in Gallegos's prose is clear, from his political writings through *Doña Barbara*. Like his literary creation Santos Luzardo, Gallegos consistently argued that Venezuela could be modernized by dedicating itself to Western-style educational reforms, advances in science, and the rule of law.

Positivism manifests itself not only in Gallegos's subject matter, but also in the very method he used to compose his novels. Gallegos's scientific approach to literary creation indicates his debt to French naturalist writers of the previous century, especially Émile Zola. While writing his famous twenty-volume Rougon-Macquart series of novels, Zola conducted in-depth field research on the environments and the people he sought to portray in his fiction. He carefully documented his investigations and claimed to have based his scientific view of literature on the physiologist Claude Bernard's *Introduction to the Study of Experimental Medicine* (1865).[4] Gallegos formed part of the Latin American literary elite that emulated the French model.[5] His sociological narrative style, his recreation of popular speech, and his research-based method of composition reveal his debt to realist and naturalist writers. Yet Gallegos's trips to the Venezuelan plains and tropical forest in preparation for writing *Doña Barbara* (eight days) and *Canaima* (three weeks) are not on the same scale as, for example, Zola's descent into the depths of French mines for the composition of *Germinal* (1885). According to Gustavo Guerrero, Gallegos visited Ciudad Bolívar and its environs in January and February 1931, during which he kept a journal with "the meticulous avidity of an anthropologist or ethnographer dedicated to the task of describing an unexplored world" (277). The resulting fifty-three pages of notes and phrases, many of which appear verbatim in *Canaima*, has been transcribed by Guerrero and reproduced in Charles Minguet's critical edition of the novel (277–300). Gallegos relied on the notebook to write the novel while living in exile in New York and Spain. Although Gallegos took copious notes on his trips through various towns in the Venezuelan forest, it is remarkable that this short visit provided the only personal experience the author had of the region he was to depict in the novel. Moreover, there is no evidence of other historical sources he may have used in the composition of *Canaima*. With the exception of Alejo Carpentier, the novelists examined in *Jungle Fever* did not study the Amazonian and Andean ethnic groups systematically, but rather found inspiration in popular (mis)conceptions about them in literature and popular media. Gallegos's presentation of the Guaraúnos and Maquiritares is therefore based largely on his own imaginings and, more important, on other literary works he had read. Foremost among these is *The Vortex*, in which Rivera describes a *ñopo* dance ceremony very similar to that of *Canaima*. Thus, while Gallegos's research in preparation for writing the novel was limited to his single trip, his decision to include verbatim expressions from his notes nevertheless demonstrates the positivist foundations of his approach to writing *Canaima*.

The best example of Gallegos's early dedication to the maxims of positivism is his tract "Necesidad de valores culturales" (The need for cultural values) published in *El cojo ilustrado* on August 15, 1912. In the essay, the twenty-eight-year-old Gallegos deplores the "miserable and tardy" cultural development of his country (439). While he is ambivalent about European investment in Venezuela and the extraction of natural resources by foreign companies, he calls for Western-style educational reforms and the promotion of "universal culture . . . with a scientific method and clear objectives" (440). Among the intellectual models he cites for Venezuela are Domingo Faustino Sarmiento, Leopoldo Lugones, the British socialist Sidney Webb and his Fabian Society, Ramiro de Maetzu, and William James. Another indication of Gallegos's foundation in scientific thought is his use of a medical conceit to frame Venezuela's problems. In the essay, the country is presented as a sick patient, and the author takes on the role of doctor, offering a diagnosis and treatment in the form of educational reforms. In using the medical conceit, he follows a trend among Latin American intellectuals of the first decade of the twentieth century. Like Alcides Arguedas's *Pueblo enfermo*, which I addressed in Chapter 3, Gallegos's argument is steeped in medical terms:

> Before we can think of a cure, we need to diagnose ourselves. Now, in our diagnosis, there are many vague symptoms that are none other than actual causes of our illness. If we would like to schematically synthesize the unifying factor in these symptoms of social ills, and at the same time discover their origins, we could express them with two antithetical terms: the city and the wilderness, and in doing so we would pinpoint

not only the places in which these ills tend to occur, but also their very nature, the circumstances that produce them, the attitudes and tendencies that give rise to them. (439)

Like Arguedas, Gallegos attributes the slow pace of Venezuela's modernization to the non-European, rural elements of society. While Arguedas explicitly blamed the indigenous population, Gallegos presents the debate in geographical and social terms. Nevertheless, both men describe the native South American population as lawless and unrefined; both also frame the issue in clinical terms. Like Arguedas, Gallegos refers to "symptoms of social ills." The employment of medical metaphors and vocabulary initiated here would become a hallmark of Gallegos's future writings. Some of his early short stories feature doctors and patients, such as in "Un caso clínico" (A clinical case, 1915), "El piano viejo" (The old piano, 1916), and "El esfinge" (The sphinx, 1915).[6] In fact, the presence of medicine and sickness in his novels and short stories is so prevalent that Dr. Jesús A. Yerena has published a catalog of their occurrence in Gallegos's work. In *Doña Barbara*, Gallegos uses medical terms to describe Venezuela's ills, which are embodied in specific characters, and he promotes education as a means of remedying those ailments. For example, Lorenzo Barquero, destroyed by his passion for Doña Bárbara, is described as a "physiological ruin" with a "fundamental decay of the will; his mouth was deformed by the rictus of sodden debauchery" (110–11).[7] Barquero's demise serves as an allegory for the dangers of contact with barbarism confronting the Venezuelan nation.

Canaima exhibits many signs of Gallegos's dedication to rationalism, positivism, and the advance of science, even in the post–World War I intellectual climate that called Western progress into question. Like other tropical quest narratives addressed in this work, *Canaima* presents the wilderness as the locus of various physical maladies, all described with scientific terminology. In his evocation of Guyana as a sick place, Gallegos produces a litany of the forest inhabitants' common afflictions: beriberi, snake bites, dysentery, malaria, tuberculosis, various plagues, yellow fever, hallucinogens, and the rare *carare* (scabies) of José Gregorio Ardavín (Yerena 119). The use of disease in the figurative sense is even more common. For example, in the chapter from which the book takes its name, trees are described as *raquíticos* (scrawny); the etymological root of the word anthropomorphically associates the trees with rickets, a disease characterized by a softening of bone and caused by a lack of vitamin D. This medical characterization extends to people in the novel as well, as evidenced by Sute Cúpira, whose first name (a synonym for rickets) connects illness directly to the wilderness itself when Gallegos describes him as the "personification of the monstrous jungle" (201).

Like other Latin American intellectuals such as Arguedas and César Zúmeta, Gallegos used medical language and a diagnostic approach in seeking out the causes of what he perceived as Latin America's failure to modernize at a pace in keeping with other nations in the hemisphere.[8] Like Arguedas, Gallegos attributes Latin America's economic and social conditions to the indigenous population, but Arguedas viewed the natives as an irrevocable impediment to political, social, and scientific advancement. Gallegos differs significantly from Arguedas and other sociologists of the era in that he placed more importance on the transformative powers of education than the inalterable fate of genetic heredity, as evidenced by his description of Marisela in *Doña Barbara* as "a personification of the soul of the race, open as the prairie to every improving action" (185).[9] This concept of a Venezuelan *raza* (race) that can be improved by education is a constant in all of Gallegos's writings leading up to *Canaima*, but, as we will see, comes to be questioned in the novel.

Gallegos's early article on the need for cultural values also sheds light on his intellectual formation, particularly his understanding of the nascent practice of psychology. The author's background in psychology has gone largely unremarked by critics because psychology—and psychoanalysis in particular—never gained the popularity in Venezuela (or most of Latin America) that it enjoyed in Argentina, which was home to the notable psychologist José Ingenieros (1877–1925). Yet Gallegos formed part of the intellectual minority that engaged in the budding field. Despite the apparently rudimentary state of the field in Venezuela during the first decade of the twentieth century, Gallegos nevertheless read the publications of important figures in the discipline.[10] In "Necesidad de valores culturales," Gallegos inaugurates a creative method he would later use in his novels: he interprets psychological theories and applies them to Venezuelan culture and politics. For example, he deplores the "mental state" of the nation and maintains that its ills are rooted in psychology rather than economics or politics (439). Gallegos paraphrases William James in writing of the paradoxical need to model Venezuelan traditions on other cultures, stating that where homegrown innovation is lacking,

> Imitation … comes in to fill the void. Imitation is, according to James's apt expression, the nerve of all human societies. In effect, just as the physical body is the nervous system that receives and transmits external impressions to the consciousness, through imitation the social body receives the influences of foreign civilizations in the form of social heredity in which the most ancient or advanced civilizations transmit their institutions, their arts, and their scientific and industrial achievements to the young and the unlearned. (439)

This passage is a nearly direct translation from the seventh chapter of James's *Talks to Teachers on Psychology and to Students on Some of Life's Ideals* (1899). Gallegos's approach to describing the human psyche, molded in large part by James, shapes the psychological portraits of several characters in *Canaima*.[11] The new scientific approach to the mind also affects the philosophical undertone of the novel, which is not surprising given the continuities between psychology and philosophy at the turn of the century. James's most influential work, *Principles of Psychology* (1890), was written at a time when the two disciplines were taught in the same department, and James himself refused to separate his interest in spiritual matters from any concept of empirical science in light of his interest in the soul and the nature of consciousness. As Gerald E. Myers has stated: "William James's thought epitomizes the ambivalent bonding between philosophy and psychology. . . . His life and thought were motivated by the need to find a place for religion in a Darwinian era, to view the world as being morally modifiable, to discover ways of making 'sick' souls into healthy ones, to uncover the hidden powers of the human psyche" (xix). *Canaima* reflects a similar point of view—namely, that spirituality (specifically mysticism) and science (specifically psychology) need not be mutually exclusive; in fact, each field complements the other. Like James, Gallegos also frequently uses metaphysical terms like *alma* (soul), and *espíritu* (spirit) alongside clinical descriptions in his writing. Much of his writing also presents the world as "morally modifiable." For example, both Marisela in *Doña Barbara* and Marcos Vargas in *Canaima* are open to a variety of influences on their conduct, which can be dictated by education or the lack thereof. Despite Gallegos's decision at a young age to follow Europe's positivist, scientific model for the education of Venezuela's citizenry, it is still possible to detect his interest in the mystical, metaphysical side of human nature. This tendency toward the spiritual would come to fruition in *Canaima*.

Gallegos's turning away from the adulation of rational, Western society in *Canaima* twenty years later is indicated by a speech he gave while he was writing the novel. On September 1, 1931, during his voluntary exile from Venezuela because of the dictatorship of Juan Vicente Gómez, Gallegos addressed the Federación Latinoamericana de Estudiantes (Latin American Student Federation) in New York. In his sweeping oration, "Las tierras de Dios" (The lands of God), which was reminiscent of Rodó's *Ariel*, it is possible to perceive some of the themes that would appear shortly in *Canaima*. For example, Gallegos told the students that "in our lands of impressive silence and tragic solitude, one feels that the sixth day of Genesis is not yet over, and that the winds of the creator still circulate in them" (117). This sentiment found a more lyrical expression in his novel four years later: "An unsettling landscape . . . where the primeval fear on the first morning of the world still rules" (*Canaima* 4). The idea of Latin America as a vibrant space that was in contact with the elemental forces of life and open to new creation was popular during the interwar period, and it would be repeated in Carpentier's *The Lost Steps* when the narrator finds himself "in the first chapters of Genesis" (167).

In the mid-twentieth century, several European philosophical texts presented Latin America as occupying an earlier position in the scope of human development, and therefore a future hope for human civilization. Oswald Spengler's oft-cited *The Decline of the West* posited that while European society was past its zenith, the cultures of the New World were on the rise. Count Hermann Key-serling maintained that "it is possible and even probable that the next rebirth of that spirit which made possible in ancient times the Greek miracle ... will arise in South America, for the salvation of all men and to redeem them from savagery" (*South American Meditations* 238). According to Julie Skurski, "Idealist and 'irrationalist' currents of thought ... made a strong intellectual impact on the metropolitan centers in this period. These currents challenged the determinist evolutionary concepts that guided ruling groups in much of Latin America while valorizing the spiritual and instinctual dimensions of life, which had long been disdained by liberal republicanism" (606). In his speech in New York, Gallegos does not urge his Latin American public to use European or North American methods to improve their home countries, which he had done in "Necesidad de valores culturales"; rather, he seeks to "defend our way of life," which he sees as the "individualism of the man of the tropics" ("Las tierras" 125). He explicitly rejects the mentality of those who think that "we will be neither great nor happy as long as we have no skyscrapers" (125). Gallegos's shift in orientation regarding Venezuela's modernity is manifest in the difference between his evaluations of Latin American imitation of Western traditions in his article from 1912 and his speech in 1931. In the earlier publication, Gallegos had exhorted his reading public to emulate other nations in order to achieve economic and political modernity. Nearly twenty years later, however, Gallegos announces that "it is now known that imitation of the foreign brings only dilettantism, and thus mediocrity. That no matter how gilded and praised the foreign may be, ... it will never be recommendable as the objective of a people" ("Las tierras" 128). His speech is also peppered with religious references that indicate a retreat from the vehement anticlericalism that characterized early twentieth-century positivism in Latin America. Gallegos's remarkable shift in political and aesthetic orientation marks both his nonfiction writings and his novels, as seen in the striking differences between *Doña Barbara* and *Canaima*.

Of course, Gallegos was not alone in his revalorization of the American continent as a site of spiritual and cultural renewal. The *novela de la tierra*, whose parameters encompass *The Vortex* and *Canaima*, was the literary fruit of this search for homegrown cultural inspiration. The disillusionment with the positivist goals of order and progress provoked by World War I triggered a retreat from scientific rationalism among European and Latin American intellectuals. As Skurski demonstrates: "Latin American thinkers applied the European challenge to positivism toward the revaluation of Latin American culture's spiritual character. The quest by social thinkers for these sources [of creative power and imagination], the turn toward the primitive occurring in the European arts, and the search by mystical thinkers for terrains that would be receptive to the development of esoteric knowledge converged to reconfigure Latin America as a privileged site of spiritual revitalization" (627). In Gallegos's novel, Marcos Vargas represents many of these facets: in turning away from education and his learned friends, he embodies the "turn toward the primitive," the intuitive apprehension of reality, and "spiritual revitalization" that seemed possible in Latin America. Marcos Vargas rejects the emulation of North American and European customs that Gallegos criticized in his 1931 speech, but—as will become clear—his transformation is not entirely positive. Disillusionment with positivism in Europe and Latin America had other repercussions. Roberto González Echevarría has noted: "The crisis of the West … removed natural science as the mediating discourse in Latin American narrative, and made way for a new one, that of anthropology" (*Myth* 150). The anthropological gaze is certainly evident in Gallegos's descriptions of the ñopo dance in *Canaima*, in which the Guaraúnos inhale hallucinogenic powder and sing and dance, to give just one example. Yet even more important in *Canaima* is the shift to mysticism instead of anthropology as a new means of describing the Latin American tierra. The true innovation in *Canaima* lies not in the exchange of positivism for anthropology but rather in Gallegos's turn toward mysticism and, in consequence, his exploration of the limits of language. Thus, while *Canaima* may narrate Marcos Vargas's failure to modernize Venezuela, it more importantly attempts to articulate the spiritual conversion in which Marcos becomes one with the forces of nature, specifically during the famous chapter "The Storm." Like *The Vortex*, *Canaima* attempts to describe the madness resulting from that conversion—to narrate what Gallegos's narrator declares cannot be narrated.

Throughout *Canaima*, Gallegos's reappraisal of non-Western modes of thought manifests itself in the competing discourses of rationality and madness. In this respect, the differences between *Doña Barbara* and *Canaima* could not be starker. In the former, Gallegos maintains the sharp dichotomy between learned reason and superstitious barbarism; in the latter, he erodes the distinction between them. For example, in *Doña Barbara*, madness is incarnated solely in Barbara's messenger, Juan Primito. He is unequivocally representative of the brutality of barbarism, and his only redeeming feature is his kindness to Marisela. There is no exploration of his psyche as there would be for the madmen in *Canaima*: Juan is simply "a simpleton with a tendency to fits of madness" (191). He is characterized solely by the negative aspects of insanity: "frenzied madness" (194), "superstitious fear" (195), and "unconditional submission" (195). Madness is thus present in both *Canaima* and *Doña Barbara*, but in the latter it is conquered, subjugated, and made sane when Santos Luzardo vanquishes Doña Bárbara and marries Marisela. In *Canaima*, however, madness becomes a mystical source of spiritual knowledge.

Gallegos constructs a veritable mosaic of madness in *Canaima*, ranging from the drunken raging of José Francisco Ardavín, which eventually leaves him drooling in the bush, to Ricardo's insanity following the theft of his bottle of gold nuggets; from Mister Reed's near-complete isolation from human contact to Giaffaro's withdrawal from the world and his fits of irrational shouting. Marcos Vargas, of course, experiences the most detailed descent into what

Gallegos depicts as irrational behavior, by abandoning the society of Ciudad Bolívar and living in the wilderness with his indigenous bride, Aymara. In exchange for discarding the trappings of civilization, Gallegos implies, Marcos Vargas achieves a spiritual gain and deep understanding of his soul. These diverse forms of lunacy all fall under the umbrella of Canaima, the malevolent spirit of the forest who drives men mad: "The malign one, the dark divinity of the Guaicas and Maquiritares, the furious god, the source of all evil and the cause of all ills, the one that fights for the world with Cajuña the Good. The demoniacal, with no form of its own and able to take on any appearance, Arimán [*sic*] of ancient Persia reborn in the Americas" (176). Gallegos's description of this indigenous spirit of the wilderness reveals his interest, both aesthetic and spiritual, in Eastern philosophies of the occult, which were gaining admirers in Latin America in the 1930s.[12] Skurski has noted that Gallegos was influenced by the "Romantic, phenomenological, and idealist thought of the period, as inflected by elements of mysticism" (633). For example, in Zoroastrianism, the ancient religion of Persia, Ahrimán was the personification of the devil. Neil Whitehead describes the Guyanese concept of *kanaimá* as a "dark shamanistic complex" and an "ancient form of sorcery" (i). Gallegos's version is similar in that the spirit of Canaima can possess individuals, transform them, and infuse them with supernatural powers. It is in the fascination with madness and barbarity that *Canaima* differs most significantly from *Doña Barbara*. While Doña Bárbara's conversations with a devilish spirit are scoffed at by the narrator as a veil for Bárbara's machinations and thievery, Marcos Vargas's communion with elements outside the realm of logical thought is upheld as part of the attractive enigma of the wilderness. Thus, despite his positivist dedication to education, Gallegos implies that in shunning the intellect and embracing the elemental spiritual forces of the forest, it is possible for a man to gain a "full sense of himself" (220). Gallegos does not fully explain what he conceives of as this greater mystical truth, which is one reason he was criticized by Balza for his "light approach to the symbolic depths" (xvi). Read within the context of other tropical adventure novels, it is clear that the appeal of Canaima resides in the possessed's ability to shed the confines of socially appropriate behavior and act in brutal, irrational ways.

In *Canaima*, both the revolting and the fascinating aspects of madness stem from the forest, just as they do in the novels of Conrad, Malraux, and Rivera discussed earlier in this book. Freed from the societal restraints that direct human thought and behavior in a linear fashion, characters who enter the wilderness in these novels get lost and lose themselves in the fullest sense of the term. Following Rivera's famous *tambocha* ant invasion passage in *The Vortex*, Gallegos also deftly merges spatial disorientation with mental disarray. He describes the tropical forest as "the green inferno where those who are lost wander in desperate circles retracing their own footsteps over and over again, accompanied by the larvae of ancestral terror, not daring to look at each other, until suddenly in the petrifying silence comes the sound, even though no one has said it, of the enormous terrible syllable that releases their madness: 'Lost!'" (175). The wanderers are turned into "delirious and solitary creatures" in their lack of orientation, and it is only a few minutes until "their instincts return down the path of the centuries" (175). The turn to madness caused by Canaima is at once attractive and repulsive; it is "inhuman" but also contains "secrets of the millennia" (173).

The common association between the madman, "primitive man," and a spirituality inaccessible to rational individuals provides the inspiration and vocabulary for some of Gallegos's most lyrical passages. In *Canaima*, the irrationality of the wilderness takes on the form of spiritual iconography. The author describes the forest floor and canopy in terms that evoke religious imagery, speaking of: "the virgin forest, like a cathedral with millions of pillars, the ground free of underbrush where the dense foliage above does not allow the rays of the sun to penetrate, solemn and submerged in a mysterious penumbra with deep, hallucinatory perspectives" (174). The rainforest becomes a possible site of spiritual ecstasy, displaced from the church onto the fertile soil. Yet this release from rational civilization also creates the opportunity for "the dehumanizing influence of the brutal solitude, which had produced in those men a dark tendency that was characteristic of the jungle: seizures of cruelty" (213). The removal of social restraints ultimately allows for both extremes of exaltation and perversion. The dangers of Canaima are both psychological and corporeal, and Gallegos mixes scientific and spiritual language to convey them.

Despite Gallegos's turn toward mysticism in the novel, he nevertheless continues to use scientific metaphors and vocabulary as a descriptive tool. The mental and physical illness of almost all the characters in the novel serves as an allegory for Venezuela's political and social problems. For example, Gallegos shows that the Venezuelan tradition of *caciquismo* (caciquism), embodied in the Ardavín family, is in its final death throes. José Gregorio, the eldest brother and patriarch, suffers from the "revolting carare disease," which he picked up living among the Guaraúnos (47). *Carare* is a Venezuelan term for *sarna*, translated from Spanish into English as *scabies*, which is an infectious and itchy skin condition. José Gregorio has retired to his ranch to die, and his brothers Miguel and José Francisco struggle to replace him as caudillo. José Francisco is a virtual portrait in clinical psychology: Gallegos describes him as cowardly yet vainly ambitious, "his rashness increased to the near pathological" (49). As the youngest Ardavín, he is both mentally and physically disturbed: he suffers from "physiological fear—uncontrollable nerves, quivering flesh," and he is a "delirious soul" haunted by "the ghost of himself" (49). Gallegos gives him a lengthy, detailed psychological portrait that is surpassed only by that of Marcos Vargas:

> The atmosphere created by the falsehood of his invented courage and
> the necessity of having to actually back it up one day with real, and
> fatal, action soon filled him with a morbid fear of himself, of the reck-
> less actions that might occur to him—the false man of courage who was

coming loose, day by day, from the other, the one he had submitted to. But as he made room in his soul for these reflections and was pervaded now by feelings of secret duplicity, he did not interpret as false the man of courage trying to manifest itself in him, but the other, the shaking and sweating self, fearful of the first, so he failed to see himself as the man he really was. Finally this notion of becoming two, already one step too many across the threshold of madness, materialized itself one morning after a night of wild drinking into a feeling that his body had split into two, one half departed with all the vital heat and energies of his spirit, and he was left with the illusory other half, paralyzed with fear and sense of oncoming death. (49)

The characterization of Ardavín as a "delirious soul" who is "already one step too many across the threshold of madness" demonstrates the affinity between Gallegos's method of psychological description and that of William James. Both merge the philosophical and the metaphysical with the medical in their approach to human psychology. Gallegos describes Ardavín as a split personality whose weakness leads him over the threshold of madness. There are echoes of Zola in the clinical tone of his description, yet Gallegos also employs a spiritual vocabulary common to writers such as Rodó and Vasconcelos. Accordingly, Ardavín's madness robs him of "vital heat" and the "energies of his spirit." References to *espíritu* and *alma* amplify the spiritual nature of Gallegos's prose. Ardavín's ailments surpass any medical issue and come to be more spiritual than physical: he seems possessed and lies uncontrollably. Like Arturo Cova in *The Vortex*, Ardavín finally unravels in drunken hallucinations such that

he no longer knew from one moment to the next if [his soul] remained in his body or was floating away from him in the shadow of the ghost. . . . Then, sober again and having no memories of his deliriums, but as though they themselves were radiating reinforced vital energies— invisible coals in the darkness where there had once been live ones—a euphoria of exaggerated self-confidence overcame him, and feeling as though he were at the height of his powers . . . he let himself be lulled into dreams of greatness by those shameless flatterers still around him. (225–26)

Gallegos juxtaposes this technical description of grandiosity with his lyrical prose, thus demonstrating the unusual mix of the clinical and the spiritual that characterize the novel. It is significant that the use of "vital energy" here is same as in Marcos Vargas's mental unraveling. For Gallegos, madness is Janus-faced in that it can lead to spiritual exaltation or mental collapse. In his final moments, José Francisco Ardavín achieves a modicum of spiritual and mental clarity similar to Marcos Vargas's later conversion in the wilderness. He suffers convulsions and seizures like those who speak in tongues in moments of religious ecstasy. Ardavín experiences:

> A flow of words that revealed a deep cerebral upheaval, without the usual coarse jokes for the benefit of the crowds, but on the contrary with a certain distinction and even elegance of thought and expression not known in him previously. . . . At times he would falter, he would raise his voice too high and incoherencies would escape him, or he would tremble, shaken by involuntary shivers, but then he would recover himself at once, although through an effort of spirit that was visible in the contractions of his facial muscles and in the pallor that flashed across his face, and return to his refined and animated conversation. . . . His beguiling spirituality made his friends think of those mysterious flames of lucidity which, erupting suddenly out of the coma before death, precede and announce the final snuffing out of mortality. (234)

In this passage, Ardavín exhibits the vacillation between a spiritual exaltation that manifests itself in his "elegance of thought" and the descent to abject, incoherent ramblings that is common to all those who go mad in the novel. Madness encompasses both of these possibilities: a character who goes mad could either attain a plane of higher spiritual understanding, like Marcos, or he could end up like Ardavín, found wandering the fields near Tumeremo, "stumbling and falling in his drunkenness, fleeing haltingly before his persecutorial obsession, jaw hanging slack, mouth drooling, eyes clouded with madness" (237). Both Count Giaffaro and Marcos Vargas undergo conversion experiences similar to Ardavín's: driven mad in the forest, both lose the ability to speak and act rationally, but in return they gain spiritual lucidity. Madness, Gallegos implies, is transformative and can lead to a deep insight into human nature. It is, however, ultimately destructive: Giaffaro remains isolated in the wilderness, Ardavín never recovers his lucidity, and Marcos abandons the civilized world.

Gallegos's characterization of Count Giaffaro as the archetypal "civilized European" (182) epitomizes the change in the author's estimation of European science since his early writings. Whereas Gallegos had previously advocated for the transplantation of foreign scientific methods and theories to Venezuela, in *Canaima* he parodies the European habit of collecting, classifying, and studying the American continent. Giaffaro's cabin in the woods is described as a tiny European outpost in a savage land:

> The lank, narrow-faced man lived in a rude but comfortable house, with fruit and vegetable gardens, in the middle of the untamed jungle, where, in a small museum, he had gathered indigenous artifacts, birds, and other animals of the jungle that he had dissected and scientifically classified, as well as the masterwork of his embalmer's art—the mummy of an

Indian who had accompanied him and served him for many years and who now, with the permanence of an incorruptible being, presided over the entire collection. (180)

The comically macabre image of Giaffaro's mummified servant provides a pointed critique of the role of Western science in the history of Latin America. Gallegos uses Giaffaro's prized collection to parody the European practice of gathering and preserving indigenous specimens in the New World—be they flora, fauna, or human individuals—since the time of the Conquest. He sarcastically spoofs the positivist method of scientific inquiry that considers the Indian merely another element of nature. Giaffaro's museum thus marks a significant shift in Gallegos's attitude toward the maxims of scientific progress that he had advocated earlier.

Despite this scientific tendency to classify, preserve, and display the world in a hierarchical fashion, Giaffaro too has become affected by the spirit of Canaima. Specifically, after fifteen years in the wilderness, the Count "had lost the habit of discursive thought and acquired in its place that of immersion into his deepest intuitions, those that could not be expressed except, at best, as the Indian did, with a single word in the midst of silence that enveloped it in a halo of significations that had only been suggested, and so the effort the count had to make to express himself in complete and coordinated sentences was obvious" (180–81). This passage demonstrates that the true discovery to be made in the forest is not the collection and preservation of artifacts but rather the access to "deepest intuitions" that this supposedly primordial space offers. Gallegos asserts that the benefits to be derived from the wilderness are not scientific but spiritual. Here he suggests that newcomers to the wilderness should emulate the Indians in their manner of thought and expression, which is not linear and discursive but rather an allusive halo of signification. Most important, true wisdom is not accessible via traditional forms of language. According to this logic, comprehension of the natural world and the deeper truths it offers are only attainable through surrender to Canaima.

The failure of language to communicate the protagonist's experience in the forest is a common thread among all the novels examined in this work. Just as Conrad constructed *Heart of Darkness* so that Kurtz rarely speaks directly, thereby making his experience inscrutable and incommunicable, Gallegos intimates that the madness and conversion to irrational thought experienced by Ardavín, Giaffaro, and Marcos Vargas cannot be conveyed in a discursive manner. For example, while alone on his property, Giaffaro expresses himself in single words, occasional shouts, and bouts of incoherence. He tells Marcos Vargas that for him the forest serves as an "escape valve" from the chaos and spiritual contamination of contact with other individuals (182).

Giaffaro is not the only character to suggest that the sole means of achieving the "periodic cures" offered by the wilderness lies in the indigenous mode of thought and expression (182). Throughout *Canaima*, Gallegos paradoxically depicts the Guaraúnos both as members of a degenerate, vanishing race and as silent carriers of a truth inaccessible to modern man. Marcos Vargas's fascination with the indigenous inhabitants of Guyana thus encapsulates Gallegos's conflicted relationship with science and mysticism, and with rational and irrational patterns of thought. In these passages, Gallegos seeks what González Echevarría has called "not so much knowledge about the Other but knowledge about the Other's knowledge" (*Myth* 150). In *Canaima*, the degenerate and the mystical qualities of the Guaraúnos go hand in hand: Gallegos suggests that the indigenous characters possess an alternative way of knowing precisely because they are biologically distinct and mentally irrational. According to Gallegos, all those who enter the forest are perverted by Canaima in that they revert to their prehistoric state and become like "the Indians, with the amazing subtlety of their senses and experts in understanding that world" (176). The descriptions of indigenous people throughout the novel reflect both the scientific and mystical orientation of Gallegos.

In the passages that align the Guaraúnos with decay and disease, Gallegos the scientist shines. For example, the indigenous Guaraúnos are "degenerate descendants of the fierce, legendary Caribs" (5). For the author, they represent the Guyana "of the native abandoned to his primitive conditions, declining and dying out as a race before ever existing as one of the peoples in the life of the nations. Venezuela of the Discovery and the Colonization ... unfinished still" (8). Here Gallegos reinforces the idea of the rainforest as the site of an earlier chronological era, and its inhabitants, therefore, as genetic relics who are wasting away. While he is sympathetic to the plight of indigenous groups who are threatened with extinction, he nevertheless makes it clear that they have no role in the Venezuela of the twentieth century. In some passages, he approaches them as Giaffaro does—as specimens to be preserved as they approach annihilation. Indeed, Gallegos's description of the ñopo ceremony is an anthropological interlude tinged with nostalgia and disgust: "The Guaraúno were there in all their barbarism. If not total savages, they were like all other Venezuela aborigines who, under the regimes of the colonial encomiendas and missions, had lost the vigor and energy of their original condition, forced as braceros into mind-dulling work far removed from their own needs, work whose human relevance was a mystery to them and whose technique, when there was one, was never taught them" (207). Gallegos laments the loss of racial vigor among the Guaraúnos, which implies that their original condition must have contained positive attributes. Gallegos further uses the ñopo ceremony to expound in a sociological tone on the participants' "delirious and bestial intoxication" (208) and to sound "the abyss of inertia in which the native soul languished" (208). In this respect, he adheres to the theories about the degeneration of indigenous peoples of the American continent propounded by Latin American eugenicists during the early twentieth century.[13] Gallegos's presentation of the effects of Canaima is ambiguous. To Marcos Vargas, it may offer a spiritual truth, but indigenous individuals are irredeemably backward. Despite his claim that a mystical truth lies in the forest, Gallegos nevertheless participates in the scientific racism of his era. This contradictory and hypocritical stance is reflected in the novel's depiction of the ñopo ceremony.

There is an element of mystery in Gallegos's ostensibly anthropological description of indigenous rites: he seeks to uncover the original vitality of the Guaraúnos and to thereby gain access to their mystical realm of truth. This desire is evident in the description of the indigenous ritual dance, which Gallegos presents as a voyage back through time for the Indians. In their intoxicated state, they regress from their current status as a vanquished people through their enslavement in the colonial era and on to their irrational prehistoric state. In this scene, the rise of the moon and the setting of the sun parallel the simultaneous metaphorical passage of the Guaraúnos back through time. The image of the moon frequently signals madness in Western literature, and it does so here. The rising moon inaugurates the irrational behavior in the most elemental sense of the term *lunacy*; it serves as a symbol of regression to a primal state. Indeed, past and present merge just as day and night do at the beginning of the dance: "And the full moon began to rise just as the sun went down, the hour to begin the fiesta" (208). In the first phase of the ritual, the participants perform "the lascivious, artless dance, pure bestiality" (209). Then the Guaraúnos relive their defeat by conquistadores and missionaries in the form of a "funereal dance and the lamentation for the dead of the community and for their great disappearance into the eternal, moonless night" (210). This second phase coincides with the continuing rise of the full moon: "The moon illuminates the savage scene with hallucinatory splendor and decorates the misery of the filthy bodies" (210). The third and final phase is the war dance in which the Guaraúnos "reproduce the ancient shouts of combat" until they lose all their vestiges of humanity and become "a filthy, panting mass" (210–11). By this point, the moon has risen fully, and the participants have reached the cumulative point of the dance: "The spectral glow of the moon shines over the pile of bodies overcome by the dehumanizing ñopo" (211). Barely human, the dancers are transformed into mere bodies without individual thought or will. Most important, they have lost themselves in the ritual and receded to a prehistoric moment unknown to the racionales. Alongside the apparent disgust the narrator uses to depict the Guaraúnos lies a fascination with the convergence of celestial and human bodies. The Guaraúnos' tragic and dehumanized dance is, Gallegos implies, a prerequisite for accessing their spiritual realm of truth.

Gallegos thus creates in *Canaima* a mystique of hidden wisdom inherent in indigenous modes of thought. According to Gallegos, those who live in the forest in close contact with the indigenous tribes have abilities and spiritual depths inaccessible to the racionales. For example, Marcos's mentor Manuel Ladera calls Juan Solito a "philosopher" with "the power of witchcraft" (30). Marcos's later contact with Solito provokes a "moment of madness" and leaves him on "the verge of a spiritual cataclysm, and the feeling was so strong that his heart was still hammering and he could feel his face had gone pale" (123). The same sensation overtakes Marcos Vargas following the ñopo ceremony: the dance provokes a "mental storm" (209) that leads to his angry outburst. As in the other novels examined in this work, the protagonist witnesses the indigenous rite and is both horrified and attracted by the base irrationality of the scene. Conrad's Marlow senses the appeal of the African drumbeats, but in the homologous scene in *The Vortex*, Arturo Cova is cured of a gunshot wound by an indigenous healing rite and his incredulity gives way to fascination (Rivera 79). For Marcos Vargas, in turn, the ñopo ceremony marks the beginning of a spiritual and political conversion. Moved by the Guaraúnos' lament, he decries their abuse by "bandits" such as Sute Cúpira and begins his own journey back through time (211). This episode is immediately followed by the chapter "The Storm," in which Marcos Vargas permanently abandons urban society and remains in the wilderness, naked, fearless, barbaric, and mad.

"The Storm" is the most famous chapter in *Canaima*, and the best piece of prose in all of Gallegos's writing. It gains its force from the overpowering, lyric evocation of the elements and Marcos's reaction to them. In these passages, Gallegos revels in the poetic possibilities of nature and humanity untethered to any progressive goal, such as harnessing the power of the great river for electricity or improving humanity through education. Through the course of the chapter, Marcos sheds the trappings of civilization: he gets lost in the forest, which, as we have seen, symbolizes the loss of sanity: "A sudden absence of self had left him at the mercy of the mesmerizing jungle ... He chose one path at random, abandoning himself to the delicious thrill that the fear of getting lost had brushed across him" (215; ellipsis in original). He is driven mad by an insensible rage at two rubber workers, one whose eyes are "glazed in madness" and is about to chop off his index finger because of an infecting worm (216). As in the ñopo ceremony, the light in the forest reflects the merging of present and past—the sane and the irrational—in its evocation of the storm: "The trunks of the trees turned spectrally pale in the diurnal gloom that was advancing through them" (217). The "diurnal gloom" heralds Marcos Vargas's own regression to a primal state similar to that achieved by the Guaraúnos. When the storm finally descends, Marcos quickly becomes part of the earth itself: "The deepest roots of his being were buried in stormy soil, the surging streams of blood in his veins still howled through him, in the depths of his spirit he was one with the nature of the furious elements, and before the overpowering spectacle offered by the satanic earth he found his essential self, cosmic man, stripped of history, reintegrated into the very first footstep at the edge of the abyss of creation" (219). This passage condenses the diverse elements that give *Canaima* its mystical, magical quality. Gone are Gallegos's positivistic concerns about Guyana's wasted potential or the description of its residents' medical ailments. Instead, Marcos Vargas undergoes a spiritual conversion and becomes an allegory for Original Man—present at the moment of creation, spiritually whole, and lacking the taint of history. This process culminates in Marcos Vargas's ability to transform himself into a tree, according to his comrades. He is literally one with nature, in contrast to the adversarial relationship that Western man has with his surroundings.

It is clear that both Gallegos and his critics have accepted the conception of the tropical forest as a primordial, prelapsarian space in which it is possible to regain the lost unity of the cosmos. Just as the author proclaims Vargas to be a "cosmic man," Orlando Araujo maintains that *Canaima* is a "Homeric novel, the epic of a continent in the first day of Creation, which reveals … the depths of the telluric mysticism that brings Marcos Vargas to identify with the forces of nature and a form of communication forgotten for centuries, and which guides him to the discovery of the perfect lost unity of the cosmos" (14). The desire to reconnect with a pristine past unmarred by modern, corrupt society permeates the novel and seduces author and critic alike. For them, the forest becomes the wellspring of mysticism and irrational thought and offers the capacity to restore humanity to what Gallegos perceived as a pure state in which positivist rationality is subsumed by a deeper spiritual truth.

The notion that premodern humanity thrived in a social realm in which rationality was not yet dominant is promulgated by Michel Foucault, who maintained in his *History of Madness* that in ancient times there was no division between madness and sanity, and that a barrier was constructed between the two only with the advent of the modern mental institution. According to Foucault, it is only by excluding madness that modern society can define itself. As I noted in the Introduction, Foucault idealizes a premodern time in which madness and reason were not always antithetical. This same idea reemerges as a deeply attractive and yet unsettling prospect in tropical quest narratives of the twentieth century. In *Canaima*, the regression to this *undifferentiated experience*, to use Foucault's term (xxvii), presents the protagonist with a complex dilemma. Lunacy becomes something of a siren song: it offers Marcos Vargas the appealing possibility of becoming a "cosmic man" and achieving a "full sense of himself" (219) via a mystical connection with the forces of the earth. And yet madness is profoundly dangerous for all the characters in the novel: José Francisco Ardavín, despite a few moments of clarity, is lost to alcohol-induced dementia forever; Count Giaffaro remains isolated, pacing and shrieking in his cabin; and Marcos Vargas gives up wealth, marriage to the upper-class Aracelis, and the opportunity to modernize his nation. After four years in the forest, Marcos's "sunken eyes flashed fleeting glances, his hair was turning gray, and instead of that expansive character and aplomb and self-control before others, he was now reserved and shy, to the point of greeting Arteaguita with the formal [form of address] 'Usted'" (260). Gallegos reinforces the traditional association between clothing and civilization when Vargas signals his complete abandonment of Western society by admitting that he isn't sure he can wear shoes anymore (263). Marcos's metamorphosis into primeval man is apparently complete; he has achieved the state of "unreason" that Foucault imagined in his history of madness (xxix).

Yet the secondary protagonist, Gabriel Ureña, who is widely considered to be a fictionalization of the author, cannot quite relinquish the idea that the barbarism of the jungle cannot be tamed like that of the plains. Ureña urges Vargas to channel his newfound spiritual power for the good of the nation:

> You can ... hear the voice crying out in the wilderness, and all you have to do is prepare yourself intellectually. Read a little, develop yourself, civilize that barbarous force inside you, study the problems of this land, and take on the attitude your character obliges you to. When life grants someone talents—and, I repeat, you have them—it gives responsibilities as well. This country expects everything of a man, of the Hombre Macho as he is now called—and you, why not?—could be that Messiah.
>
> And this was, in words, what Marcos Vargas had felt so suddenly revealed to him, intuitively and confusedly, so violently on that night of the storm.... Once again his soul had been revealed to him in an unexpected way; and when this happens to someone like him, in whom the force of the spirit quickly overwhelms everything, little room is left to receive what comes from the outside, and so Ureña's words were heard only vaguely and distantly. (249–50)

Rather than becoming another Santos Luzardo, Marcos retreats to the prehistorical (or perhaps ahistorical) realm with his companion, Aymara. They wed in a traditional Guaraúno ceremony that involves the groom whipping the bride, and Marcos gives up on the civilizing project Ureña has suggested. Rather than pushing for further reforms, Gallegos finds the solution to Venezuela's intractable challenges to modernization in the large communal tent, an emblem of the simplicity of indigenous living habits: "Everyone consumed equally what was produced by them all; all shared the same life, and the *churuata* was an appropriate symbol: it belonged to all of them, all contributed to its raising, and individual rights were acquired only at night beneath its roof" (275). This recognition of the worth of indigenous cultures was common among socialist Latin American intellectuals in the 1930s: writers such as Vasconcelos argued that the future of Latin America lay in the revalorization of indigenous customs. Skurski writes, "Rather than being viewed as a threatening source of anarchy, societies and peoples associated with barbarism were regarded from this perspective as sources of creative power and imagination waiting to be tapped" (627). Like Marcos Vargas, it seems that Gallegos himself is tempted by the simplicity and spirituality of his own literary wilderness.

The presentation of the tropical forest as a mythic, irrational, prehistoric space devoid of the complications of modern life is a constant in twentieth-century tropical novels, which Alejo Carpentier wistfully parodies in *The Lost Steps* (1953). The quest narrative in which the protagonist searches for both material and spiritual wealth in the wilderness is also a common thread.[14] Where does this mythical, literary jungle come from? As González Echevarría has noted, the protagonists of these tropical quest narratives are surrounded by a forest made of books.[15] He also observes that "the jungle of the Americas was described by the chroniclers of the Discovery and the Conquest, by the infinite number of European travelers who passed through it in the last century in search of the origins of all of nature's phenomena—Darwin sought the origins of species in the New World. The jungle also appears in the sacred books of indigenous peoples, and in the powerful verses of Genesis" ("Introducción" 47). Although Gallegos seeks to portray the mythic quality of nature as stemming from the wilderness itself, the concept has a textual origin, in books already written about the region. The forest—supposedly a preliterate, wild space—is in fact a palimpsest on which scores of writers have already projected their judgments of the New World and their aspirations for it. Gallegos illustrates this literary origin of his telluric mysticism through Gabriel Ureña. For the telegraphist, the appeal of the forest comes from "the mystical readings, under whose influence many of those words came to acquire a religious significance: Erevato, Merevari, Roraima, Duida, became the rivers and jungles of a sacred land he was able to imagine only in the glow of a tragic sunset and which were, at the same time, cabalistic words of a great voice crying out in the wilderness" (64–65). The sickly attraction of the "measles of mysticism" is thus felt even by the bookish Ureña, who, like Gallegos, had thought of becoming a priest before his disillusionment with Christianity (97).

The literary roots of the forest seep into Gallegos's description of the landscape. The uncivilized wilderness is evoked using distinctively literary terminology that celebrates "the drama of the virgin forest, the desolate plains, the unexplored jungle, and the unused rivers, a grandiose and epic panorama in whose vast silence the cries of a race had died, a race whose culture had been destroyed and had not yet been replaced by another" (65). The narrator notes, however, that "these same realistic notions continued to reflect also the gleams of the flames of mysticism: the calamities of this region removed from progress and abandoned to the satanical rule of violence had the nature of a biblical curse" (65). The use of literary terms such as *epic* and *drama* implies that the new telluric Latin American literature will not come from the scientific maxims of "order and progress" but rather from the intoxicating mysticism of the indigenous past. Gallegos's task, then, would seem to be the creation of a new literary jungle—to inscribe on the palimpsest left by the explorers, conquistadores, and poets before him his narration of the mystical conversion of the criollo Marcos Vargas.

And yet, like Conrad's Marlow, Marcos Vargas finds that his epiphany in the forest is incommunicable. Arteaguita wants to know what Marcos has found in the forest, but the narrator states that "what Marcos brought back from the jungle was not something that could be told in stories. His experiences had been fused into the emotion of the storm, the fullest and most intense sense of himself he had ever felt, and it could neither be held in his memory nor communicated to anyone else" (232–33). Marcos Vargas—like Solito and Giaffaro, like Malraux's Perken, and like Kurtz and Cova—is faced with the prospect of expressing an irrational experience in a discursive fashion. The act of narration is an inherently rational practice in which the elements of a story are organized hierarchically and related in chronological fashion. Narrative discourse, then, is for the sane—for the mundane physical world rather than the spiritual world accessible to Marcos Vargas after the storm. Thus, in the deepest substratum of the novel lies a questioning of the act of narration and the ability of the written word to convey the meaning of the mystical telluric experience.

Gallegos, like other so-called regionalist novelists, conceives of the tierra as the source of original Latin American literature. The struggle to find the correct language—be it scientific or mystical—in which to express what he viewed as the essence of the selva forms the core of Gallegos's literary style in *Canaima*. I argue that this struggle is present in all the novels discussed here, and forms a hallmark of the tropical quest narrative. The authors seek to answer the question: How to explain the unexplainable? How to subject madness to a rationalizing discourse and still express it? How to narrate what "no era para narrado"? This crisis of expression plays itself out in the repeated failure of the written word in the novel: rational discourse bends under the weight of the forest. Throughout *Canaima*, the written word is proved to be fallible, and in some cases even fraudulent, as evidenced by the creation of the marriage license granted posthumously to José Gregorio Ardavín and the episode of the treasure seeker's map. With the help of Apolonio Alcaraván, Marcos Vargas forges the matrimonial document of the recently deceased José Gregorio Ardavín to his longtime indigenous companion in order to secure her some of his assets. Alcaraván, who inserts a clause guaranteeing himself a healthy kickback, exalts the malleability of the written word: "Oh, what we can do with paper, Marcos Vargas! What a great invention!" (150). The disconnect between what is written and what is truthful casts the validity of written expression into doubt. In the latter incident, Marcos and his companions poke fun at the townspeople of Upata who are gullible enough to believe that an Andalusian known as El Españolito is in possession of an authentic map marking buried treasure in their area. The written word, Gallegos shows, is no guarantee of authenticity. Moreover, it is of little service in the wilderness, as Marcos prefers "the living geography, learned through the tales of the caucheros. For the dead geography they taught him in school—or for anything else they might try to put in his head—he had no interest at all" (11). This remarkable phrase represents a complete reversal from Gallegos's former celebration of education as a means of overcoming barbarity. Marcos Vargas, the incarnation of a possible messiah for Venezuela, turns away from writing in favor of the unwritable forest.

In contrast to written documents, both the jungle and the Indian are portrayed as silent, impenetrable, and illegible entities. Their meaning cannot be read easily but rather must be deciphered like the "halo of significations" that surround Giaffaro when the spirit of Canaima overtakes him (180). The narrator describes "the enigma of the millennial jungles," which are encompassed in

the graveyards of vanished villages where now there are only uninhab-
ited forests, and in the monumental stone petroglyphs cut into the
granite stones of the great waterfalls, symbol inscriptions of an unknown
race from a truncated civilization. The Indians living here now do not
know how to interpret them, and when they have to pass nearby they
rub a burning chile around their eyes to ward off the malevolence of the
taboo, for the characters contain the mysteries of the tribes that were
lost in the great, moonless night. (175)

For Gallegos, the act of narrating the enigma of the jungle entails the literary
expression of the mysterious symbols of ancient Amerindian people. His lyrical
passages describing the forest and Marcos's conversion are therefore more akin to
the petroglyphs than a rational narrative discourse. As in *The Vortex*, the novel
we read—particularly the chapter "The Storm"—becomes the literary fruit of the
protagonist's unnarratable adventure. For Gallegos, only non-Western vocabulary can express the new Latin American literature.

Similarly, Gabriel Ureña recognizes the seductive literary possibilities of
indigenous modes of expression as he examines a map of the region: "The native
words—evocative words from barbarous tongues stretched out over mysterious
lands—and the geographic terms for rivers, caños, and jungle mountains all exer-
cised a magical power on his imagination" (64). Ureña feels the "old emotion
of the magic words when the peons revealed the secrets of things, expressing
themselves in the lively and suggestive language of men who are in touch with
nature" (243). *Doña Barbara* and *Canaima* both locate the tierra as the source of
poetry, which is allusive rather than discursive thought. As González Echevarría
has observed, Gallegos shares a revalorization of indigenous culture and its poetic
possibilities with Pablo Neruda's "Canto General" ("Canaima" 381). *Canaima*
is Gallegos's best work precisely because in it the moralizations of Gallegos the
educator cede to the more lyric and artistic expression that he finds in *la barbarie*. While *The Vortex* is a more radical text because the madman narrates his
own mental dissolution, Gallegos makes in *Canaima* an important jump from a
consistently didactic tone to one that evokes the poetic appeal of the wilderness,
thereby anticipating the later poetic directions of Pablo Neruda and Octavio Paz.

As in the rest of *Jungle Fever*, I am interested in the intersections of madness,
wilderness, and writing. *Canaima* is a powerful and seductive work precisely in
the passages in which Gallegos's carefully tended philosophy of order and progress gives way to the more interesting attraction of the base and the regressive,
which for Gallegos is embodied in the tropical forest and the Guaraúnos. By
approaching the irrational through the lens of psychology, Gallegos acquires a
legitimate reason to explore insanity in its many different guises—and, indeed,
to revel in it. As a result, his descriptions of men driven mad by Canaima are a
mix of clinical and lyrical elements. *Canaima* challenges Gallegos's reputation as
a positivist, progressive educator and politician because it offers him the chance

to indulge (in novelistic form) in the pleasures of what he perceived as his country's irrationality and barbarity. Indeed, *Canaima* allows him to challenge the inherent primacy of reason and to delve into the psychology of the pathological. It enables him to parody the maxims of progress he espoused in his political life. Through Marcos Vargas, he rejects the value of a formal, Western-style education. Even the well-educated, rational bourgeois Gabriel Ureña is tempted by the "mysterious lands" (64), though he does not succumb to them as do Count Giaffaro, José Francisco Ardavín, and of course Marcos Vargas.

Like *The Vortex*, *Canaima* is also a narrative of failure in the sense that Marcos Vargas, who presents a great hope for the future of Venezuela, does not combat the exploitation of the peons or lead his country from barbarism to civilization. Instead, he goes native, disappears into the vegetation, and marries an indigenous woman instead of the blonde, wealthy Aracelis. This symbolically dire ending is only nominally mitigated by the final page of the novel, when Vargas's son appears on Ureña's doorstep, sent by his father to be educated. Like José Vasconcelos and other Latin American intellectuals of the 1930s, Gallegos argued that the *mestizaje* would be the solution to the civilization-barbarism divide that had riven Latin America. While in this way *Canaima* is more optimistic than Rivera's novel (in which Cova and his son are both presumed lost), the hasty, brief, and palliative finale does not really lessen the impact of Vargas's total metamorphosis. Instead, it reifies Gallegos's lifelong ambivalence regarding the merits of rational progress and the destructive seduction of irrationality. Yet Gallegos has not so much narrated a failure as redefined success as a mystical conversion that is inexpressible except in poetic language. The departure from scientific rationalism is groundbreaking in a novel by a politician who was known as the Teacher throughout his life. *Canaima* is Gallegos's own moment of lyrical madness in an otherwise civilized and rational body of work.

Chapter 5

Surrealism, Science, and Sanity
in *The Lost Steps*

I HAVE SELECTED ALEJO CARPENTIER'S *THE LOST STEPS* TO CONCLUDE THIS exploration of madness in tropical quest novels because it marks the total reversal of the conventional opposition between "sane Europeans" and "irrational savages." This subversion begins implicitly in *Heart of Darkness* when Marlow's exclamation "An appeal to me in the fiendish row—is there?" signals the demise of Western rationality in the tropics (140). André Malraux and José Eustasio Rivera both reveal the irrationality inherent in the minds of their ostensibly civilized protagonists as they lose themselves in the tropical forest, and Rivera and Rómulo Gallegos transform that irrationality into wellsprings of artistic creation. Like the other two Latin American authors discussed in this book, Alejo Carpentier also capitalizes on the literary potential of the American wilderness. In *The Lost Steps*, published in 1953, he makes complete and explicit the reversal of the Manichean opposition between the civilized metropolis and the barbaric wilderness. Whereas the other authors examined in this study portray the forest as a site of madness, for Carpentier it is a locus of sanity and natural order. Indeed, in *The Lost Steps*, Western civilization becomes emblematic of the irrational and the destructive forces of humanity. For the narrator-protagonist, there is no one more sane than he who lives simply in the wilderness, and none who live so madly as the city dwellers.

Carpentier's inversion of this now-familiar dyad is contemporaneous with widespread intellectual disillusionment toward Western civilization in the wake of the brutalities of World War II. Following the narrator's return from serving as a translator in the war, he works as a composer for various commercial enterprises. Dissatisfied with his profession, his marital life, and the dissipation of his own ambitions, the protagonist flees his North American city on the pretext of locating indigenous musical instruments in an unnamed South American country on behalf of a museum. Once in the wilderness, he seeks solace in what he perceives as a more natural way of life, which presents a marked contrast to the violence and irrationality of the modern world.

Yet it is not the trauma of world war alone that is responsible for turning the city=sanity and forest=madness dynamic on its head. Carpentier's association of civilization with disordered insanity stems from his participation in the surrealist movement. His protagonist's search for an ordered utopia in the community of Santa Mónica de los Venados is a direct result of his rejection of the European avant-garde. The protagonist's frequent dismissal and condemnation of surrealism make the artistic movement a recurrent presence in the novel. The presence of surrealism is particularly apparent in the role medicine plays in Carpentier's work. This rather surprising connection derives from the affinities between surrealist art and the medical profession, as will become clear shortly. In *The Lost Steps*, a society's healing traditions are as fraught with cultural signification as its art, literature, architecture, and music. Accordingly, Carpentier's protagonist denigrates Western medicine and the surrealist fascination with the irrational in favor of traditional healing rites embodied in the Shirishana shaman's death chant in chapter 23. The protagonist, however, is unable to free himself from his own surrealist aesthetic upbringing, especially as his interest in the Shirishana and Guahibo peoples converges with his former surrealist interest in ethnography. Similarly, he is unable to maintain his illusion of the forest as a place of health and order; irrationality and illness seep into his literary, fabricated world despite his best efforts to banish them. In the following discussion, I will trace the dynamic relationship between science and surrealism and the way it shapes the portrayal of the tropics in *The Lost Steps*.

Before delving into the interrelations of science and surrealism in *The Lost Steps*, it is important to consider how the novel both adheres to and departs from the tropical adventure conventions I have considered thus far. *The Lost Steps* shares a basic structure and core motifs with the tropical quest narrative, but like *Heart of Darkness*, the work presents a turning point for this subset of the adventure novel genre. After *The Lost Steps*, the physical journey—replete with its standards of time, geography, and space—becomes a metaphor for voyages that are entirely interior, timeless, and metaphysical, as is the case in Wilson Harris's *Palace of the Peacock*, as I will show in the Conclusion. Carpentier's novel is an intermediary waypoint in the evolution of the adventure novel: it conforms to the conventions of an adventure novel in order to parody them and ultimately to expose the foundations of the flawed and futile desire to "go native."

In terms of plot structure, *The Lost Steps* mimics the traditional format of the other novels examined in this book. Like Malraux's Claude, the protagonist of *The Lost Steps* tries to remove valuable cultural artifacts from their places of origin. Like Arturo Cova and Marcos Vargas, he derives spiritual and artistic inspiration from his time spent in the wilderness. Like Kurtz, he turns his back on Western society and attempts to remain in the forest with a woman who is neither his betrothed nor his wife. Like all the protagonists, this narrator gets lost, undergoes a spiritual conversion, and perceives his journey into the wilderness as a voyage back through time as well as space. By the time Carpentier was writing *The Lost Steps*, in the late 1940s and early 1950s, all these elements were commonplace in adventure novels, which he well knew; he had even published a review of *The Way of the Kings* in *Social* in 1931 ("André Malraux"). His departure from these novels comes not in terms of plot but in the self-reflexive, intertextual references the narrator makes throughout the work, thereby acknowledging his debt to previous adventure narratives and the impossibility of his quest to flee the written word.

Carpentier presents an ironic tribute to and parody of previous journey narratives throughout *The Lost Steps*. It has already been noted that Homer's *Odyssey* is a foundational literary basis for *The Lost Steps* (Rosman 41). Yet the narrator is a parody of Ulysses because he fails the tests placed before him. For example, he cowers in fear during a thunderstorm rather than assisting the crew: "My reason gone, unable to control my fear, I clung to Rosario, seeking the warmth of her body, no longer as a lover, but like a child clinging to its mother's neck" (169–70). Moreover, at the conclusion of the tale, he remains divorced and childless because Rosario refuses to wait for him—to be his Penelope, as another character notes (276). The narrator is painfully aware of his failings and of his clear imitation of other adventure narratives, and in response he crafts an extended parody of the adventure novel with himself as its antihero. To wit, when the protagonist ultimately returns to Western civilization, he plots to pass off his own fictitious adventure narrative as a true account of his sojourn in the wilderness. In an intertextual twist, the protagonist invents a story based on a famous novel he carries in his suitcase, one that gives "the names of animals, trees, native legends, long-forgotten events, everything needed to lend a ring of authenticity to my narration" (243). While Roberto González Echevarría argues that this unnamed novel is *Canaima* ("Canaima" 332), the parodic description has more in common with *The Vortex*. It was Rivera, not Gallegos, who took the unusual step of including a glossary of indigenous words for the flora and fauna used in his novel, as well as interpolating into his narrative the legend of Mapiripana and "long forgotten" events such as the massacre of Venezuelan rubber workers by Coronel Funes in 1921.

Carpentier's tongue-in-cheek nods to other tropical narratives are repeated in the depiction of several characters in *The Lost Steps*. Like his counterparts in the other tales, the protagonist attempts to shed his urban, urbane persona as he travels farther from "civilization." During his journey, he meets several European transplants to the forest; indeed, many of the characters in *The Lost Steps* are clear tributes to other characters of tropical adventure novels. For example, Doctor Montsalvaje is the lonely Westerner in the tropical outpost, risible and pathetic because he resists adaptation to the wilderness. Even his name, which can be rendered in English as "Savage Mountain" is a comic misnomer. Montsalvaje is a parallel figure to *Canaima*'s Count Giaffaro, who creates a botanical and ethnological museum in the depths of the forest. He is also like the accountant in *Heart of Darkness*, who insists on keeping urban standards of appearance even "in the great demoralisation of the land"; as Marlow notes sarcastically, "His starched collars and got-up shirt-fronts were achievements of character" (118). Doctor Montsalvaje spends his time attempting to classify the wilderness. The protagonist calls him a "scientist-adventurer, collector of curare, peyote, ñopo, and all the herbal poisons and narcotics of still unknown properties he was studying and experimenting with.... The herbalist overwhelmed us with Latin terminologies designed for fungi never before seen" (140). Carpentier's oblique nods to other tropical narratives heighten the meta-literary intertextuality of his own novel. At the same time, Carpentier seems to be parodying himself in his lack of originality in describing the supposedly pristine wilderness. The depiction of the guide known as the Adelantado explicitly points up the relationship between Carpentier's novel and its predecessors.

The central character who founds Santa Mónica de los Venados, the Adelantado, shares certain characteristics with Conrad's Kurtz. Carpentier's indirect reference to *Heart of Darkness* signals that *The Lost Steps* will become a palimpsest of tropical narratives: "It was said that the Adelantado ... had made himself king of a group of Negroes who had run away to the forest three hundred years before, and who, some said, lived in a settlement defended by stakes in which drums could be heard booming day and night" (127).[1] The similarities to Kurtz are unmistakable: the rumor that a treasure-seeker has "gone native"; the sound of the drums in the night; the cabin surrounded by heads on stakes. Arturo Echavarría has shown that while Carpentier does not explicitly mention Conrad in any of his works, there are clear resonances between the narratives. The most important of these similarities is the increasing alienation and isolation of Kurtz and that of Carpentier's narrator from Western society as he reaches the furthest point of his voyage (168). Lesley Wylie has argued that Conrad, Rivera, and Carpentier all employ what Homi Bhabha calls *colonial mimicry*, a tactic that destabilizes and undermines imperial categorizations of nature. While Wylie is convincing in her claim that both the Latin American authors capitalize on and celebrate myths of "telluric horror," I disagree with her contention that neither Rivera nor Carpentier is "successful at conveying the reality of tropical nature" (113). As I have shown throughout this work, the Latin American authors seek to overcome what Wylie calls a "linguistic impasse" (113) by employing the trope of madness and the lexicon of medical science, thereby creating their own highly literary jungle rather than seeking a realistic depiction of the wilderness; their works belong to the modernist rather than the realist tradition.

The Lost Steps follows the conventions of the adventure novel in another crucial instance: the moment of disorientation, when each protagonist becomes physically lost and consequently undergoes a spiritual conversion. In positions of great weakness, the protagonists show themselves to be most open to radical life changes. These passages destabilize the otherwise determinedly idyllic portraits of life in the wilderness. They demonstrate the book's affinity with *Canaima* and *The Vortex*. Specifically, the link between the main character's physical disorientation and his mental unbalancing is a motif that Rivera, Gallegos, and Carpentier all use with great success. In these moments, the protagonist's façade of order is peeled away to illustrate each character's lightly concealed mental and social alienation. For Carpentier's protagonist, this moment comes as the group travels through narrow canals in search of the entryway that will lead them to Santa Mónica de los Venados.

> After sailing for a time through that secret channel, one began to feel the same thing that mountain-climbers feel, lost in the snow: the loss of the sense of verticality, a kind of disorientation, and a dizziness of the eyes....As the trees, the sticks, the lianas were refracted at strange angles, one finally began to see nonexistent channels, openings, banks. With this succession of minor mirages, my feeling of bewilderment, of being completely lost, grew until it became unbearable. It was as though I was being spun round and round upon myself to make me lose my bearings before bringing me to the threshold of some secret dwelling....I was beginning to be afraid. Nothing menaced me. All those around me seemed calm, but an indefinable fear out of the dim reaches of instinct was making me short of breath, as though I lacked air. (161)

The loss of spatial orientation is a commonplace in twentieth-century tropical narratives, and here, as in other works, it heralds the protagonist's incipient internal disorientation. The disintegration of his carefully constructed jungle foreshadows his own eventual return to the city because it reveals the chimerical nature of his utopia. The ever-shifting forms of the forest result in a profound ambivalence in the protagonist's assessment of the wilderness. Like other writers who have described tropical nature since antiquity, Carpentier vacillates between portraying the wilderness as tranquil or as menacing: "The jungle is the world of deceit, subterfuge, duplicity; everything there is disguise, stratagem, artifice, metamorphosis" (166).[2] The discovery that all is not as it seems in the forest provides the same creative spark to Carpentier's narrator as it did to Arturo Cova in *The Vortex*. While Cova used the horrors of the selva to inspire his ragged and lyrical diary, Carpentier's narrator uses a dense, baroque prose to express the exuberant vegetation and geological features through which he travels.

In fact, the forest, home of "artifice," displays the same values and characteristics as the neobaroque, the literary and artistic style that Carpentier would explicitly adopt in a later essay as "lo barroco americano" (the American baroque) and for which he would advocate as the necessary style for Latin American authors in his "Problemática de la actual novela latinoamericana" (The problem of the contemporary Latin American novel; *Obras* 13: 21). The narrator describes his urban life as "useless," filled with "tumultuous days" and "reckless nights" (22). His disillusionment (known in Spanish as *desengaño*) is a hallmark of the baroque. Later in the novel, Carpentier's descriptions of granite monoliths as part of a great gothic cathedral and of the vegetation itself as baroque are his own original contribution to the literary creation of the wilderness (233). Steve Wakefield has argued that the use of baroque prose in *The Lost Steps* functions as a self-parody in order to avoid the question of authorial intentionality (99). While parody is undoubtedly used to obfuscate the differences between author and narrator, fiction and autobiography, in the case of *The Lost Steps* baroque parody is Carpentier's response to the recognition that any description of the wilderness will be merely a rewriting of texts that have come before. His inability to write the original autobiographical narrative of his failed *El libro de la Gran Sabana* (Book of the Great Plains; González Echevarría, *Alejo Carpentier* 172–75) manifests itself in the narrator's incapacity to describe the wilderness without baroque, parodic descriptions of the surroundings that are either explicit or implicit references to other works.

Another manifestation of ironic parody in the novel is the structure of the narrative. On a formal level, *The Lost Steps* takes the shape of a diary, though like the narrator himself, it is ironic, flawed, and self-reflexive. At first, the novel is simply a first-person narration. Once the protagonist begins his voyage, it contains dated diary entries, much like Arthur Conan Doyle's *The Lost World* and other adventure tales. As Silvia Rosman notes, the protagonist tries out different narrative stances in the novel: he is at turns tourist, discoverer, adventurer, ethnologist, novelist, and journalist (40). The most significant element of the diary has been pointed out by Eduardo González, who uses textual references and dates to place the historical time of the novel as the last six months of 1950, thereby dividing both the year and the century. He further shows that the novel begins on a Sunday and ends on the last Saturday of 1950, thereby offering a simultaneous ending and new beginning to the week, the century, and the protagonist's life. Moreover, González shows that the chronological diary entries skip over two Mondays in the course of the novel. This fact highlights the liturgical and secular significance of this gap: by skipping Mondays, the protagonist evades the working world, and each Sunday is endowed with magical value, which is represented in the ability to access a previous historical moment (González 590).[3] Gustavo Pérez Firmat has shown that the very language in which the protagonist writes is open to question, further freighting the diary with ambivalence and equivocation (193). The subtle changes made to the diary form indicate Carpentier's simultaneous engagement with and self-distancing from the epistolary form used in traditional adventure novels. The emphasis on precise dates and days that are nevertheless intentionally incorrect is a manifestation of the tension in the novel between the mythic and concrete aspects of the voyage put forth by the author. Just as the diary is specific and yet imprecise, the author's note included with the novel suggests the names of the rivers depicted (indicating that they were traveled by Carpentier himself) and undermines Carpentier's insistent refusal to name the cities, people, and geographical features mentioned in *The Lost Steps*. This ambivalence is a reflection of Carpentier's unsettled relationship with his own creation. He seeks to write an adventure novel, and yet ends up writing a meta-adventure novel. Faced with the conventions of the genre that make his protagonist's adventure seem repetitive and unoriginal, Carpentier responds by parodying that adventure in both the form and content of his own novel.

One way in which Carpentier escapes the conventions of the adventure novel, however, is by positing the forest as a place of peaceful order and the city as a realm of disorganized violence. While this reversal of the traditional opposition was begun in *Heart of Darkness*, it comes to full fruition in *The Lost Steps*. A major component of this reversal is embodied in the pivotal role played by medicine in the narrator's journey. In Carpentier's case, the close ties between surrealism, medicine, and the liberation of the irrational side of the mind influence the protagonist even as he explicitly rejects them in favor of what he sees as the logic and artlessness of life in the wilderness. For Carpentier, the medical and literary fields are linked; many of the surrealists he knew in Paris between 1928 and 1939 had either been trained as doctors or were themselves chronically ill patients.[4] Members of the movement shared an interest in the creative possibilities of psychological pathology; Antonin Artaud proclaimed, "We affirm the absolute legitimacy of [the madman's] concept of reality, and of all acts resulting therefrom" (qtd. in Matthews 12). The surrealists' leader, the poet André Breton, had studied to become a doctor, and during World War I he had served as a medical orderly in a ward for patients with mental disturbances at the hospital in Saint-Dizier. Breton later brought his clinical perspective to bear on the creation of literature: automatic writing and dream analysis both demonstrate a methodical, scientific approach to unleashing the artistic power of the irrational inside each individual. Other aspects of medicine also interested the group: the trope linking the dissection of human bodies and the disarticulation of language was common, and even Lautrèamont's famous description of finding beauty in the chance encounter of a sewing machine and an umbrella on an operating table stimulated the close ties between surrealism and medicine.[5]

Carpentier's early writings reveal his involvement in the literary avant-garde. For example, the story fragment "El estudiante" (The student, 1929) is both surreal and medical: the title character is a medical student who passes through the Parisian Hôtel-Dieu while doctors and patients operate on motionless, possibly deceased bodies. As I will demonstrate shortly, Carpentier explicitly connects surrealism to madness and medicine in other articles written for Cuban publications. Even his earliest work makes the relationship between the seemingly disparate fields of Western art and science clear. While Carpentier would eventually distance himself from his early work, his later novels nevertheless evince some continuity with his first writings.

In *The Lost Steps*, the narrator-protagonist rejects the author's youthful interests as "surrealist bargain basement" (25). As the novel progresses, he turns away from both Western literature and medicine, which he associates with Breton's obsession with the irrational, in favor of indigenous rituals, which he sees as imbued with logic and order. The figure of the *Hechicero* (often capitalized in Carpentier's novel, and translated by de Onís as "shaman") demonstrates Carpentier's abiding interest in the rites of the New World as a source of artistic creation.[6] In the Orinoco river basin, the protagonist discovers the link between indigenous song and medicine in the threnody (death dirge) sung by the shaman. The protagonist's rejection of Western art and medicine paradoxically inspires him to compose his own threnody based on Shelley's *Prometheus Unbound* (1898). Ironically, the protagonist's utopian quest to remain in the wilderness is thwarted by the very things he sought to leave behind. In the absence of books and paper, the protagonist cannot complete his composition; in the absence of medicine, the utopia is destroyed by the leper Nicasio, whose rape of a young girl brings an end to the Edenic quality of Santa Mónica de los Venados. The idyllic vision of Santa Mónica is also belied by the moments in which the forest does not conform to the protagonist's expectations, informed as they are by literary texts. In the end, the impact of surrealism on Carpentier's work is as indelible as the protagonist's need for paper and ink.

The use of medical metaphors and disease imagery in literature is certainly nothing new; the surrealists, however, are exceptional within the tradition because they incorporate pathology and medical praxis into the creation of art itself, rather than merely using them in metaphors and similes. They were interested in both mental and physical disease, though their fascination with mental pathology is perhaps better known because of André Breton's early reading of Freud.[7] Surrealism exalted mental illness as a means of unlocking the artistic potential of the brain. In addition, members of the movement found significant parallels between bodily dissection (such as the flayed bodies in Salvador Dalí's work) and the fragmentation of reality. They employed physical and linguistic disarticulation to produce aesthetically arresting images (Orban 45). Just as a body could be meticulously dismembered by science, so too could reality be dismantled and language picked apart, reconfigured, and juxtaposed for maximum artistic impact. The surrealists' literary modernity thus stems from their connections between science and the dissection of language. As Clara Orban contends in *Surrealist Case Studies: Literature, the Arts, and Medicine*, "Disease imagery becomes a signpost for the cultural shift" of the literary vanguard of the 1920s and 1930s (8). It is no coincidence, therefore, that many surrealists were in some way involved in the medical profession, as both doctors and patients (Orban ch. 1). Among the latter, we can count the previously mentioned Artaud, with whom Carpentier collaborated on projects for French radio.[8] Artaud spent almost ten years confined in a mental institution, and his condemnatory "Lettre aux médecins-chefs des asiles de fous" (Letter to the heads of insane asylums) was published in *La révolution surréaliste*. Unlike

Artaud, most surrealists were not mentally unbalanced, but rather had a scientific and artistic interest in the insane.

André Breton had a well-documented background in medical and psychological matters. As noted earlier, the surrealist leader had been a medical orderly during World War I, and he had served as an intern for Dr. Raoul Leroy in the Hôpital du Collège in Saint-Dizier. While there, he had interacted with patients with mental disorders, and he later stated that this experience had provided him with "almost all the working material of surrealism" (qtd. in Matthews 13). Breton's interest in insanity was artistic rather than clinical, as Matthews points out; the surrealist leader said he sought no less than "the total recuperation of the original powers of the mind," which had thus far been limited by the constraints of logic (qtd. in Matthews 14). His prose often betrays a clinical tone—a meticulous rhetorical strategy even as he advocates for disorder. In the first manifesto of surrealism (1924), Breton praises the ability of hallucinations to free the mind from rational thought: "I could spend my whole life prying loose the secrets of the insane" (5). He rails against "the absolute rationalism that is still in vogue" because it "allows us to consider only facts relating directly to our experience. Under the pretense of civilization and progress, we have managed to banish from the mind everything that may rightly or wrongly be termed superstition, or fancy; forbidden is any kind of search for truth which is not in conformance with accepted practices" (9–10). Although Freud never recognized any connection between Breton's work and his own, both were deeply interested in the irrational impulses that drive human behavior: "If the depths of our mind contain within it strange forces capable of augmenting those on the surface, or of waging a victorious battle against them, there is every reason to seize them—first to seize them, then, if need be, to submit them to the control of our reason" (Breton, "Manifesto" 10). Subsequent literary and artistic works by the surrealists sought to explore the irrational side of the mind through automatic writing and the "exquisite cadaver" game of group literary composition. Breton's most in-depth exploitation of madness for its artistic value can be found in *Nadja* (1928). This novel left a strong impression on Carpentier, as he recorded in his December 1928 article "En la extrema avanzada" (In the extreme vanguard): "André Bretón [*sic*] has just let loose a book of contemporary magic; a book as full of mystery as it is of faith, a book steeped in the belief in a higher reality: *Nadja*" (131). *Nadja* chronicles the relationship between the unnamed narrator and the title character, whose madness makes the narrator believe that Nadja was born to serve the cause of "human emancipation in every sense" (143). As he had in the first surrealist manifesto, Breton extols insanity as a liberation from the constraints of logical thought: for him, it is essential to thrust "one's head, then an arm, out of the jail—thus shattered—of logic, that is, out of the most hateful of prisons" (143). Breton shocked the bourgeoisie and the medical community by having the narrator declare, "I know that if I were mad, after several days of confinement I should take advantage of any lapses in my madness to murder anyone, preferably a doctor, who came near me" (141). Breton's willingness to defend the free expression of the irrational to the point of violence arises from his outrage at any type of confinement, especially that suffered by literary figures such as Baudelaire, Nietzsche, and Sade—all surrealist favorites.

For Breton, insanity offered a path to poetic liberation. Yet, as he recognizes in *Nadja*, total madness makes true poetic creation impossible, as the author had undoubtedly witnessed among the World War I soldiers confined in Saint-Dizier. Instead of extolling madness as an end in itself, Breton sought to explore madness as an artistic medium through the empirical structures of medicine, such as hypotheses and documented experimentation. As Clara Orban notes, "The dissection table, the laboratory for testing hypotheses, and the rigor of precise language even in automatic writing exercises, could all become part of the avant-garde literary landscape" (61). This unique blend of authorial precision and uninhibited expression became a hallmark of surrealist creations. In their art, both Dalí and Breton sought a sort of controlled delirium; as Dalí put it, his work aimed to "systematize confusion and to contribute to discrediting the world of reality totally" (qtd. in Matthews 52). Dalí's "paranoia-critique" theory demonstrates his interest in a clinical examination of the irrational: "Paranoiac-Critical Activity reveals … new and objective 'meanings' of the irrational, and it makes the very world of delirium pass tangibly to the level of reality" (qtd. in Orban 49). J. H. Matthews emphasizes: "It is solely the liberative effect of mental derangement, as made concrete in the imagery presented by certain insane artists, that the surrealist prizes. Insanity appeals to him only when and as it frees pictorial and verbal expression from unwelcome rational restraints that he deprecates as anti-poetic in essence" (140). This clinical approach to irrationality would have a lasting effect on the young Carpentier.

Recent Carpentier scholarship has shed light on the author's participation in the surrealist movement and its lingering impact on his later work. Anke Birkenmaier's *Alejo Carpentier y la cultura del surrealismo* (Alejo Carpentier and the culture of surrealism, 2006) is particularly useful for this study because it distinguishes between Carpentier's self-proclaimed break with the movement in the famous prologue to *The Kingdom of This World* and the actual continuity of surrealist motifs throughout his work (32). From his earliest collaborations with faithful and dissident surrealists in 1928 through his retrospective writings on the movement, Carpentier's particular engagement with the Parisian avant-garde displays an abiding association between medical science and the surrealist interest in the irrational. Though he would later parody Breton's praise of madness in *The Lost Steps*, his early publications show him to be a surrealist enthusiast.

As his biographers note, Carpentier arrived in Paris in 1928 and was an active member of surrealist factions until 1933, when he began working in radio full time.[9] Of the surrealists, he was closest to Robert Desnos; in 1931, the two were so poor that they shared a pair of shoes (Conley 73). Accordingly, in January 1930, Carpentier sided with Desnos when he signed "A cadaver," the open letter to André Breton in which several dissident surrealists, among them Georges Bataille and Michel Leiris, declared their independence from the movement's founder (Conley 66). Carpentier wrote for several French publications associated with current or former surrealists: *Documents, Bifur, Le cahier* (Birkenmaier 36). He also wrote prolifically for various Spanish-language magazines and journals back in Cuba, most frequently for *Social* and *Carteles*, and in *El nacional*, for which he had a column entitled "Letra y solfa" (Lyrics and musical notation) from the late 1940s to 1959. Intimately involved with the French cultural scene, Carpentier served as an unofficial cultural emissary who could keep the Cuban public abreast of the latest developments in Continental art, music, and literature.

While most of his publications from the 1920s and 1930s focused on music, art, and ethnography, Carpentier did try his hand at writing fiction in the surrealist style. One of the resulting works, the previously mentioned "El estudiante," reflects his early participation in the surrealists' interest in medicine. While "El estudiante" was not published until 1989, when it appeared in *La gaceta de Cuba*, Carpentier had written it in 1929 during his time in Paris, possibly in French (Birkenmaier 32). The brief story fragment is both surreal and medical: the title character is a medical student who "mentally calculates how much cocaine would be necessary to anesthetize the Niagara." Once inside, he watches doctors and patients operate on motionless bodies: "Held on the metal table by ten icy pins, the patient had felt rubber gloves passing through his entrails, and in less than twenty-two seconds, his midsection had been sewn up, with a gesture like that of a tailor bent over his table, while the thread went through balls of flesh, and the needle shone, between thumb and forefinger, under the glare of the lightbulbs."[10] He ends up in an operating theater populated by a Greek chorus who perform surgery on a *bacalao* (codfish). Before the chorus can speak, Prometheus appears in chains. Then a fisherman throws the *bacalao* over his shoulder and leaves the Hôtel-Dieu, followed by the student. The story is truncated shortly after the protagonist enters a funeral home and asks for something to eat.

This brief window into Carpentier's early fiction reveals a writer who has not yet found his own voice. The seemingly random, frenzied action and the juxtaposition of disparate elements indicate Carpentier's emulation of surrealist style and imagery. Despite its clumsiness, "El estudiante" bears the hallmark of thematic elements that Carpentier would use in his later work. In particular, the proliferation of literary and mythological characters in this short text foreshadows *The Lost Steps*, which is saturated with references to Greek literature and, significantly, *Prometheus Unbound*. Additionally, Carpentier's passion for music is apparent in the song of the Greek chorus, whose voices are "made of silence and mystery," and who "tuned the nerves" of the body they dissect ("El estudiante"). Most importantly, Carpentier's earliest work makes the connection between the disparate fields of Western literature and medicine clear. The eerie medical setting of the story and its precise, bizarre details align Carpentier with the surrealist artists of the era. The residue of this early style is palpable in *The Lost Steps*, namely in the way its narrator-protagonist rejects both surrealist writing and medicine; their presence is only magnified by his ostensible rejection.

Another article of Carpentier's that was published in *Carteles* in the same year as "El estudiante" sheds further light on the extent to which insanity and surrealism contributed to his artistic formation in the 1920s and 1930s. "El arte de los locos" (The art of the insane) is a review of an unnamed Parisian art gallery that had recently opened an exhibit of drawings and sculpture produced by the insane. Carpentier calls this type of art "serious" because mad artists "put forth extraordinary problems, whose solutions are far from known. This obscure yearning for creation is governed by mysterious laws that touch on the enigma of true poetic creation that was of such interest to the ancient philosophers" (12). He goes on to quote Plato, Socrates, and Cicero, all of whom maintained that madness was often a manifestation of divine poetic inspiration.[11] While he recognizes the affinities between madness and artistic creation, Carpentier is more circumspect about the inherent artistic value of any object created by the mentally unstable, noting that "their inspiration is unhinged and uneven" (3). Carpentier compares "the art of the mad" to so-called primitive art:

> Their works are similar to those of the primitive Flemish and Italians, especially when they want to present religious themes. What similarities can there be between the mind of a contemporary madman and the mind of a medieval stone worker? It is very difficult to say. But there frequently are similarities, as can be seen in the various examples of a new crop of *primitivismo* in the strange exhibition that is the topic of this review. (12)

He acknowledges that writers such as Gérard de Nerval have produced great literature while insane, but reaffirms that "today's mad writers are much more modest" (12). In the latter portion of the review, Carpentier speaks to the topicality of the exhibition in the contemporary Parisian artistic climate, which was, of course, dominated by the fractious surrealists: "The rather ugly platitude that states that modern art has contact points with the art of the mad is well known" (50). He calls that notion an "overly simple fantasy" (*fantasía demasiado fácil*; 50). Here Carpentier is undoubtedly referring to the common misperception that surrealists, because they sought to exploit the artistic potential of the irrational, were necessarily mad themselves in some form or another. Matthews offers a corrective to this common myth: "Surrealists may aim to emulate the results that insanity can bring, but do not intend to shut themselves up in the state of mind that has bred these results" (140). The surrealists were interested in sounding the depths of the human psyche for art, and they were interested in the art created by the nonrational parts of the mind. Carpentier's sensitivity to this "ugly platitude" reveals his sympathy with the avant-garde's exploration of madness for artistic purposes.[12]

During the aftermath of the disputes between Breton and his followers, Carpentier contributed to the surrealist publication *Documents*, along with Robert Desnos and Michel Leiris (Leiris, along with Georges Bataille and Roger Caillois, would later found the Collège de Sociologie). He wrote an article on Cuban music, in keeping with the publication's interest in non-European cultures. *Documents*, subtitled "Archaeology, Fine Arts, Ethnography, Varieties," marked a shift in the former surrealists' interest from medicine and psychology to ethnography. Although its focus had shifted, the group nevertheless maintained its clinical perspective. As Allan Stoekl has written about the Collège de Sociologie: "Finally, it seemed, the avant-garde was becoming scientific; or rather, it was learning that it had been, even in its wildest ravings, scientific all along" (931). As Birkenmaier has noted, what James Clifford has called *surrealist ethnography* "seemed to offer a scientific solution to the conflict between an insider's perspective and an outsider's" (26). The dissident surrealists' turn toward ethnography, especially in *Documents*, furthered both a scientific approach to art and an artistic approach to science. Given their pessimistic view of European culture as decadent and disconnected from any sense of unity, the surrealists' embrace of ethnography, which offered the possibility of a closer relationship to the sacred and the collective, is hardly surprising. This aesthetic orientation would leave a lasting impression on Carpentier's work. In *The Lost Steps*, it is possible to see Carpentier's disenchantment with surrealist ethnography and his difficulty in freeing himself from it. His disdain for this sort of anthropology, which he himself had practiced in the novel *¡Écue-Yamba-O!* (Lord, be thou praised), is virulent in *The Lost Steps*, as only the atheism of a former believer can be.

Carpentier's own contribution to the aesthetic shift from psychology to ethnography is found in *¡Écue-Yamba-O!*, which he began in a Cuban jail in 1927 and completed and published in Paris in 1933.[13] In the novel, Carpentier contrasts Western medicine and Afro-Cuban healing rites, just as he would later compare European science and indigenous rituals in *The Lost Steps*. The first of two rites discussed in *¡Écue-Yamba-O!* occurs during the protagonist Menegildo's childhood, after he is bitten by a diseased crab. The second takes place years later, after he is beaten by the Haitian husband of his lover, Longina. In both cases, which are described in chapters respectively called "Therapeutics (a)" and "Therapeutics (b)," Menegildo is attended by the "wise *curandero*" (104), a shaman named Berúa who has been the "doctor of the family for four generations" (29). Berúa "knew of practices that stimulated the deepest and most primordial elements of the human being," and the narrator praises the healing rituals in a didactic tone: "Men of color are capable of continuing the great tradition of a science handed down over centuries, from fathers to sons, from kings to princes, from initiators to the initiated; they know that the air is a tapestry of seamless threads whose task is, at heart, that of condensing a higher mystery in order to direct it against or in favor of something" (59). Carpentier's valorization of Afro-Cuban "science" demonstrates the impact of surrealist ethnography on his work.[14] The former surrealists' privileging of non-Western cultures and the use of surrealist imagery permeates *Écue*, and even though Carpentier would later parody their interest in the exotic in *The Lost Steps*, it nevertheless forms an essential part of that work as well.

Carpentier scholars have been divided regarding the legacy of surrealism on Carpentier's later work, particularly in *The Lost Steps*, his most frequently studied novel. The author himself sought to give the impression that surrealism was a mere phase that he had overcome early in his career: in an interview with César Leante in 1964, Carpentier declared, "My surrealist efforts seemed to be in vain. I was not going to add anything to that movement" (qtd. in Chiampi 36). More recent scholarship has demonstrated the continuities between Carpentier's early enthusiasm for surrealism and his later works.[15] Indeed, Carpentier's famous rejection of the European avant-garde in the prologue to *The Kingdom of This World* is belied by the dominant tension of *The Lost Steps*: the protagonist's struggle to free himself from his past. This struggle ends, of course, in failure, as nearly every critic of the novel has mentioned since González Echevarría's *Alejo Carpentier: The Pilgrim at Home* (1977). Just as Carpentier recognized that he was a man chained to the printed word ("encadenado a la letra impresa"; "El Kodacrome" 106), so too was he inextricably linked to surrealism.

Despite Carpentier's claims to the contrary, *The Lost Steps* is marked by surrealism in both patent and subtle ways. Some nods to the movement are oblique: the interlocking Vs that mark the passage to the Santa Mónica de los Venados are identical to the title of the surrealist magazine *VVV* that Breton, Marcel Duchamp, and Max Ernst published in New York from 1942 to 1944.[16] More obviously, there are several instances in which the narrator resorts to surrealistic imagery in his attempt to describe the wilderness. In one instance, the sight of his expedition party aboard their riverboat evokes for the protagonist a much-beloved surrealist image, the *Ship of Fools* (*Nave de los Locos*):

> With its cargo of bellowing bulls, coops of chickens, pigs running about
> the deck under the hammock of the Capuchin and getting tangled up
> in his rosary of seeds, the song of the Negress cooks, the laughter of the
> Greek diamond-hunter, the prostitute in her mourning nightgown bath-
> ing in the prow, the guitar-players making music for the sailors to dance,
> this ship of ours made me think of Bosch's *Ship of Fools*. But a ship of
> madmen now taking off from a shore that defied ubication; for though
> the roots of what I had seen were grounded in styles, reasons, myths I
> could identity, the final result, the tree that had sprung up on this soil,
> was as disconcerting and new as the huge trees that began to hide the
> banks, and which, in groups at the entrance to the channels, stood out
> against the setting sun. (119)

The surrealists were interested in this painting by Hieronymous Bosch (c. 1450–1516) because of its wildly diverse passengers, such as the monk and the prostitute, and the base, sensual pleasures in which they are engaged. This view of the ship, with its juxtaposition of incongruous elements and Dionysian revelry, makes it a natural surrealist object.[17] Bosch was a favorite painter of the surrealists because he shared with them what Ismael Fernández de la Cuesta has called "the prestige of madness" (149). The madness of surrealism thus follows the protagonist into the wilderness because he has internalized it. The Ship of Fools is also an excellent example of Carpentier's *lo real maravilloso* (the marvelous real), indicating that Carpentier's famous autochthonous literary innovation has its roots in surrealism.[18]

The most profound legacy of surrealism persists in the novel in the contrast Carpentier creates between Western medicine and indigenous rituals such as the Shirishana shaman's death song. Like the surrealists, the narrator of *The Lost Steps* associates Western medicine with European art, finding both artificial in comparison with the simple rites of the Shirishana. The depiction of science and medicine in the novel bears witness to their relationship to avant-garde literature and art: both are presented as unnecessary foreign contaminants to the forest. Paradoxically, it is the need for these two very elements, books and medicine, that destroys the utopia of Santa Mónica de los Venados and drives the protagonist out of the wilderness. Surrealism and Western medicine thus serve as the background that throws the unity, authenticity, and sanity of the wilderness into relief in *The Lost Steps*. The surrealists capitalized on the affinities between bodily dissection and the fragmentation of reality, and the consequent disarticulation of language for artistic purposes. The forest, in contrast, becomes the site of prelinguistic unity—of wholeness unassailed by either language or Western medicine. The protagonist's rejection of Breton's revindication of the irrational causes him to portray the Shirishanas and Guahibos as the polar opposites of city dwellers. If New York is sick and deranged, Santa Mónica de los Venados must be healthy and sane. The idea of the wilderness as a rational place is clearly a projection of the narrator's anxieties regarding Western civilization; this reactionary construction occasionally falters, revealing a complex world that at times overwhelms the literary jungle the narrator has created for himself.

Carpentier's ostensible rejection of the surrealists' interest in the exotic and his concentration on logical, purposeful, Shirishana rituals in *The Lost Steps* is, in fact, in keeping with the rise of ethnography among former and dissident surrealists such as Michel Leiris and Georges Bataille following the dispersion of Breton's group. Leiris, for example, traveled to Ethiopia, while Bataille sought to reintroduce the sacred into Western society.[19] As Mercedes López-Baralt has shown, ethnography pervades *The Lost Steps* on many levels.[20] Even the protagonist's infatuation with Rosario arises not only from sexual desire but also from his anthropological curiosity. I do not maintain that Carpentier wrote *The Lost Steps* in conscious emulation of the French avant-garde, but rather that his early participation in the surrealist movement marked his literary foundation indelibly. In his eagerness to escape European aesthetics, the protagonist flees to the wilderness and finds there the subjects of study of interest to Europeans.

Once in the forest, the protagonist cannot free himself from the sort of surrealist ethnography Carpentier practiced in *Écue* and *Documents*. The legacy of surrealism in *The Lost Steps* manifests itself in the recurring dichotomy between the rejection of Western medicine and the attraction of ethnographic study of indigenous rites for the protagonist.

Carpentier's interest in medicine carries over from his earliest fiction, "El estudiante," to his later work. Yet in *The Lost Steps* medicine is not a surrealist topos but rather a useless cultural relic when practiced in the wilderness. Medicine forms part of the world the protagonist leaves behind because Western medicine is ill suited to the tropical environment. This is clear from the very beginning of his arrival in Latin America. The unnamed South American city is pervaded by a malignant pollen that wreaks havoc in the hospitals, and the Rubens in the National Museum is eaten away by an unknown parasite (39). In this neat juxtaposition, Carpentier shows that medicine and art are equally out of place in the unruly environs of the tropics.

The most important symbol of surrealism and sickness in the novel is the narrator's French lover, Mouche, who repeatedly serves as his surrealist punching bag. Mouche, the figurehead for all things European, is unsuited to the new environment. When the revolution takes place in the city, Mouche suffers a nervous breakdown and, after several days in the wilderness, "she felt as though she was losing her mind" (148). Shortly thereafter she is stricken with malaria, which the protagonist sees as fitting because the modern, avant-garde Mouche is culturally and physically ill equipped for life in the prehistoric world: "It had taken only a few days for a powerful, heartless nature to disarm her, wear her out, make her ugly, break her spirit, and, now, deal her the *coup de grâce*" (149). Her illness also perpetuates one of the most commonly held assumptions about the survival of white women in the tropics. During the first waves of colonial occupations by European powers, white women were thought to be unsuited to the tropical climate. As late as 1931, Europeans still maintained that white women suffered more in the tropics than either men or indigenous women: "Life [in the tropics] is more difficult for European women. . . . The bites of mosquitoes, the plagues of flying animals of every description that come with the rains, the feeling of discomfort with wet clothes, . . . until nervous exhaustion drives them home" (Toms 1091). Mouche's illness is therefore frustrating but not surprising to the narrator, and he uses her sickness as an excuse to seduce Rosario. Mouche's illness gives rise to one of the most pathetic scenes in the novel, in which the protagonist and Rosario make love for the first time on the ground beneath Mouche's hammock. A drooling, Gorgonesque Mouche hurls insults at them, and Rosario merely kicks her until she recedes back into the fog of fever. Mouche eventually returns to the South American city with the gentlemanly Doctor Montsalvaje; both figures are archetypes of the adventure novel that are neatly done away with by following the conventions of the genre.

While the protagonist forcefully rejects Mouche, his approach to his new surroundings is not so different from hers. As González Echevarría first noted, the narrator frequently voices the same thoughts for which he has just excoriated her ("Introducción" 109). Indeed, the protagonist's effort to free himself of surrealist influence is unsuccessful; when the narrator attacks Mouche, it is really Carpentier attacking his former self, the Carpentier of the 1920s and 1930s, still naively in thrall to the surrealist aesthetic. Mouche's early return to civilization because of malaria foreshadows the protagonist's own eventual inability to adapt to Santa Mónica. Like Mouche, he cannot do without the "surrealist bargain basement" (25). There is, of course, a certain amount of tongue-in-cheek self-recognition and self-criticism in the protagonist's disdain for Mouche, since the young Carpentier participated in precisely the same activities that the protagonist now lambastes. For example, he parodies the South American musician, painter, and writer who are enthralled by Mouche in Los Altos because of her connection to Paris. The narrator notes that they remain oblivious to the "authentic" artistry of the local harp player (74), and are interested only in Europe:

> Depending on the color of the day, the topic of conversation would be the longing for evasion, the advantages of suicide, the need to slap the face of corpses or of taking a shot at the first passer-by. Some high priest of delirium would initiate them in the cult of Dionysus, "god of ecstasy and fear, of brutality and liberation; a mad god whose mere sight throws living beings into a state of delirium," though without telling them that the one who invoked this Dionysus, the officer Nietzsche, had had himself photographed on one occasion in *Reichswehr* uniform, sword in hand, and helmet on a console table of Munich style, like a prophetic prefiguration of the god of horror whom reality would unleash in the Europe of that *Ninth Symphony*. (72)

This passage is extremely revealing in regards to the narrator-protagonist's relationship to European culture. Each phrase is laden with meaning: first, the phrase "the longing for evasion" (*el anhelo de la evasión*) is a perhaps unwitting reference to the review of *The Way of the Kings* that Carpentier published in *Social* in May 1931. Titled "André Malraux, o el anhelo de la evasión," the review is an unqualified rave. Carpentier praises the current generation of artists for their desire to escape decadent Western society, specifically citing the surrealist "evasion of an absurd ethic, [seen] in the state of lyric paranoia illustrated by Salvador Dalí" (37). Revealing his youthful enthusiasm for the aesthetic attitude of the avant-garde, Carpentier proclaims that "any chance is preferable to the despicable order they try to impose upon us" (37). The great irony of *The Lost Steps* is that the adventure the protagonist seeks demonstrates precisely the "longing for evasion" that he parodies when the Latin American artist and composer speak to Mouche. This review confirms that Malraux's novel serves as a model for *The Lost Steps*, further strengthening the ties to Europe that Carpentier sought to sever. Similarly, the narrator is also scornful of the idea of slapping corpses and shooting pedestrians. This last activity is a clear allusion to Breton, who is also the "high priest of delirium" that the narrator now views as ridiculous. Ironically, Breton's scientific fascination with the irrational—especially his "praise of madness" (*elogios de la locura*), are rejected by Carpentier's narrator even as his work is influenced by surrealist imagery (309). The sardonic comment about Nietzsche wearing "the *Reichswehr* uniform" seeks to portray the surrealists as naive: Carpentier emphasizes that Nietzsche influenced not only the surrealists and their followers, who emulated his interest in Dionysus, but also Hitler, who was inspired by Nietzsche when he wrote *Mein Kampf*. The bitterness of his protagonist's derision betrays the depths of Carpentier's own disillusionment with the surrealist movement, and simultaneously his inability to escape the surrealist frame of reference.

Western medicine figures importantly in the protagonist's condemnation of the brutalities of the modern world. He catalogs the horrible kinds of deaths produced by the Nazi regime in World War II: "Everything bore witness to torture, mass extermination, crematories, all set in walls spattered with blood and ordure, heaps of bones, human dentures shoveled up in the corners, not to mention even worse deaths accomplished coldly by rubber-gloved hands in the neat, bright aseptic whiteness of operating-rooms" (94). According to the narrator, European science is thus complicit in the attempted extermination of an entire people; their deaths are worse than executions because they are used for scientific experiments as if they were animals. Whereas in "El estudiante" the operating theater evokes the famous operating table of Lautrèamont, in *The Lost Steps* Carpentier links the "operating-rooms" to the Nazis' genocidal experiments. While he does not imply that surrealists were in any way complicit with the Nazis, there are clear parallels between their fascination with dissection and the murders carried out amidst the "aseptic whiteness" of the German death camps. Despite this strong condemnation, surrealist imagery pervades *The Lost Steps*. By repeatedly rejecting the European avant-garde, the protagonist makes it an essential component of the novel. Raúl Caplán has noted that the protagonist's chance encounters with the Curator and Rosario are an example of the "fruits of chance so dear to Breton" (157). Although the narrator disparages Mouche for buying a hippocamp (seahorse) because it reminds her of Rimbaud, he too views his new surroundings through European cultural lenses.

Carpentier repeatedly demonstrates the uselessness and even fecklessness of scientific endeavors in the wilderness, such as Montsalvaje's occupations. In addition, while on a bus, the protagonist overhears the story of members of a scientific expedition who were stranded on a mountaintop and froze to death, their faces transformed by "a transparent death mask" of crystal (80). These scientists, like Mouche, had been unable to cope with the new environment they set out to explore. This passage prefigures the narrator's turn away from Western civilization and toward indigenous rituals in the transformation of the scientists' faces into funeral masks. Yet despite the protagonist's enthusiasm for his new environment and his disdain for those who fail to acclimatize to it, he still cannot escape his own European perspective. Like Montsalvaje, he views his new world through old scientific eyes. As much as he attempts to eschew Western modes of thought, his impression of Rosario is predetermined by scientific theories: "There was no question but that this living sum of races had an aristocracy of her own. . . . I even asked myself whether certain blendings of minor races, without a transplanting of the parent stock, were not preferable to the fusion of Celts, Negroes, Latins, Indians, even 'New Christians,' that had taken place on the great meeting-ground of America in that first encounter" (82).[21] This passage shows that even though the protagonist ostensibly rejects Western medicine and its theories of race and culture, he nevertheless describes Rosario in just these terms. Medico-cultural texts are just some of the "thousand books I had read and of which she knew nothing" that separate him from his love object (171).

While many scholars have noted that Rosario symbolizes indigenous culture for the protagonist, she becomes not just his lover but his anthropological object of study. In contrast to Mouche and Ruth, with their reliance on the artificial world of art and theater, Rosario offers him the ability to access the healing powers of the natural world, such as when she shows him plants and roots that can serve medicinal purposes (149). Sex with her offers him an approximation of the lost world he wishes to inhabit. With her, the protagonist is able to flee his world of books momentarily, finding instead "the syntax of our bodies. . . . From the mutual apprenticeship that this forging of a couple carries with it, a secret language was born" (156–57). Just as the protagonist will later find solace and inspiration from the Hechicero's death ritual because in it he witnesses the birth of the Word, in his relationship with Rosario he seeks out the prelinguistic dialogue of bodies.

Rosario is similar to other female figures in tropical adventure narratives. As Eugenio Suárez-Galbán Guerra has noted, while Mouche is similar to Kurtz's Intended, Rosario is similar to Kurtz's African lover, whom Marlow glimpses in the forest near the Inner Station. Both Rosario and the African represent barbarism, and are subservient to their white lovers (Suárez-Galbán Guerra 194). In addition, Rosario bears important affinities to Rima in Hudson's *Green Mansions*, which I discussed in the Introduction. She is attractive to the protagonist because she has an aura of another age and place. For example, she exhibits a "mythological concept of human physiology" (132) in which humors of the blood, a medieval concept, play a major role. For the protagonist, her mentality shows that she lives outside of time (*fuera del tiempo*; *Lost Steps* 83; *Los pasos* 148).[22] Rosario, like Rima for Hudson's Abel, becomes the vehicle through which the protagonist can travel back through time. Just as Mouche embodies European artistic fads, Rosario becomes the incarnation of the timeless forest.

The persistence of the surrealist-ethnographic approach to Amazonian cultures is evident in the importance given to the interconnected issues of music and death rituals in the novel. As the protagonist voyages farther from civilization, he also moves back in time toward the birth of music, which is his ultimate goal. The funeral for Rosario's father is one step back toward the song of the Hechicero. The protagonist feels that death in Western civilization has become "sordid" and "petty," but in the tropics he feels the ancient and magical presence of death awaken in him "obscure memories of funeral rites" (131). The lost sacredness of death in the twentieth century that Carpentier laments here was a theme common to European intellectuals in the wake of the world wars. In "The Storyteller," for example, Walter Benjamin notes that "dying was once a public process in the life of the individual, and a most exemplary one. . . . In the course of modern times dying has been pushed further and further out of the perceptual world of the living. . . . Yet, characteristically, it is not only a man's knowledge or wisdom, but above all his real life—and this is the stuff stories are made of—that first assumes transmissible form at the moment of his death" (151). The poignant loss of sacredness in this ultimate rite of passage that the protagonist feels so acutely is one further ramification of the legacy of European culture in the novel; Georges Bataille voiced concerns similar to Benjamin's in his "Attraction and Repulsion" lectures for the Collège de Sociologie on January 22 and February 5, 1938 (Surya 261).

Similarly, Carpentier infuses the Shirishanas and Guahibos with an awareness of the sacrality of life, and with an ordered and logical existence. Like Gallegos and the other authors of all the works studied here, Carpentier projects on the wilderness and its inhabitants those values he finds lacking in his own society. Thus, while his own existence is marked by national and linguistic rootlessness, the indios are a sedentary people (*gente asentada*; *Los pasos* 255). In the same way, "a certain animism lived on in [the inhabitants of the region], an awareness of ancient traditions, a living memory of certain myths which indicated the presence of a culture more estimable and valid, perhaps, than that which we had left behind" (*Lost Steps* 123). Indigenous characters step in to fill voids in the lives of the protagonists. In all the tropical adventure novels examined in this book, the dichotomy between rational and irrational thought is at the core of the issue. *The Lost Steps* is, in a sense, the outlier among the novels under consideration here in that it is urban society that is portrayed as savage, and the wilderness that is the epicenter of order. Yet despite the narrator's desire for the forest to embody the virtues of rationality, a disconcerting tendency toward disorder encroaches on his sojourn in the wilderness, as we will see.

The depiction of indigenous rites is a commonplace in tropical adventure narratives and reveals much about the author's attitude toward both the culture he inhabits and the one he visits. For example, *Canaima*'s ñopo ceremony shows Gallegos's conception of the Guaraúnos' reversion to their primordial, irrational state. For Arturo Cova, the natives' dance fuels his incipient madness. For the narrator of *The Lost Steps*, however, the ritual stimulates his artistic creation and represents the connection with elemental forces that modern life has lost. The indigenous ritual performed by the shaman following the hunter's death gives rise to the birth of music

(184–85). In "André Malraux, o el anhelo de evasión," Carpentier had praised novels of adventure because in them "death shows its horrendous, naked face, without any of the tricks of civilization that attempt to soften it in order to make man live a truncated, reduced existence, with only the slightest amount of liberty" (75). Here, Carpentier has clearly emulated Malraux's depiction of death in the tropics in his own jungle novel. The Hechicero's lament is both medicinal and artistic: it reveals to the protagonist the origin of music, which will serve as inspiration for his own threnody. Ironically, his inspiration in the indigenous healing rituals is not truly different from that of the former surrealists who traveled to Africa in search of the collective sacred rituals that Europe had lost. Indeed, Carpentier's description of the threnody bears a resemblance to the anthropological studies of the occult that were popular in Paris during the first half of the twentieth century. Mircea Eliade observed the popularity of studies of the occult (such as his own) for the French intellectuals of the nineteenth and twentieth centuries: "From Baudelaire and Verlaine, Lautréamont and Rimbaud … to André Breton and his disciples, all these artists utilized the occult as a powerful weapon in their rebellion against the bourgeois establishment and its ideology" (qtd. in Rabinovitch 64). González Echevarría notes that Carpentier was very interested in the occult and the Cabala, frequenting Parisian bookstores in search of works about those subjects (*Alejo Carpentier* 33, 96). Thus, even this ritual that the narrator presents as an organic, natural occurrence in the forest has its roots in Carpentier's varied readings.

The most important passage regarding shamanism in *The Lost Steps* reveals much about Carpentier's conceptualization of indigenous death rites and deserves to be quoted at length. The black, swollen body of a hunter who has been dead for several hours is brought into the village, and the Hechicero attempts to "drive off the emissaries of Death":

> There was a ritual silence, setting the stage for the incantation, which raised the tension of the spectators to fever pitch. And in the vast jungle filling with night terrors, there arose the Word. A word that was more than a word.…This was something far beyond language, and yet still far from song. Something that had not yet discovered vocalization, but was more than word. As it went on, this outcry over a corpse surrounded by silent dogs became horrible, terrifying.…I tried to remain outside, to establish distances. And yet I could not resist the horrid fascination this ceremony held for me. In the mouth of the shaman, the spell-working orifice, the *Threne*—for that was what this was—gasped and died away convulsively, blinding me with the realization that I had just witnessed the Birth of Music. (184–85)

This description of the threnody (funeral song) has much in common with Mircea Eliade's famous theory of *hierophany*, which Wendy Doniger summarizes as "the sudden irruption of the sacred in the profane world, sacred time opening to the transcendent, resulting in radical discontinuities" of time (qtd. in Eliade xiii). The shaman's song is precisely one such irruption of the sacred, and it allows the protagonist to witness the birth of music and the origination of language. This passage occurs precisely when the narrator proclaims they are in the fourth day of Genesis: "What lay before our eyes was the world that existed before man" (186). In a certain sense, this arrival at the origin of language is the final culmination of the process begun by the protagonist's union with Rosario: it is the point furthest from the protagonist's idea of Western civilization. This location is akin to Conrad's Inner Station, the hut situated in the inaccessible depths of the wilderness that Marlow implies is the antithesis of Kurtz's European roots. The Inner Station is also a metaphor for the interior of an individual's consciousness, his soul.

Bobs M. Tusa has investigated the similarities between Carpentier's novel and the work of Mircea Eliade, specifically regarding the shamanic rite and the differing concepts of time in indigenous culture.[23] Eliade was a lecturer at the Sorbonne's École des Hautes Études and published his major works in Paris between 1949 and 1952, just as Carpentier was revising and rewriting *The Lost Steps*. Tusa demonstrates that Carpentier was familiar with Eliade's publications. In his article "El mito paradisíaco" (The myth of paradise), Carpentier refers to Eliade as "the Romanian psychologist" and paraphrases his theory of "the persistent 'nostalgia for a lost Paradise' in all human societies" (qtd. in Tusa 49). Eliade's work thus forms one more tree in the forest of books that surrounds the protagonist. Eliade and Carpentier were both interested in the myth of the eternal return, in the idea that what Eliade called "archaic" peoples coexisted with modern civilization, and in the extraordinary power of the shaman.[24] Eliade's work is significant to this study because Carpentier found in it evidence of a spiritual order in indigenous peoples that he felt was lacking in the Western world.

In addition to the work of Eliade, Carpentier's involvement in the publications, conferences, exhibits, and research trips of the Venezuelan Servicio de Investigaciones Folklóricas Nacionales (SIFN [National Folklore Research Service]) shapes the presentation of indigenous rituals and musical instruments in *The Lost Steps*. The first indication of Carpentier's familiarity with SIFN lies in his "Nota" at the end of the novel. Carpentier writes, "The Indians described in chapter 23 are *Shirishanas* from the Alto Caura. An explorer made a phonographic recording of the *Threnody* of the Shaman, which now resides in the folklore archives of Venezuela" (*Los pasos* 332).[25] Elsewhere, I have uncovered previously unknown articles and book reviews that Carpentier published in several Venezuelan folklore journals while he lived in Caracas from 1945 to 1959.[26] This new evidence shows that Carpentier based the shaman's song not on a ritual he witnessed on his trips into the Venezuelan interior, but rather on his research in Caracas. He then used that research in writing *The Lost Steps* to demonstrate that the origins of human music lie in death rites. In this sense, Carpentier is like his Doctor Montsalvaje, more accustomed to classifying indigenous peoples than living with them. His investigations with SIFN led him to believe that indigenous Amazonian cultures practiced cultural rites infused with logical customs rather than brutal primitivism.

A close reading of *The Lost Steps* makes it clear that *reason* is precisely what the protagonist searches for in the wilderness, in contrast to the exotic barbarism that Carpentier accuses the European intelligentsia of seeking out:

> For more than twenty years a weary culture had been seeking rejuvenation and new powers in the cult of the irrational. But now I found ridiculous the attempt to use masks of Bandiagara, Africa *ibeyes*, fetishes studded with nails, without knowing their meaning, as battering-rams against the redoubts of the *Discourse of Method*. They were looking for barbarism in things that had never been barbarous when fulfilling their ritual function in the setting for which they were designed. By labeling such things "barbarous" the labelers were putting themselves in the thinking, the Cartesian, position, the very opposite of the aim they were pursuing. (254)

In this passage, Carpentier accuses Breton (whose apartment on rue Fontaine was famously decorated with art objects from all over the world) of a total lack of actual acquaintance with the falsely named *barbarie* that he praised in other cultures. The protagonist thus distances himself from his European nemeses by virtue of his own presence in the wilderness: "I saw how unfounded were the speculations of those who feel that they can grasp the beginnings of certain of man's arts or institutions without knowing prehistoric man, our contemporary, in his daily life, in his healing and religious practices" (199–200). The protagonist thus reinforces the dichotomy between the artifices of surrealism that he has left behind and the ordered, logical, simple, seemingly authentic world he has entered. Yet that very world is his own invention, created through the books he has read and the very surrealist ideas that he has sought to escape. Ultimately, his search for the sacred and his inspiration in the death chant is not a rejection of surrealism but rather its greatest fruition.

The desire to occupy contradictory positions simultaneously is evident throughout *The Lost Steps*. The protagonist seeks to be autochthonous and anthropological at the same time—to be both a believer in and a recorder of shamanic rites. The contradictions embodied in the protagonist's desire both to remain in Santa Mónica de los Venados and to share his musical discovery with the Western world reflect the impossibility of the anthropologist's task. As Mercedes López-Baralt has proved, *The Lost Steps* dramatizes the crisis of anthropology. She maintains that Carpentier recognizes "the terrible putting into question all of Western anthropology, condemned to sterility by its ethnocentrism, which underlies the failure of the protagonist's journey" (89). The conclusion of the novel indicates that the protagonist is aware of this paradox: his ethnographic way of viewing the foreign culture is not lost on him. This, indeed, is the central difference between the role of ethnography in *¡Écue-Yamba-O!* and *The Lost Steps*. In the latter, the narrator becomes cognizant of the "impossibility of epiphany, which impedes the return to the sought culture" (López-Baralt 85). The insertion of the first-person, self-conscious narrator, in contrast to *¡Écue-Yamba-O!*'s omniscient narrative voice, signals Carpentier's realization of the impossibility of gaining access to the realm of the sacred. In *The Lost Steps*, Carpentier has passed beyond *¡Écue-Yamba-O!*'s naive enthusiasm for ethnography's ability to comprehend fully its object of study. Instead, the narrator of the later novel has recognized the inherent flaws of anthropology and yet cannot escape them. Western science is indeed imperfect, but unshakable. The narrator is, as González Echevarría has noted, "unable to be autochthonous at the moment of writing" (*Alejo Carpentier* 154). Carpentier remains "chained to the printed word" (*Obras* 15: 106), unable to free himself of the scientific desire to write, to record, to catalog—in sum, to submit human action to a system of classification. The narrator's struggle with his anthropological perspective makes *The Lost Steps* a major departure from the conventional adventure tale. Gone is the fresh, unselfconscious sense of discovery that imbues earlier tropical quest novels and communicates the thrill of the unknown to the armchair traveler.

In contrast to *Écue*, in *The Lost Steps* the narrator is aware of his inability to plumb the depths of the Other's psyche. He is careful to shy away from making the Shirishanas spiritually enigmatic, setting him apart from Gallegos's treatment of the Guaraúnos in *Canaima*. In fact, *Canaima* is probably one of the texts implicated when Carpentier's narrator states:

> Those Indians, whom I had always seen through more or less imaginary reports that looked upon them as beings beyond the pale of man's real existence, gave me the feeling here, in their own setting, in their own surroundings, that they were complete masters of their culture. Nothing could have been more remote from their reality than the absurd concept of *savage*. The fact that they ignored many things that to me were basic and necessary was a far cry from putting them in the category of primitive beings. (173)

Carpentier goes to the opposite extreme of portraying the Indians. His indigenous characters are not wild and undomesticated but flawlessly rational; their "harmonious concert of duties" have a purposeful and deliberative quality (173). They are, to wit, everything that Breton and the surrealists are not. If Conrad's Africans are archetypes of an unknowable irrationality, Carpentier's Shirishanas inhabit the other end of the spectrum, but Carpentier's utopia is just as artificial and novelistic a creation as Conrad's dystopia.

In contrast to the Dionysiacal ravings and massive destructive powers of civilization, the protagonist is determined to find solace, order, and artistic inspiration in the forest. Consequently, the threnody that he composes in Santa Mónica is perfectly logical and obeys "the most valid laws of music" (216). Like the Europeans he disparages, the protagonist finds the rejuvenation for Western music in indigenous rituals. His composition of the *treno* is based explicitly on the song of the Hechicero:

> The *Threnody* had been inside me all the time, but its seed had been resown and had begun to grow in the night of the Paleolithic, on the banks of the river inhabited by monsters, when I heard the medicine man howling over a black, snake-poisoned corpse.... At the memory of an authentic threnody, the idea of the *Threnody* revived in me, with its statement of the cell-word, its verbal exorcism turning into music when confronted with the need for more than one intonation. (216–17)

The protagonist thus believes that his threnody is capable of capturing the essence of the origins of music without the mediation of the composer's own aesthetic perspective, just as the contributors to *Documents* sought to publish accounts of non-Western artifacts and rituals without the intervention of Western aestheticism. The narrator criticizes himself for the prelude he had written before coming to the tropics, a piece in which

> like so many others, I had tried to revive the health and spontaneity of a craftsman's art—the work begun on Wednesday to be sung at the Sunday service—borrowing its formulas, its contrapuntal devices, its rhetoric, but without recovering its spirit.... Now, far from concert halls, manifestoes, the unspeakable boredom of art polemics, I was inventing music with an ease that astounded me as ideas, descending from my brain, crowded my hand, falling over one another to reach my pencil. (220–21)

This moment of epiphany, or what Eliade would call *hierophany*, inspires the protagonist to transcribe his own *treno*. Ironically, it will be this desire to record, to enter himself into history—in a word, to write—that will expel him from Paradise.

In her insightful article, López-Baralt mentions the important connections between writing and anthropology.[27] She notes that "writing—that essential instrument for the transmission of ethnographic information—is also the Achilles' heel of anthropology, since it alters the original field work (oral and dialogic), in order to textualize the experience and transform it into a silent monologue" (91). In the case of *The Lost Steps*, we could say that the anthropologist is he who composes; the protagonist derives artistic inspiration from the rudimentary instruments he finds, just as the ethnographer uses the foreign culture as his inspiration. Likewise, in the same way that the ethnographer's presence alters the subject he attempts to describe, the narrator's composition will also destroy the very spirit that he hopes to capture in his work.

As in *The Vortex*, writing comes to the fore as the protagonist reaches the heart of the wilderness. González Echevarría reads the novel as a desire to "return to a moment of original innocence before the duplicities and ambiguities of language that metaphor and simile attempt unsuccessfully to obliterate" (*Alejo Carpentier* 171). Again, surrealism is implicated in the duplicity of language: the protagonist associates modern urban life with Mouche and the "mental gymnastics" and "acrobacy of culture" of her friends (30). Surrealists fetishized language; the proliferation of automatic writings and literary word games reveal the avant-garde's desire to disarticulate and reconfigure language, and make the narrator realize "how vertiginous is the elliptical process of thought and language" (30). The narrator's attempt to free himself from the ambiguities of language is thwarted by his stronger desire to transcribe his *treno*. His composition that is supposed to embody a prelinguistic unity is thus a paradoxical and flawed return to the ambiguities of language. The necessity of this return is rooted in both his pride and his own inescapable reliance on language and literature.

At the climax of the novel, medicine and science reassert their essential presence in modern life for the protagonist. Disease plays a significant role in the destruction of the utopia when the incursion of the leper Nicasio into the community heralds its demise. While leprosy can be easily treated with modern medicines, in the prehistoric world of Santa Mónica, it still signifies the specter of death-in-life: "I did not know what to do about this living corpse, gesticulating, moving stumps of fingers, before whom Rosario knelt on the floor, mute with terror" (227). Guillermina de Ferrari has written that Nicasio presents a threat to the utopia on a most elemental level, and that "in *The Lost Steps* sickness attains the biblical proportions of leprosy" (223). Rosario's medieval conception of human illness may appeal to the narrator, but the lack of treatment for Nicasio's leprosy illustrates the dark underside of scientific ignorance.

Paradoxically, even though Nicasio represents a threat to Santa Mónica, he is also responsible for its cohesion as a group: a community becomes such by excluding others, much as the Adelantado excludes gold seekers from his village. De Ferrari observes: "For the community, Nicasio represents the fear, real or imagined, that one of 'us' could become one of 'them.' The presence of Nicasio on the margins of society is encouraged because he serves the purpose of distinguishing between the normal and the abnormal in the community" (223). As de Ferrari cogently explains, Nicasio must be sick so that others can be healthy; he must be a pariah so that others can be citizens. Madness and sickness are thus constitutive elements of society, forming the backdrop against which people define themselves. Foucault recognized the power of illness to delineate and divide society; in *The History of Madness* he notes that in Paris, the institutions used to house leper colonies were converted to insane asylums once leprosy was eradicated (5). The leper colonies and the mental institutions serve the same purpose: to divide the healthy from the unhealthy. They provide a physical barrier—and more importantly, a psychological one—between members of the community and those who are ostracized by it.

As a result, the narrator cannot kill Nicasio because on the deepest level, Nicasio's status as a pariah holds the community together: "The physical disintegration of Nicasio is accompanied by a semantic disintegration because when he dies, so does the structuring taboo of the utopia" (de Ferrari 225). In a novel that places so much importance on rituals of death, it is significant that Nicasio is denied a confession, despite his pleas to the contrary. Instead, he is devoured by vultures in the wilderness. The most basic rites, such as those the protagonist has just praised as natural and germane to the wilderness, are thus shattered. This final apparition of disease prefigures the protagonist's sudden and unhappy return to Western society: Nicasio's deformed, melting figure is reminiscent of a Dalí painting. In fact, members of the European avant-garde such as Filippo Tommaso Marinetti and Tristan Tzara used leprosy as a poetic motif (Orban 41). Only moments later, the airplane passes overhead in search of the narrator, thereby heralding the end of his stay in the forest. The lack of medicine and literature, the very things the narrator disparages, has driven him out of his utopian jungle and back to civilization.

On his return, the entire unnamed city seems diseased: "On my return I found the city covered with ruins that were more ruins than those considered as such. Everywhere I saw sickly columns and dying buildings" (252). He arrives at the Venusberg, his old bar, and finds a surrealist compilation of objects in total disorder, including a photo of André Breton, "the King whose praise of madness had made him fashionable among certain circles—now old hat" (253).[28] Carpentier also uses the phrase "praise of madness" (*elogios de la locura*) to dismiss the surrealists in his seminal article "Lo real maravilloso en América." Breton's legacy haunts Carpentier years after his departure from Paris. Despite his repeated declarations of independence from European aesthetics, Carpentier returns to them time and again, as does the protagonist of *The Lost Steps*.[29]

In a sense, the return to the city in *The Lost Steps* is the protagonist's true return—not to a prehistoric state of unity, but rather to Carpentier's own literary and aesthetic roots: his prickly relationship with surrealism. The protagonist pompously recognizes that the world of Santa Mónica de los Venados is closed to him because of his need to compose: "None of this was for me, because the only human race to which it is forbidden to sever the bonds of time is the race of those who create art" (278). Even though Carpentier's protagonist is harshly critical of both surrealism and Western science, he cannot escape their frame of reference. Just as his interpretations of the forest are colored by the books he has read, so too does he view the people he encounters through an anthropological lens. Moreover, he supposedly turns away from surrealism and Western medicine by becoming fascinated with the shaman's song and the curative natural herbs that Rosario offers. Yet in turning toward the Shirishana rite, he nevertheless fulfills a stated goal of the French intellectuals he ostensibly left behind: as members of the Collège de Sociologie advocated, he finds vitality and artistic inspiration in indigenous rituals, though he cannot become one of the natives. This is the legacy of surrealism and its concomitant interest in ethnography that leaves its mark on *The Lost Steps*.

The narrator-protagonist's forays into the wilderness reveal Carpentier's own ambivalence regarding his intellectual roots and his incomplete participation in cultures of the Old World and the New. Like the author, the protagonist is content neither in the cosmopolitan city nor in the remote tropical locale. While he finds artistic inspiration in the Shirishana rite, he is constantly reminded of his role as an outsider there. Carpentier scholars have noted that the protagonist's alienation is a driving force in the novel.[30] Indeed, Carpentier's narrator flees the metropolis for the wilderness in the hopes that he can escape his own misanthropy, failed marriage, and professional dead end. He is alienated in the fullest sense of the term; that is, he is estranged both from the societies he inhabits and from himself.

The protagonists of the novels I have studied find in the forest whatever it is they are seeking, though Carpentier's narrator eventually becomes aware of the tautological nature of his own quest. The selva is a space of freedom, lacking any social constraints. For most, the wilderness becomes a place of the irrational and the diseased, but also a place of artistic creation. Carpentier fittingly concludes this study because he deftly reverses those tropes: in *The Lost Steps*, the city is diseased, maddening, and irrational. He seeks to heal the wounds of violent surrealist juxtaposition in the rational, natural environment. Yet the protagonist nevertheless carries a bit of madness within him, as his irrational fear during the storm shows, proving that a tendency toward madness is inescapable in every human. The protagonist's failure to remain in the wilderness is not so different from that of the protagonists of the other novels, because in them the forest always represents what the protagonist is not: it is a blank, ahistorical canvas onto which they project their unconscious dreams, hopes, fears, and deepest anxieties.

Conclusion

MADNESS HAS LONG BEEN A HALLMARK OF GREAT LITERATURE, FROM CERVANTES to Poe to the Brontës. The tropical narratives discussed in this book form part of that tradition by exploring the act of going mad in the wilderness. This common thread implies that the forest—rather than individual psychosis, societal pressures, or literature itself—causes insanity. Yet in the course of this study it has become clear that the destructive irrationality that encroaches on the protagonists of these adventure tales reveals more about them than about their tropical environs. More than a mere physical endeavor, the voyage into the wilderness symbolizes a journey back through both time and space toward the origins of human existence. It is also an exploration of the protagonist's mind, even more so than of his surroundings. As a result, the fact that a tendency toward madness and self-annihilation is found within the protagonist himself as he reaches the depths of the forest indicates that irrationality, rather than sanity, lies at the core of human nature.

The descent into madness experienced by these protagonists critiques the nineteenth-century adventure novel tradition by undermining the assumption that colonizers bring Western rationalism to non-Western, irrational places. The insane and uncivilized behavior of the adventurers signals the twentieth-century writers' skepticism regarding narratives of tropical excursions in which Westerners easily subdue wild peoples and nature. Beginning at the turn of the century, adventure novels emerged as detractors rather than supporters of European empires; while earlier texts narrated the exciting act of bringing Western civilization to barbarous natives, these works told of the discovery of irrationality and cruelty within the Western or Westernized individual. This shift was not a radical about-face, but rather a dawning realization that all humans share destructive and irrational impulses. Although the protagonists of these works undoubtedly endure physical hardship, the more arduous journey is internal. The characters gradually begin to doubt their intrinsic superiority over the indigenous people they encounter and become aware of their own erratic and uncivil behavior. This literary trend mirrored the contemporary political one: imperial designs came under increasing scrutiny both in the centers of empire and in their (former) colonies around the turn of the twentieth century. The resulting cultural introspection intensified as the supposed civility of the Western world was belied by the ferocity of two world wars. At the same time, the protagonists of tropical adventure tales explored their own psyches in the wilderness, and what they found was a terrifying tendency toward madness, irrationality, and self-destruction within themselves. This is not a quality inherent in tropical nature, but rather in human nature, which is revealed to the protagonists only when they shed the physical and mental trappings of society. The madness glimpsed by the protagonists transforms their infatuation with the imperial project into disillusionment, which is a distinguishing characteristic of tropical narratives of the twentieth century. While the spread of Europeans into lands as diverse as Africa, Southeast Asia, and South America undoubtedly served as inspirational fodder for these writers, the philosophical and literary significance of their adventure tales goes beyond the realm of colonial and postcolonial meditations. More than an expression of ambivalence about the supposed civilizing of indigenous peoples, these books expose the incivility and the tendency toward irrationality at the root of humanity.

Medical terminology permeates all these novels but plays a different role in each of them, as exemplified in their presentations of mental illness. Throughout the colonial period, European scientific and medical theories frequently depicted the tropical wilderness as insalubrious and maddening, and colonized peoples as inferior to their would-be masters. According to these theories, the inhabitants of the tropics were in need of Western scientific, medical, and political advances. Particularly during the nineteenth and early twentieth centuries, medical writings contributed to the imperial project, such as in the pamphlets circulated at the 1931 International Colonial Exposition. The novels of Conrad and Malraux both participate in and challenge the medical theories of their day. They do so by revealing the concern that their protagonists, rather than dominating the tropics and its inhabitants, would be dominated by them. Furthermore, the protagonists suffer from degeneration, tropical neurasthenia, and even madness once they are removed from the civilizing forces of the Western world. The myth that the environment is capable of making a sane Westerner "go native" and thus attain a deeper spiritual understanding of human nature is rooted in cultural prejudice, geographic ignorance, and scientific racism. The authors derive the central literary and philosophical tensions in their works from the perceived medical causes of their protagonists' madness in the wilderness. In *Heart of Darkness* and *The Way of the Kings*, insanity is portrayed as resulting from a combination of climate and contact with indigenous peoples. In both works, time spent in the tropical forest seems to imbue the mad characters with a dark, enigmatic secret about human nature that they struggle but ultimately fail to disclose before dying. In the European novels, medical terminology is used to describe the plight of the protagonists as their rational discourse is silenced by the maddening power of the wilderness; Kurtz's famous last words—"The horror! The horror!"—remain the mere echo of his interior transformation.

Latin American authors also appropriate medical conditions and terminology for their own artistic and ideological purposes. Yet in their novels, the madness of the protagonists is associated not with failed communication and silence, but rather with artistic creation in the form of writing and music. While the environment impedes both the spoken and written word for the European protagonists, the Latin Americans find their creative fires stoked by their surroundings. In *The Vortex*, madness in the wilderness is the driving force behind both the plot and the structure of the narrative. *Canaima* achieves its most lyrical passages in describing Marcos Vargas's irrational, mystical experience of "going native" in the chapter entitled "The Storm." Carpentier's protagonist finds that the inspiration for his musical masterpiece is awakened only when he takes the irrational step of deciding to live in the forest forever in *The Lost Steps*.

This creativity in the depths of the wilderness within the literary works provides a stimulus to the Latin American authors' conception of their own role in literary history. While some medical and anthropological theories treated them as different, inferior, or imitative, the authors deftly transform these qualities into the source of their originality. Thus, the wilderness, once a symbol of the irredeemable barbarism of Latin Americans, becomes the wellspring of literary creativity. The vision of the Latin American landscape as the defining subject of the region's literature has often been noted with respect to the *novelas de la tierra*, namely Gallegos's *Doña Barbara*, *The Underdogs* (*Los de abajo*, 1915) by Mariano Azuela, Rivera's *The Vortex*, and *Don Segundo Sombra* by Güiraldes. Yet the once-insalubrious Latin American tierra continues to be a source of literary fertility late into the twentieth century.

Beginning with the short stories of Horacio Quiroga and flourishing in *The Vortex*, Latin American authors celebrate the dark side of the protagonists' psyches, transforming supposed defects into the basis of Latin American innovation. In later tropical novels such as *The Lost Steps*, the supposedly inferior indigenous culture comes to represent an authenticity now lost to Western civilization. These later tropical narratives continue to rewrite the encounter between the Westerner and the native, and the former's process of "going native." For each author, the concept of "going native," or becoming another, has different connotations. For Conrad, Gallegos, and Rivera, for example, "going native" implies what the authors depict as a mental degeneration and insanity that results from participating in African and Amazonian rituals, such as possible cannibalism in *Heart of Darkness* and the ñopo ceremony in *Canaima* and *The Vortex*. For Carpentier, "going native" signifies a return to a state of cultural purity absent in the modern world.

Given the repetition of these motifs, tropical narratives of the second half of the twentieth century thus become palimpsests of their predecessors. Many of them, such as Mario Vargas Llosa's *The Storyteller* (*El hablador*, 1987), specifically mention *The Vortex* in describing the voracious quality of the jungle (94).[1] Other novels that dramatize the Hispanophone wilderness are Luis Sepúlveda's *The Old Man Who Read Love Stories* (*Un viejo que leía novelas de amor*, 1989), Severo Sarduy's *Colibrí* (1972), Vargas Llosa's *The Green House* (*La casa verde*, 1965), and Álvaro Mutis's *The Snow of the Admiral* (*La nieve del almirante*, 1987) and *Amirbar* (1980). Shortly after winning the Nobel Prize for Literature in October 2010, Vargas Llosa published yet another novel set in the tropics, *El sueño del celta* (The dream of the Celt). In these novels, the authors all seek to rewrite the narrative of the encounter between two worlds and to explore the temptation to "go native."

In the second half of the twentieth-century, tropical adventure narratives both converge and diverge from earlier texts. Two novels in particular are representative of major divergent trends in tropical adventure fiction: the Guyanese writer Wilson Harris's *Palace of the Peacock* (1960) and Mario Vargas Llosa's *The Storyteller*. Based in this tradition of tropical adventure novels, many late twentieth-century works continue tropes begun decades and even centuries earlier, while others transform the failed tropical quest into a fantastical allegory of place, nation, and identity. *The Storyteller* is representative of the former tendency, *Palace of the Peacock* of the latter.

Harris's *Palace of the Peacock* repeats many motifs set forth in earlier narratives, though reality melds with dreams in what Harris calls "a mixed futuristic order of memory and event" (48). While in previous novels the physical journey had been paralleled by an internal one, in *Palace of the Peacock* the division between reality and the dreamworld is effaced. The entire voyage is shrouded in dreams, visions, and a sense of the uncanny. The novel is narrated in the first person by an unnamed individual referred to as the Dreamer, who describes the river voyage led by his twin brother and double, Donne, from the Guyanese savannah into the forest. As in *The Vortex*, the trip begins as a search for a woman, Mariella, who is simultaneously a person and a mission settlement in the forest. As Mark McWatt has noted, Mariella is transformed in the novel from the subservient mistress of Donne to a destination and finally to a powerful and elusive force of nature (78).[2] The journey into the interior of the *mother*land functions as a metaphor for the journey to the source of human creation, and, as in Carpentier, both time and space are described in explicitly biblical language.[3] Harris's novel also offers a panoramic biological mosaic of Guyana in the racial makeup of the boat's crew. Donne represents the white settler intent on dominating human, plant, and animal life, while Cameron, whose great-grandfather was a Scot and great-grandmother an "African slave and mistress," is symbolic of racial mixing in the Guyanese population (39). Once they reach "the soil of Mariella," Donne forces an ancient Arawak woman to guide them and convinces the rest of the crew to continue upriver in search of laborers to work on his plantation (42). When they stop at a river camp in the course of their journey, the crew becomes aware that their names are identical to those of a previous crew who perished in the rapids.

Their own deaths are therefore predestined, and the mission is guaranteed to end in failure, as are all twentieth-century tropical quest narratives.

As in early twentieth-century novels, the instances of disorientation, sickness, and madness continue to haunt *Palace of the Peacock*. The narrator suffers from vertigo and faints after being "overwhelmed by a renewed force of consciousness of the hot spirit and moving spell in the tropical undergrowth" (28). The wise and wizened Schomburgh observes that on entering the wilderness, every man takes on a "dead risk" (29).[4] This risk is found not only in the physical surroundings, but also in the "tropical fever that blew out of the Mission in an ague of fears, shaking the leaves of the dreaming forest" (41). While characters of previous tropical adventure novels such as Arturo Cova and Mouche are afflicted with malaria or other fevers, in *Palace of the Peacock* the illness has been transformed into a metaphor that is no less dangerous for being part of the forest dreamscape created by Harris. Indeed, madness and irrational behavior continue to be tropes in the wilderness, though here they are provoked only by other men. One crew member, Wishrop, is said to be mad for having killed his wife and her lover. He represents the base and homicidal instincts that would soon be unleashed in the wilderness, reflecting "the desire [the crew] too felt—in their vicarious daydream, to kill whatever they had learned to hate. This wish was the deepest fantasy they knew mankind to entertain" (56). The fantasy is soon played out as the group nears their destination. Like Conrad's protagonists in the story "An Outpost of Progress," the crew members grow to distrust each other. Their frustration at being lost and at feeling that their fates are sealed leads the men to kill each other senselessly in a maddened rage. Wishrop falls overboard and is eaten alive by carnivorous fish, the same fate that befalls the villain Narciso Barrera in *The Vortex*. Their quest in the wilderness is described as a "mad pursuit in the midst of imprisoning land and water and ambushing forest and wood" (27). While Harris repeats several of the motifs employed in early twentieth-century tropical quest novels, his work is explicitly postmodern in that it mixes dreamworlds with reality and merges past, present, and future events. The instances of madness and sickness are no longer based in medical writings, as in earlier texts, but rather are internalized and allegorical manifestations of man's mortality.

When the boat founders in the War Office rapids, the surviving crew members ascend a rock face and enter the Palace of the Peacock, which offers "the undivided soul and anima in the universe from whom the word of dance and creation first came" (116). Antonio Benítez Rojo's excellent chapter on Harris and Carpentier in *The Repeating Island* reads the quests in both *Palace of the Peacock* and *The Lost Steps* as a search for origins, which lies at the heart of Caribbean literature (177–96). He characterizes that literature as "the persistent discourse that travels toward a rediscovery of the divided Self, or better, toward a Utopian territory with an Arcadia where one might reconstitute his Being, might all be explained in relation to the known cultural fragmentation which, because of the Plantation, is the experience of every man and woman in the Caribbean" (187).

While the cultural fragmentation of Carpentier's protagonist is not due to the plantation but rather to the uprootings produced by the world wars and economic migrations of the twentieth century, it is clear that all protagonists of Caribbean quest novels of the last century are intent on seeking out the originary moment of existence. The mystical union achieved in *Palace of the Peacock* exactly parallels the musical epiphany achieved by the protagonist of *The Lost Steps*. In both novels, the moment of spiritual revelation proves to be fleeting. While Carpentier's utopia is shattered by the protagonist's decision to return to the city to acquire books and paper, Harris's palace of the peacock is attainable only in death. Death, rather than creation, is the ultimate result of the search for origins, thereby revealing that a return to the source is not possible in life.

If *Palace of the Peacock* is a fantastical allegory for the Caribbean search for origins in which the protagonists attain their goal by dying, other late twentieth-century tropical novels repeatedly present the possibility of "going native" as a viable quest.[5] In this vein, Mario Vargas Llosa's *The Storyteller* self-reflexively follows the general trajectory of the tropical adventure narrative. Like its predecessors, *The Storyteller* presents the jungle as the locus of originality for Latin American literature. For Vargas Llosa, the promise of literary innovation in the wilderness resides in the narrative possibilities offered by Amazonian myths as retold by Saúl Zuratas, a half-Jewish Peruvian who lives among the Machigenga people (known in Spanish as the Machiguenga). The novel has two narrative perspectives. The first is a first-person narrative by a Westernized Peruvian who suspects that his friend Saúl has "gone native" and is living as a Machigenga storyteller. The second story thread is the third-person narration of supposedly indigenous creation myths, presumably told by Saúl in his new identity as a Machigenga. Vargas Llosa's novel is similar to Gallegos's *Canaima* in that Saúl, like Marcos Vargas, does indeed integrate himself into the indigenous community and turn away from Western civilization. It goes against *The Lost Steps* in positing that it is possible to "go native," and in this respect, *The Storyteller* is a decidedly less complex and intriguing narrative.

Throughout the novel, Vargas Llosa repeats several motifs that have been constant in this study: the notion that Congolese, Shirishana, Maquiritare, Machigenga, Guaraúno and Guahibo peoples occupy a Hegelian place outside of history, and that they live in a state of prehistory untouched by the conveniences and corruptions of the modern world. The notion that the indigenous peoples inhabit a prehistorical realm thus never wavers throughout the twentieth-century tropical novel. In *The Storyteller*, it continues: "When we reached the tribes, by contrast, there before us was prehistory, the elemental, primeval existence of our distant ancestors: hunters, gatherers, bowmen, nomads, shamans, irrational and animistic" (73). Common too is the idea that these peoples share a secret, hidden knowledge that is inaccessible to contemporary civilization, which is part of what inspires the protagonist to "go native." It is important to note that in *The Storyteller*, as in *Canaima*, the protagonist still associates native peoples with irrationality, which is linked to a hidden source of knowledge unattainable by modern man. In an echo of Carpentier's protagonist, for the narrator, the Amazonian people all share "the wisdom born of long practice which had allowed them, through an elaborate system of rites, taboos, fears, and routines, perpetuated and passed on from father to son, to preserve that Nature, seemingly so superabundant, but actually so vulnerable, upon which they depended for subsistence" (27). This type of statement shows that myths regarding Amazonian people's proximity to the past remain vibrant, if clichéd, throughout the twentieth century. Finally, later tropical adventure novels continue to portray the wilderness as a sickening, dangerous place. Like the authors of tropical tales before him, Vargas Llosa depicts the jungle as a sick and sickening place in *The Storyteller*. The wilderness is characterized by "unhealthy forests" (93) and leprosy, here known as *la uta* (167). Although *The Storyteller* was published twenty-seven years after *Palace of the Peacock*, it is a much less radical and postmodern novel because it perpetrates rather than questions basic assumptions about indigenous peoples and their tropical environs.

Most of the characteristics mentioned above originated in early tropical adventure novels and have been dutifully repeated for years, long after being debunked as wildly inaccurate and degrading. To wit, Vargas Llosa follows Rivera in including ostensibly indigenous myths in his narrative, yet postcolonial scholars have excoriated him for presuming to speak for the Other. This gesture has been viewed as a further cultural theft that robs the Machigenga of their narrative agency even as it seeks to make room for traditionally marginalized voices.[6] As Doris Sommer notes, Vargas Llosa makes "authoritative, enlightened, and despotic choices for others. He tends to speak for them in general" ("About Face" 313). Vargas Llosa has similarly been criticized for making a "calculated appropriation of indigenous culture" (Kokotovic 454).[7] With varying degrees of severity, this same accusation must be leveled at all tropical adventure novels written in the twentieth century. Indeed, for the Latin American *novela de la tierra*, literary originality stems from this appropriation even as the Western narrators dictate the structure and content of the novel. Moreover, none of the novelists conducted lengthy research in preparation for depicting indigenous rituals or speech.[8] Rather, their knowledge is based on brief sojourns into the wilderness—exploratory trips that lasted merely days (Gallegos), weeks (Carpentier), or months (Rivera) rather than years. Their wildernesses are truly literary jungles in the sense that they are laden with a hodgepodge of common suppositions, superstitions, and assumptions about the cultures their protagonists encounter.

One central question that arises from the longevity of such fabrications even when they have patently been proven false is: why have these myths endured? What perpetuates this vision of the wilderness as a site of timelessness, of danger, disease, and sensuality? Simply put, these narratives allow the reader to vicariously experience the process of "going native" alongside the protagonist. She or he, too, is offered the chance to cast off the confines of appropriate behavior and to become another. For a contemporary first-world reader, these narratives also provide a voyeuristic glimpse into societies characterized by poverty, low life expectancy, and social marginalization caused by the ever-expanding reaches of political and economic globalization.

Lest the reader think that the allure of the jungle has been demystified in the twenty-first century, a brief look at a popular "reality" television program will demonstrate the endurance of this myth in the present time. From February 8 to March 29, 2009, the Travel Channel aired an eight-episode series based on the adventures of two men, Scottish Mark Anstice and British Oliver Steeds, called *Mark and Olly: Living with the Machigenga*.[10] For four months, they lived in a community of thirty Machigenga people called Koran Korata on the shores of the Urubamba River in Peru. While the show purports to be a transparent documentary, the footage has clearly undergone extensive editing to produce a carefully crafted narrative structure, and thus deserves to be analyzed as a work of fiction rather than a testimonial text.[9] An unseen camera crew and translators follow Steeds and Anstice as, according to the show's promotional materials, they "battle severe weather, harsh living conditions, and savage wildlife" ("Strangers").

The marketing apparatus of the program takes advantage of all the clichés about life in wilderness in order to attract a broad viewership. For example, the introduction to the series carries a warning of "indigenous nudity and extreme rituals," presumably to pique the interest of the spectator. Anstice declares that "the jungle has eyes" ("Strangers"), and yet it is simultaneously a "magical paradise" ("Trouble"), where "they all live in peace and harmony" ("Trouble"). As in other adventure narratives, the community is barely accessible and can be entered only after the men posing as explorers pass "the last place on the map" ("Strangers"). The Machigenga, like Gallegos's Guaraúnos and Carpentier's Shirishana, are portrayed as having an innate biological connection to the land; as Anstice declares, "This land is in their blood" ("Trouble"). Sensuality is a prime component of the community in the eyes of the Westerners. Referring to the sex act, Steeds exclaims, "They're constantly at it" ("Interviews"). Steeds calls the community of Koran Korata "untouched by the outside world" ("Strangers"). In the opening sequence of each program, the narrator declares that the Machigenga have lived this way for "over four thousand years" and tantalizes the viewer with the possibility of vicariously visiting "one of the Earth's greatest tribes, while they still exist" (*Mark and Olly*).

Ironically, the Machigenga are members of the same ethnic group that Vargas Llosa's character Saúl Zuratas infiltrates, and like Vargas Llosa and so many other writers and explorers of previous centuries, the creators of the show declare that this may be the last chance to record Machigenga experience "before it disappears forever" ("Strangers"). Of course, even Vargas Llosa noted he was not the first to come across these groups when he was there in the 1950s; Spanish missionaries had long preceded him. In a way, the afflictions of Western civilization wrought on the Machigengas present a panorama of colonialism in microcosm: first they were subjugated and indoctrinated by missionaries; then by scientists, anthropologists, and linguists who wanted to study and "improve" them; and finally by reality television crews, who seek to exploit these now long-discovered groups for lucrative entertainment purposes.

The similarities between Anstice and Steeds and earlier tropical adventure novel protagonists abound: they travel up a river into "hostile territory" to reach a "mysterious tribe" that "lives in isolation" and "doesn't like strangers" ("Strangers"). Like the other novelistic adventurers, they declare the trip in the wilderness "was like traveling back in time" ("End of the Affair"). Their express purpose is to "become part of the traditional Machigenga tribe"—in other words, to "go native" ("Strangers"). Like Kurtz, Perken, Cova, Marcos Vargas, and Carpentier's protagonist, Steeds and Anstice also observe and even participate in drumming and dancing ceremonies. They get lost, and they must pass "tests" in order to stay in the village, just as Carpentier's narrator-protagonist passes through several trials on his way to Santa Mónica de los Venados. Like their literary predecessors, they make a pilgrimage to the region's shaman and drink his black *ayahuasca* brew to induce hallucinations ("Heaven or Hell"). The fear of cannibalism is sublimated but persistent: when the men are asked to eat monkey hands, Anstice compares it to eating a child's hand ("Strangers").

The Machigenga, however, are clearly far savvier than the visitors comprehend. The requirement to eat monkey hands in order to join the group is a farce that reveals that the people living in Koran Korata are clearly aware of and sensitive to Western stereotypes about forest-dwellers. One also wonders how many other rituals are concocted for the benefit of the cameras. The viewer familiar with the plight of indigenous communities around the world feels an acute sense of injustice as the white men set up camp in a village that does not want them because of centuries of similar incursions and the resulting violence and destruction; the reader of tropical adventure novels feels an ironic sense of victory when they are teased and treated like defenseless children by the community. At first Anstice, Steeds, and their camera crew are rejected by the community because the Westerners are thought to be after rubber, food, or their children (the kidnapping of children, particularly girls, continues to afflict indigenous groups in the area). When it is clear that they want to stay with the group for several months, they are rejected again; the leader declares, "I have too many children already" ("Strangers"). It quickly becomes clear why: the British men are unable to forage for their own food and do not respect the rites of the village, such as when they repeatedly attempt to enter a hut in which a woman is giving birth. They are nearly expelled from the village after violating a taboo that prohibits deer meat from entering the community, and are punished by having their hands pressed against the Tangaranga tree, which is crawling with poisonous ants ("End of the Affair"). Even as Steeds and Anstice recognize that the Machigenga have endured centuries of oppression, they do not view their own trespass as a similar affront because they seek to "learn from them" ("Strangers"). There is no engagement with the ethical principles being violated in the name of ethnography; Steeds and

Anstice are never concerned that their presence and attempt to record Machigenga customs will further erode what they view as Koran Korata's fragile way of life. Moreover, the premise that they seek to learn from the Machigenga is completely debunked by an interview Anstice gives just before embarking on the trip. Rather than learning the group's customs, Anstice stated that he "didn't want to know too much" before meeting them ("Interviews"). The program deftly uses the façade of anthropology to exploit a non-Western population for the titillation of the gawking viewer.

Despite the show's faithful adherence to fixed assumptions about the natural beauty, innocence, isolation, and simplicity of life in the wilderness, a counternarrative emerges over the course of several episodes. Just as in the tropical adventure novels of the twentieth century, a sense of disconnect between what the adventurers expect to find in the wilderness what they actually encounter pervades the series. The supposedly isolated Machigenga all have Hispanic names: José, Rosita, Fabiana, Luciano, and Jacinto. The "medicine man" Juan and two other village residents speak Spanish fluently. When Juan speaks Spanish for a few moments in one episode, the camera cuts away, and in the next frame he speaks Machigenga again. One wonders what transpired off camera to make Juan conform to the producer's vision of Machigenga "reality." In fact, after the narrator declares that the community has been living this way for "centuries," the village leader José reveals that he founded Koran Korata only eighteen years ago, after Spanish-speaking Peruvians forced his father to work for them and then killed him. José and his family were driven off their farm and into the wilderness. Nor is the family's presence in the forest guaranteed to be permanent: José's eldest son has abandoned the forest community to live with other Machigenga in the neighboring town of Timpía, where there are markets, health care, and schools, so that his children can learn to read and write.

The only occurrence in the series that cannot be adapted to maintain the illusion of Machigenga isolation and tranquillity is the sudden entrance of a group of armed Spanish-speaking men into the village. The gunmen offer to buy José's thirteen-year-old daughter, yet in the presence of the camera crew claim to be tourists who were simply lost in the area. José explains that such men frequently raid places like Koran Korata for children, who are forced into the sex trade. Their parents are often murdered. In fact, Koran Korata was founded as a refuge from this violence. In this way, the settlement is similar to Carpentier's Santa Mónica de los Venados, because it was begun as a conscious attempt to found a utopian community free from exploitation and crime in more established areas. The community members inform the armed men that they are prohibited from entering the area because it is a reserve for Machigenga protected by the Peruvian government. It is thus revealed that the group lives within the "Reserva Comunal Machigenga," which was formally established as a protected zone in 2003, and had been part of the national forest preserve since 1963 ("Reserva"). Anstice and Steeds are not at all "off the map" or even in "total isolation," as they claimed ("Strangers"). Although Anstice and Steeds lament the harassment of the Machigenga by such criminals, they do not spend much time decrying these abuses, unlike Rivera's efforts in *The Vortex*. Instead, they continue fabricating the charade of Koran Korata as a bucolic realm free from brutality. They persist in playing games, taking canoe rides, and domesticating baby monkeys in the wilderness, rather than taking any action to protect the people of the community. The most poignant, tragic aspect of the series is arrived at inadvertently: the show makes clear not the pristine nature of life in the forest, but rather the persecution of the people by Spanish and English speakers, be they gunmen seeking to plunder the village and steal children, or pseudo-explorers looking to exploit Machigenga life for entertainment purposes.

Despite this sobering and foreboding sequence of events, the show doggedly presents every other aspect of Koran Korata as happy and tranquil; for example, Anstice states that carrying logs through the forest "sure beats getting stuck in a traffic jam on the way to work" ("Boys"). What is the attraction of the narrative presented in *Mark and Olly*? How does this sanitized vision of the wilderness persist, even given direct evidence to the contrary? In the most immediate sense, the series undoubtedly attracted viewers because of the comic drama inherent in the conflicts between the cultures: Steeds carries a large, black, wood-handled umbrella for the first few episodes, and grimaces for the camera while eating live cicadas. The differences in diet, clothing, and custom (not to mention female nudity) in Koran Korata shock the viewer and are intended to provide a sense of superiority. The series promotes a condescending, idealized belief in the fragile endurance of "primitive" people who need to be protected by Westerners, as when the camera crew ejects the "colonistas" from the camp. In addition, the show offers the spectator an escape from an increasingly homogenized, automated society, similar to that sought by the protagonist of *The Lost Steps*. Indeed, the show reinforces the notion that because of his advances in engineering, man (and not woman) has been weakened by modern civilization. An episode of *Mark and Olly* entitled "Boys to Men" chronicles the protagonists' attempts to be declared "men" by the village elders, as opposed to the helpless children they are at the opening of the show. The final cliché that endures is that of the protagonists coming to understand that they share more in common with the "remote" community than they had initially assumed. In *Mark and Olly*, Marlow's "An appeal to me in the fiendish row, is there?" is reduced to a saccharine Hollywood conclusion: "We found out we weren't so very different. In the end we became part of the family." This fantasy of inclusion in another society also links *Mark and Olly* to the tropical narratives of the twentieth century; Anstice and Steeds seek to be like Marcos Vargas, who remains in the forest, or Carpentier's protagonist, who imagines an alternate life for himself in the Orinoco River basin. Yet, like Carpentier's narrator, they must eventually leave the wilderness as well. Their membership in the tribe is, after all, simulated for entertainment purposes.

All these elements common to tropical adventure narratives remain vibrant and potent in the twenty-first century: the protagonist's flight from the metropolis, the encounter with another culture that is either idealized or disdained by him, the temptation to "go native," the sometimes grudging recognition of similarities between the two cultures, and the inevitable return to the city. In addition, the travel narratives published after *The Lost Steps* share the flawed desire to explicate—indeed, to narrate—the full process of "going native" in the wilderness. This desire is flawed because the attraction of the tropical adventure tale is precisely the temptation of uncovering the jungle's unknowable, mysterious core. The appeal of the adventure rests on the prospect of encountering the unknown, be it in the wilderness or in the protagonist's own mind, but not on the act of actually laying bare what the Westerner perceives to be the enigma of indigenous culture. Accordingly, Steeds's declaration that he and Anstice have become "part of the family" is blatantly false, and dissipates the very allure of their adventure. In a similar fashion, the attempt by *The Storyteller*'s narrator to write *for* the Machigenga deflates the mystery of the unknown Other. In this way, adventure narratives of the second half of the twentieth century seem to herald the demise of Conrad's allusive descriptions of the wilderness. His "implacable force brooding over an inscrutable intention" (*Heart* 137) has been replaced and written over by Vargas Llosa's misguided narrative and *Mark and Olly*'s wide-angle lens. The enigma of the jungle evaporates.

Another popular media representation of the wilderness takes a very different tack in maintaining the enigma of the forest. The wildly popular television series *Lost*, created by J. J. Abrams, Damon Lindelof, and Jeffery Lieber, was shot in Hawaii and ran from September 2004 to May 2010. While both *The Storyteller* and *Mark and Olly* attempt to speak for the Machigenga and perpetuate the idea that it is possible to "go native," *Palace of the Peacock* and *Lost* treat the wilderness as an allegory that points up the metaphysical quality and psychological trauma of the tropics. If Mario Vargas Llosa and the creators of *Mark and Olly* seek to maintain the illusion of the possibility of "going native," *Palace of the Peacock* and *Lost* highlight the internal transformations of their protagonists when removed from structured society.

The plot lines of *Lost* are far too complicated and too often contradictory to outline here. The driving concept of the series is a plane crash that lands the survivors on a mysterious tropical island in which they must fight for survival not only against normal meteorological and biological elements, but also against supernatural forces that cause them to travel through both time and space. In this sense, *Lost* recaptures the attraction of the wilderness found in the tropical adventure novels discussed in *Jungle Fever*: by going to the tropics, it does seem possible to travel through time by traveling through space. In addition, various human attempts to harness the electromagnetic power of the island have resulted in disaster and oppression, just as mankind's incursion into the tropical rainforests of the earth has wrought their destruction. Once removed from society, the crash survivors behave in uncivilized ways, alternately forming alliances and violently turning on each other, much as do the characters in *The Vortex* and *Palace of the Peacock*.

The complicated desire to "go native" that runs through the novels, films, and television shows of the twentieth and early twenty-first centuries is precipitously and succinctly distilled in Jorge Luis Borges's ironic 1969 micronarrative, "The Ethnographer." Borges anticipates and surpasses later novels by perfectly capturing the incommunicability of his protagonist's time in the wilderness. It also serves as a parodic tribute to the adventure narrative genre. The elements of the traditional story are all there: the youthful flight from civilization, the indigenous rituals, the conversion experience, the crisis of ethnography, the limitations of rationality and logical thought, the inexpressibility of the experience, and the return to civilization are all present.

At this point, such commonplaces are expected in the tropical adventure narrative, and Borges alludes to them in a brief and cryptic fashion. A young American named Fred Murdock leaves civilization to study "certain tribes out West" (334). He participates in ceremonial rites and "goes native": He "came to dream in a language that was not that of his fathers. He conditioned his palate to harsh flavors, he covered himself with strange clothing, he forgot his friends and the city, he came to think in a fashion that the logic of his mind rejected" (334–35). He learns the "secret doctrine" of the tribe and returns to his university. He tells his professor that he knows the secret of the group but will not reveal it:

> "Are you bound by your oath?" the professor asked.
> "That's not the reason," Murdock replied. "I learned something out there that I can't express."
> "The English language may not be able to communicate it," the professor suggested.
> "That's not it, sir. Now that I possess the secret, I could tell it in a hundred different and even contradictory ways. I don't know how to tell you this, but the secret is beautiful, and science, *our* science, seems mere frivolity to me now."
> After a pause he added:
> "And anyway, the secret is not as important as the paths that led me to it. Each person has to walk those paths himself." (335)

Borges's micronarrative is much more consonant with Conrad's allusive tale than with Vargas Llosa's. As Rolena Adorno has noted, Borges shows that "the timelessness that emanates from the unuttered experience can be understood only through the unmediated experience itself, not through any (contradictory) interpretative utterance" (278). Like Conrad, Borges preserves the "secret doctrine" from subjugation by the written word and linear thought. Most important, he recognizes that the drama of the adventure novel lies not in revealing the secret of the Other, but in the mesmerizing transformation of the Westerner who seeks it: "The secret is not as important as the paths that led me to it." Vargas Llosa, on the other hand, destroys the mystique of the wilderness by domesticating it and by appropriating the Machigenga tales for his own literary use. Vargas Llosa, like Conrad's Marlow and *Mark and Olly*, seeks to narrate the unnarratable. For the *Lost* viewer, total incomprehension of events contributes to the show's drama. In tropical adventure novels, the appeal of the jungle lies in the fact that it is the repository of the base, the irrational, the repressed, and the inexpressible. The jungle is seductive precisely because it is the blank canvas upon which characters and even authors can project their deepest fears, anxieties, and desires. Vargas Llosa's novel and the Travel Channel series show that the urge to narrate the enigma of the wilderness transformation remains a temptation best left ungratified.

The most compelling tropical adventure tales dramatize the protagonist's internal metamorphosis in his decision to "go native"; this is the strength of "The Ethnographer." While this conversion may have outwards manifestations, such as Marcos Vargas's determination to no longer wear shoes and to take an indigenous wife, the true revolution occurs in the protagonist's mind. As the doctor in *Heart of Darkness* notes, "The changes take place inside, you know" (112). Thus, the wilderness is not the root cause of the protagonist's madness, as it would seem at first glance. Rather, it is a threshold—a mechanism that releases the irrational side of humanity in the protagonist. The true drama of the tropical adventure novel therefore lies not in the battle with unruly foliage and undomesticated natives, but within the unruly and undomesticated regions of the human mind. Through these tales, the reader can explore the dark underbelly of civilization, and his or her own psyche, without setting foot in the wilderness.

Notes

Introduction

1. I owe the definition of this subgenre of the adventure novel to Roberto González Echevarría, whose graduate course at Yale, "The Jungle Books," inspired this examination of madness in tropical adventure novels. He pioneered the literary exploration of jungle novels in "Canaima y los libros de la selva," and "*Canaima* and the Jungle Books."

2. Other jungle films include *La muralla verde* (The green wall, 1970) and *The Medicine Man* (1992).

3. This phenomenon is not true of all tropical narratives. For example, while the main character of Hudson's *Green Mansions* declares himself mad after living alone in the Guyanese wilderness, the roots of his experience lie in Romantic tropes of bereavement and isolation rather than in psychological medicine.

4. David Arnold calls this discursive representation of the tropics *tropicality* in his analysis of Pierre Gourou's *Tropical Countries* (6). Similarly, Krista A. Thompson defines *tropicalization* as "the complex visual systems through which the islands were imaged for tourist consumption and the social and political implications of these representations on actual physical space on the islands and their inhabitants" (5). Thompson's work shares with my own a focus on how the subject matter of exotic representations reacted to, adapted, and appropriated Western theories about them (11); in this book, I apply this focus to the Latin American writers of jungle novels. Denis Cosgrove unravels the development of the words *tropics* and *tropicality* in Western cultures going back to the Ptolemaic and Aristotelian cosmographies (199).

5. The widely used Köppen-Geiger climate classification system divides tropical climates into three subdivisions: tropical rainforest, tropical monsoon, and tropical savannah. These classifications were established between 1918 and 1936 by Wladimir Peter Köppen (1846–1940), who categorized climates into six broad groups according to the major vegetation types associated with them, broadly determined by critical temperature and the seasonality of precipitation. Prior to this attempt at scientific rigor, any hot, wet climate was denominated "tropical" in both popular and specialized writings (Allaby and Allaby).

6. I use the term *Western* here to refer to Western Europe's colonial powers, particularly those countries whose colonizations of the Americas, Africa, and Asia are examined in this book: namely, Spain, England, and France. This denomination, like many geographical terms, is inherently relative and occasionally misleading, as the Americas are far to the west of Europe.

7. Ileana Rodríguez underscores the idea of the wilderness as a marginal space. For her, the jungle is "constituted as a liminal border, an *orilla*. Written as forest, wood, or wilderness, jungle is a divider, and specifically refers to a ne plus ultra, a frontier, or empty signifier, at times lacking all but generic referentiality" (167). While the term *orilla* or "shore" does not share an etymological root with the words "forest" or "jungle," it does invoke the concept of being far from the center of consideration.

8. In the Latin American context, Fernando Aínsa refers to the tropical forest as a "mythical and personalized geography, a conflictive space *par excellence*" (106). His reading adds an important Hispanic dimension to the European quest narratives traced by Frye and Campbell, but he reads both *Los pasos perdidos* and *La vorágine* as quests for original sources of Latin American culture rather than interior psychological voyages undertaken by the protagonists. I argue that these interior psychological voyages result in artistic inspiration for Latin American literature of the twentieth century.

9. Rod Edmond has demonstrated that "'the tropics' is emphatically a relational term, requiring the antonym 'temperate' for its full significance" ("Returning" 176).

10. Segalen's work is not without its glaring flaws. He was apparently uninterested in the oppression of the very colonized peoples who were often deemed exotic. He also failed to consider the subject of sexual exoticization, though he listed "the opposite sex" as an exoticized type. This is perhaps due to his disregard for women in general; he referred to feminism as "a monstrous social inversion" (63).

11. In a special section of the *Dictionnaire culturel en langue française* dedicated to lengthy cultural descriptions of terms, Tristan Hordé gives several examples of the use of *forêt* from ancient Rome to Descartes. He notes that the forest is defined as a place for what remains inassimilable by man, literally outside of human knowledge: "C'est au contraire à l'abri des murs de la cité ou sous son règne qu'ont lieu les activités productives, agriculture et élevage—qui exigent la déforestation—que l'organization administrative, commerciale se construit—que l'Histoire commence" (qtd. in Rey 1108).

12. The *Oxford English Dictionary* notes the change in meaning from dry wasteland to "land overgrown with underwood, long grass, or tangled vegetation; also, the luxuriant and often almost impenetrable growth of vegetation covering such a tract . . . especially tropical" ("Jungle").

13. Lisa Makman states that "the word [jungle] continues to conjure images of imperial adventure. . . . We owe our deep association of jungles with mystery, threat, and the struggle for survival in large part to Rudyard Kipling" (xv). She calls *The Jungle Books* "perhaps the most influential mythology of the jungle written in English" (xv). Kipling's legacy in the adventure novel tradition and the depiction of the tropics will be analyzed in further detail in Chapter 1.

14. The Spanish reads, "Terreno extenso, inculto y muy poblado de árboles" ("Selva").

15. Corominas's text states: "Es de creer que SILVA (acaso junto con LUCUS) sería el viejo término heredado del latín para expresar la idea de 'bosque', pues esta última palabra es extranjerismo entrado en fecha relativamente tardía. . . . De todos modos 'bosque' ganó terreno rápidamente relegando pronto selva al terreno de lo arcaico o poético; como voz poética y noble, inspirándose en el latín, exhumó este arcaismo Juan de Mena. . . . Sea como quiera, selva nunca volvió a ser palabra del fondo popular; pero aparece en muchos textos. Del habla arcaica la toman los Libros de Caballerías, y de allí Cervantes en el *Quijote*; del lenguaje poético de Mena la heredan varios líricos del siglo XI y señaladamente Góngora, que la emplea docenas de veces, en calidad de palabra noble.

En el siglo XIX queda fijado el matiz de 'bosque intricado y muy espeso, a la manera de los tropicales" (179–80).

16. The New Revised Standard Version of the Bible renders the important passage of Genesis 2:8–25 thus: "Out of the ground the Lord God made to grow every tree that is pleasant to the sight and good for food, the tree of life also in the midst of the garden, and the tree of the knowledge of good and evil. A river flows out of Eden to water the garden, and from there it divides and becomes four branches. The name of the first is Pishon; it is the one that flows around the whole land of Havilah, where there is gold; and the gold of that land is good; bdellium and onyx stone are there. The name of the second river is Gihon; it is the one that flows around the whole land of Cush. The name of the third river is Tigris, which flows east of Assyria. And the fourth river is the Euphrates" (*New Oxford*). In *Green Imperialism*, Richard Grove argues that the search for Eden in the East shaped early Romanticism, and that the visible symbols of Eden were "frequently located in the tropics" (4). He maintains that the roots of the modern environmental movement are to be found in colonial depictions of the Caribbean as a series of "tropical island Edens," and in the subsequent destruction of the Edens by imperial powers in pursuit of financial gain.

17. Silvia Spitta calls this gulf between expectation and reality an essential "misplacement" that marks Europeans' conceptualization of the Americas from their first interactions with the region (12). While it is true that early cartographers did effectively mis-place the continents because they thought they were actually a part of Asia, European geographers effectively created (rather than misplaced) a myth of the Americas in terms of geography, language, and culture.

18. While Jack Ross has demonstrated commonalities in the South American place-myth among the novels of Joseph Conrad, Alejo Carpentier, and Wilson Harris (Ross 466), I argue throughout this work that the notion of "the tropics" is not confined to the Americas.

19. I thank Carina Ray for bringing this quote to my attention. In the case of the Americas, Hegel acknowledges that they had been populated prior to the arrival of Europeans, but he nevertheless dismisses the indigenous population by stating that "the inferiority of these individuals, in all respects, even in regard to size, is very manifest" (99). The supposed inferiority of uncolonized societies bolstered the European justification of enslavement and exploitation of non-Europeans from Hegel's time through the twentieth century.

20. Pierre Gouru, writing in the 1940s, was reluctant to accord Maya and Aztec societies "civilized" status because doing so would undermine his central argument, that of the tropics being unsuited to sophisticated economic and cultural development (*Tropical World* 61).

21. Cabeza de Vaca's *Relación* (*Narrative*) depicts the Spaniards as being ill equipped for their surroundings and unschooled in how to cope with the challenges they faced: "And having considered these and many other obstacles, and having tried many solutions, we decided upon one very difficult to be put into effect, which was to build ships in which we could leave. To everyone it seemed impossible, because we did not know how to make them, nor were there tools, nor iron, nor a forge, nor oakum, nor pitch, nor ropes, nor finally any single thing of all those that are necessary, nor was there anyone who knew anything about carrying this out" (*Narrative* 71–72). They ultimately resorted to the greatest taboo, cannibalism. The irony of the Europeans' engagement in a practice

they imagined and condemned in the indigenous peoples in what is now the southern United States is not lost on Cabeza de Vaca: "And five men who were in Xamho on the coast came to such dire need that they ate one another until only one remained, who because he was alone, had no one to eat him" (89–90). The total inversion of the traditional European fear of indigenous cannibalism is ironically underscored by the horror the native peoples express at the actions of the Narváez men: "The Indians became very upset because of this and it produced such a great scandal among them that without a doubt, if at the start they had seen it, they would have killed them, and all of us would have been in grave danger" (90). This is not the only occurrence of cannibalism described in the narrative; the survival of another Spaniard was guaranteed by his consumption of a companion, again related in the sparsest language: "And the flesh of those who died was jerked by the others. And the last one to die was Sotomayor, and Esquivel made jerky of him, and eating of him [Sotomayor], he [Esquivel] maintained himself until the first of March" (104). Thus, the narration of a gradual conversion of the protagonist from Western explorer to debased "savage" is inaugurated here by Cabeza de Vaca, and it will flourish in twentieth-century tropical adventure narratives.

22. It is worth noting that the lands Cabeza de Vaca traversed from 1527 to 1535 were, with the exception of Cuba, north of the Tropic of Cancer and therefore were not technically tropical. Yet as I have shown, geographical realities and scientific climatological distinctions (such as the Tropic of Cancer) have only a tangential relationship to the popularly imagined tropical world.

23. Malcolm Nicolson points out that for Humboldt, "the mathematical precision of the stars' orbit was just as valid a topic for study as their sparkle and its associated delights" (180). Nicolson argues that Humboldt's scientific precision is actually part of his Romantic formation, rather than a departure from it.

24. As Nigel Leask observes, Humboldt's writing reveals "a desire at once to grant America parity with Europe and Asia as an 'antique land' but also to insist upon its cultural *difference* from, and hierarchical subordination to, Europe" (258). See also Vera Kutzinski and Ottmar Ette's *Political Essay on the Island of Cuba*, part of a new series of translations and critical editions of Humboldt's work.

25. Martin Green explores gender in the adventure novel in *The Adventurous Male: Chapters in the History of the White Male Mind*, while Gail Bederman analyzes the link between manhood and modernity in the United States in *Manliness and Civilization: A Cultural History of Gender and Race in the United States, 1880–1917*. Both show that the advent of mechanized, industrialized society led to a crisis of masculinity because a large percentage of men were no longer required to perform manual labor. Adventures in foreign environments offered men a chance to prove themselves physically in a way that had become absent from contemporary Western society.

26. Indeed, the link between the two types of novels is strong: Thomas Mann once said in reference to *The Magic Mountain* that the bildungsroman was the sublimation and spiritualization of the novel of adventure (M. Green, *Dreams* 347).

27. This historical moment and rise of the novel make it clear why Spain has few adventure novels: since the Spanish Empire had largely reached the limits of its expansion by the time the novel became the dominant genre, there were few imperial goals for adventure novels from Spain to support.

28. Makman gives a partial list of popular remakes of *The Jungle Books*, including *Tarzan of the Apes* (1914) by Edgar Rice Burroughs, the first Mowgli film by Zoltan Korda (1942),

and the series of books and films by Disney beginning in 1967 (Makman xxxviii). Of these, Tarzan became an enduring cinematic and cultural figure in his own right; Kipling noted wryly that Burroughs had "'jazzed' the motif of the Jungle Books and, I imagine, had thoroughly enjoyed himself" (qtd. in Makman xxxviii).

29. Nyman demonstrates that the positive attributes of the Western colonizers are represented by "rational brown bears," while "native snakes and degenerate monkeys seek pleasure and self-gratification in denying the authority of colonial rule" (41).

30. Kipling's legacy in twentieth-century culture is at once profound and profoundly controversial. In his day, Kipling was famous for exposing the Anglophone readership to what he, and they, viewed as the exotic East. Edmund Gosse, in an early review of Kipling's work, praised the ability of Kipling's "devils of the East [to] reawaken in us the primitive emotions of curiosity, mystery, and romance in action" (qtd. in R. L. Green 108). Hannah Arendt called Kipling the "author of the imperialist legend" (169). As John Kucich notes, more recent criticism of Kipling has described his imperialism as "multivalent" (136). In his excellent summary of postcolonial Kipling scholarship, Kucich shows that interpretations of Kipling's work range from "redemptive leftist readings" that portray the author as an "avatar of Homi Bhabha" due to his examinations of racial and cultural hybridity in the Anglo-Indian colonial milieu to the more condemnatory view that despite his interest in colonial subjects, Kipling's conservative politics and propagation of British imperialism trump his sympathetic depictions of Indians (136–37). Writing in 2004, Benita Parry noted, "Now that the ideological right is on the offensive in the west, an even more favourable climate exists for Kipling's rehabilitation," stating that new editions of Kipling's work "are frequently buttressed with exculpations of his imperialist vision. Such readings draw on and abet the anti-anti-imperialism fostered by western ideologues eager to impugn postcolonial regimes, honour the colonialist legacy bequeathed by Europe and justify the continuing asymmetry between the hemispheres" (119). Contemporary critics continue to either condemn or reclaim Kipling's political and literary legacy, but none denies its potency.

31. Mount Roraima is a tabletop mountain in Venezuela on which the boundaries of Venezuela, Brazil, and Guyana converge. For such an inaccessible place, it has a rather extensive literary history. The first Westerner to see Roraima from below was the poet and explorer Sir Walter Raleigh, who determined it to be "a mountaine of Christall.... We saw it a farre off and it appeared like a white Church towre of an exceeding height.... [The guide] Berreo tolde mee that it hath Diamondes and other precious stones on it, and that they shined very farre off." (188). Later expeditions in the area fueled speculation about what the plateau might contain. In 1877, in the wake of debates over Darwin's theory of evolution in England, an editorial in the *Spectator* newspaper asked, "Will no one explore Roraima and bring us back the tidings which it has been waiting these thousands of years to give us?" (qtd. in Boddam-Whetham v). The mountain was finally scaled in 1884 by the Swiss scientist and explorer Everard Im Thurn. He later visited England and spoke at the British Geological Society and other explorers' clubs of which Arthur Conan Doyle was a member. Doyle's novel is inspired in part by Im Thurn's account of the area.

Indeed, this isolated wilderness seems fertile ground not just for scientific discovery but also for artistic creation. There have been at least four films made of Doyle's novel, the first in 1925 and the most recent in 1998. Radio shows of the Lost World have been popular as well, including one starring Leonard Nimoy. Michael Crichton's *Jurassic Park* is in part inspired by Doyle's novel.

32. Juan Durán Luzio argues that Humboldt's writings, popular in London at the time in which both Bello and Humboldt were there, were "a type of inspiration and a challenge to nostalgia, a sort of recuperation of his American life" (141). For Latin American writers, too, the sense of landscape was always tied to concepts of nationalism and personal history.

33. The full Spanish fragment reads: "Oh jóvenes naciones, que ceñida / alzáis sobre el atónito occidente / de tempranos laureles la cabeza! / honrad el campo, honrad la simple vida / del labrador, y su frugal llaneza. / Así tendrán en vos perpetuamente / la libertad morada, / y freno la ambición, y la ley templo" (Hills 40–41).

34. It should be noted that Misiones is located south of the Tropic of Capricorn, and is technically "subtropical" in climatic nomenclature. It is, however, part of the imagined geography of the tropics that I have discussed in this Introduction.

35. The translator, Earle K. James, renders "¿Qué hado maligno me dejó prisionero en tu cárcel verde?" as "What malignant fate imprisoned me within your green walls?"

36. As Andrea White has noted, "From within the [adventure] genre that had constructed the imperial subject, then, [Conrad] wrote a fiction at odds with the traditional assumptions of the genre that was being used increasingly in the service of imperial expansion" (5). See also Zweig.

37. In his biography of Rivera, Eduardo Neale Silva outlines Rivera's protests of the exploitation of rubber workers in Colombia. In his biography of Malraux, Olivier Todd recounts Malraux's public denunciation of the corruption of colonial justice that he perceived in Indochina.

38. Jennifer French admirably deconstructs the relationship between nature and neo-colonialism in *La vorágine* in *Nature, Neocolonialism, and the Spanish American Regional Writers*.

39. The Belgian Congo is now the Democratic Republic of Congo. Indochina was a French colony that in 1930 included what are now parts of Laos, Cambodia, Vietnam, and Thailand.

40. See Todd, *Une vie* 117.

41. For an excellent summary of texts that fed into the travelogue of the twentieth century, see Ette, particularly chapter 2.

42. For more on technological advances brought by colonialism, see Headrick.

43. This expression comes from Marlow's soliloquy early in Conrad's *Heart of Darkness*: "Now when I was a little chap I had a passion for maps. I would look for hours at South America, or Africa, or Australia, and lose myself in all the glories of exploration. At that time there were many blank spaces on the earth, and when I saw one that looked particularly inviting on the map (but they all look that) I would put my finger on it and say, When I grow up I will go there" (108).

44. Jorge Marcone has published an essay that is also titled "Jungle Fever." While Marcone's analysis of *Canaima* is innovative in that it examines the novel's engagement with environmentalism *avant la lettre*, my own approach differs in that I consider the text within the historical and literary context of its era.

45. Fabian defines these ecstatic states as "a dimension or quality of human interaction that creates a common ground," and argues that they are "a prerequisite for, rather than an impediment to, the production of ethnographic knowledge" (8).

46. "Il ne peut y avoir dans notre culture de raison sans folie" (Foucault, *Histoire de la folie* vi).

47. Foucault's *Naissance de la clinique* focuses on the eighteenth century in which the patient was subjected and confined by the physician's medical gaze. While not all historians agree with Foucault's assessment of the eighteenth century's confinement of madness, his approach has been of most use to literary scholars, and conforms most to my own critical orientation. For other interpretations on the history of madness and its relationship to literature, see Thiher; Sass; Rieger; Saunders and Macnaughton; Biasin; Porter.

48. Foucault maintains that "the historical ensemble—notions, institutions, judicial and police measures, scientific concepts … hold captive a madness whose wild state can never be reconstituted; but in the absence of that inaccessible primitive purity, the structural study must go back to that decision that both bound and separated reason and madness" (*History of Madness* xxxiii).

49. A. David Napier performs a fascinating analysis of the intersections of the language used to describe the foreign and the pathological in *Foreign Bodies* (25). The intrusion of a foreign body into both human individuals and a human society is described as an illness.

50. The scholars whose work on this topic is pertinent to my own include Richard Keller, Shoshana Felman, Sandra Gilbert, and Susan Gubar.

51. "Until the 1920s it was to France that Latin American students of science and medicine went if they could for their medical and biological training, and it was there that they aspired to be published and recognized" (Stepan, *Hour* 72). As the twentieth century progressed, the United States replaced France as the medical authority, but the growth of the South American medical establishment also resulted in more would-be doctors studying in their home countries.

52. For more on European sociomedical theories regarding Latin Americans, see Stepan, *Hour* 8.

53. Both Roberto González Echevarría (*The Voice of the Masters*) and Carlos J. Alonso (*The Spanish American Regional Novel*) have written on the telluric novels and their relationship to modernity.

54. Nouzeilles demonstrates with respect to the Argentine naturalist novel that "its plot develops the sequences of an irrefutable syllogism that instructs the citizen by means of a corroboration of a narrative hypothesis: the unhappy endings warn the reader of the dangers that he would confront if he violated biological laws which—according to the theories of the day, prohibited the mixing of certain bodies" (20). As I show in Chapter 3, a similar fear of racial mixing pervades *The Vortex*.

55. Marianna Torgovnick's *Gone Primitive* is a detailed study of the history and evolution of the notion of primitivism in the Western world. She notes, "Increasingly, as cultures once characterized as primitive have become actors on the world stage or come into contact with urban, technologica! societies, the word *primitive*—with its aura of unchangeability, voice-lessness, mystery, and difference from the West—has come to be understood as problematic" (20). Modernist authors and artists often presented the primitive as mad and vice versa because both were thought to operate independently of the maxims of rational thought.

Chapter 1

1. *Tropenkollered* was first used by the Danish sea captain Otto Lüken in his essay "Joseph Conrad and the Congo." Quoted in Griffith 126. *Tropenkoller* also exists as a noun with a similar meaning in German.

2. Conrad scholars have been divided regarding the academic citation of *Heart of Darkness*.

Most cite it as a book, even though it was originally published serially in *Blackwood's Edinburgh Magazine* on 22 February, 12 March, and 13 April 1899 (165: 193–220, 479–502, 634–57). It was published later as part of *Youth: A Narrative, and Two Other Stories* (1902), and many subsequent editions present *Heart of Darkness* as a stand-alone work. It is often categorized as a novella. In this study, I follow the majority of Conrad specialists in citing the text as a book, referring to the Oxford University Press edition.

3. For example, in an early essay, Barbara Gates interprets Kurtz's "moral insanity" against the background of Victorian theories of "alienation." In a more exhaustive fashion, Martin Bock thoroughly examines the impact of Conrad's medical preoccupations on the novelist's imagery of restraint, solitude, and water in *Joseph Conrad and Psychological Medicine*. Rod Edmond ("Returning Fears") demonstrates the prevalence of degeneration theory in Conrad's Malay fiction, while Robert G. Jacobs underscores Conrad's familiarity with the work of the Italian criminologist and phrenologist Cesare Lombroso, which is visible in *The Secret Agent* (Jacobs 78). Going against the common tendency to view Conrad as a nationless writer, Vilashini Cooppan shows how Kurtz's fate reverses Spencerian theories of progress and represents British fears of a "crisis of nationalism" (67).

4. Some critics construe Kurtz's madness in the wilderness as a "savage reversion" (Guerard 36), which likens him to the African population in *Heart of Darkness*. John Griffith shows how Victorian anthropological concepts such as cycles of degeneration and regeneration shape the presentation of Kurtz's decline even as Conrad mocks the notion of European progress (83–84).

5. Padmini Mongia offers an excellent summary of scholarship on race in Conrad, and she particularly critiques scholars who attempt to reduce Chinua Achebe's famous nuanced excoriation of Conrad as "simplistic" and "essentializing" (156). Cedric Watts and Hunt Hawkins both argue that Conrad was unconventionally progressive for his era, thus shielding him from charges of racism.

6. In other Anglophone fiction set in tropical locales, the menace of the jungle resides not only in the physical challenges of the climate, but also in its psychological conflicts. For example, several Kipling scholars have posited Kipling's India as a screen on which the author projects his own fantasies, fears and insecurities. Lewis Wurgaft reads the depiction of the jungle in Kipling as a veiled extension of his own psychological troubles: "Kipling's attraction to the passive and the violent elements in his nature led him to project these feelings onto India itself in a way that complemented the magical character of the colonial relationship. He produced as much a symbolic as a real landscape. The basic component of this projective process was the association of India with some primitive or elemental force" (132). Alan Sandison likewise proposes that for Kipling, India was a "symbolic screen on which the internal struggles of his protagonist were projected" (108). Their central insight—that the landscape in Kipling's stories is more symbolic than real—is the key to the far-reaching impact of Kipling's use of the term *jungle*, whose resonance and symbolism are heightened in Conrad's allusive prose. In his case, Freudian and Jungian psychoanalytic readings abound. Frederick Karl posits that the Congo exists as Marlow's dreamscape, rather than any physical location ("Introduction"). Joseph Dobrinsky reads Marlow's meeting with Kurtz as a sublimated oedipal encounter between Conrad and his father. Uzoma Esowanne argues that both of these interpretations are complicit in effacing and dehumanizing Africans in the text by willfully ignoring the geographical setting of the novel. Yet it is clear that *Heart of*

Darkness lends itself to a multiplicity of interpretations; it is both dreamscape and racist obfuscation of Africans' humanity.

7. Both Martin Green and Andrea White see Conrad as a linchpin in the transition of adventure literature from promoting to challenging the imperial project (M. Green, *Dreams* 332; White 5). Conrad's relationship to the British Empire was, however, more complex than a simple renunciation of its aims. His service to the British Navy and the Belgian Société Anonyme pour le Commerce du Haut-Congo show that he was a willing collaborator with imperial powers at the beginning of his career. His gradual evolution over the course of his life is evident in the fact that he declined knighthood shortly before he died in 1924.

8. McClure attributes the insanity of the main character of "At the End of the Passage" to his insights into his own condition: "Hummil has seen the true face behind the imperial facade; he has recognized, behind the image of the brave man with the stiff upper lip, the terrified child. And the vision drives him mad" (36). The combination of external rigidity and internal terror are typical of Kipling's protagonists even when they are not suicidal, and certainly show that while Kipling was undoubtedly a staunch imperialist, his colonial characters are not monolithic vehicles for propaganda.

9. Madness is present in the animal fables of *The Jungle Books* as well. In "Kaa's Hunting," the Monkey People, avatars of the Indian population, are portrayed as undisciplined and lawless; the jackal Tabaqui is "apt to go mad" and needs to be controlled by others (Nyman 44). In both his animal fables and his short fiction, Kipling intimates that madness is communicable, leading to fears of contamination of the colonist by the colonized. As Jopi Nyman argues, "The notion of contamination, a term with roots in medical discourse, suggests that the colonizer may not be able to govern the Other, a fear that in colonial discourse has been articulated as the fear of the uncontrollability of the natives, of their infectious panic" (45). As I will show, the protagonists of tropical adventure narratives frequently express these same fears of "going native" and of going mad, often eliding the two concepts.

10. Andrea White maintains that Conrad's narrator Marlow is different from "generic adventure heroes" because "he has been changed forever by his adventures and their attendant realizations so distance him from his audience that they can only be represented in an indirect, impressionistic telling" (181). While my work builds on her excellent comparison between Conrad's work and the adventure novel tradition, I go beyond her central thesis to show how madness is the driving force of Conrad's modernism.

11. Bock thoroughly explores Conrad's involvement with neurasthenia, water-cures, and other treatments for psychological ailments. He also traces evidence of these concerns in Conrad's fiction, most particularly the notion that Kurtz's lack of "restraint" is responsible for his degeneration (94–95). His exemplary work informs my own, but Bock fails to note the connection between Kurtz's madness and Conrad's modernism.

12. As Phillip Curtin notes, during the late eighteenth century, death rates of European troops in Africa were near 50 percent: "When the Sierra Leone Company took over the settlement [of Sierra Leone] in 1792–3, 49 percent died in the first year" (4). While the death rates during the late nineteenth century were much lower, the reputation of West Africa as the "white man's grave" was well established.

13. Fabian catalogs the extensive diseases and medications of the tropics (60–70).

14. For more on the effect of climate on colonists, see Kennedy 118–40.

15. Madness affected both upper and lower classes, but with different root causes,

according to nineteenth-century medical theories. Thiher is good in pointing out that madness attributed to degeneracy was linked to "genetically caused deviance in the poor, the hungry, and the exploited," as I show in Chapter 3. Elaborating on Morel's theory, Thiher states that "the degenerates of society are predestined to their alcoholism, crime, and insanity because their fathers were unhealthy. . . . Morel presents the interesting case in which a mediocre scientist was able to influence great writers" (204). In the case of affluent Europeans, madness was thought to be brought on by circumstance rather than birth.

16. For the impact of degeneration theory on Conrad's work, see Bock and Griffith. For an excellent study of the intersections of modernism and degeneration, see Edmond. The literary motifs of illness, degeneration, and neurasthenia were most frequently exploited by decadent writers as a reaction to the modernization of society. In female characters, illness was often called "hysteria," while in men "railway brain" was more common (Cooppan 66).

17. See Kennedy and in particular Woodruff, *Tropical Light* 3–4.

18. In *Joseph Conrad: The Three Lives*, Frederick Karl cataloged Conrad's many ailments on his return from the Congo: "Legs swollen, rheumatism in left arm and neuralgia in right arm, stomach in bad condition, hands swollen, nerves disturbed, palpitations of the heart, attacks of suffocation, malarial attack, dyspepsia" (307). Martin Bock adds that Conrad was also diagnosed with anemia, and that "if Conrad's list of physical problems seems to us so varied and complex as to defy an obvious diagnosis or course of treatment, the therapy recommended for Conrad is rather clearly in line with medical thought during the decade following his Congo voyage" (26–27). See Bock 27–30 for a complete list of Conrad's diagnosed medical ailments.

19. Conrad's original text reads, "Je pense que, vu mon séjour prolongé aux pays chauds (d'ou je viens de retourner dernièrement) et mon probable départ pour l'Afrique dans peu de mois il serait prudent de profiter du climat européen le plus longtemps possible" (Letter).

20. The letter was written on 22 May 1890, in Polish. An English translation appears in Jean-Aubry, *Life and Letters* 1: 126.

21. See Conrad's letter to Marguerite Poradowska, 26 September 1890, in Karl and Davies 1: 58–61.

22. See Woodruff, "Tropical Subjects" 773; for a discussion of the link between suicide and neurasthenia, see Bock 116–17.

23. This letter of 22 November 1898 is published in Karl and Davies 2: 121–22. Karl and Davies suggest that Conrad refers to *The Nigger of the Narcissus* in this letter (121). John Griffith dedicates an excellent chapter of his book to the intersections between Nordau's ideas and Conrad's *Heart of Darkness* (153–78).

24. Yuan-Jung Cheng argues that in *Heart of Darkness*, "madness is more enlightening than reason" (29). She reads Kurtz's madness as originating in the "alienation between head and heart" (38), and therefore disregards the historical forces, geographical realities, and medical theories at work in the novel.

25. Mikkonen incisively states that Marlow's "observing mind projects imaginary and madness-inducing qualities onto the immense forest" (303). She goes on to demonstrate similar tendencies in Céline's *Journey to the End of the Night* and Graham Greene's *Journey without Maps* (1936). While her work is perceptive, it does not take into account contemporary social theories about the ability of the forest to produce madness.

26. Passages such as these have become the subject of vigorous debate among Conrad and postcolonial scholars following Chinua Achebe's condemnation of Conrad as a "bloody racist" due to his depictions of Africans as surprisingly "not inhuman" (788).

27. I quote from Felman's preface to the second English-language edition of *Writing and Madness* (*Literature/Philosophy/Psychoanalysis*), originally published in French as *La folie et la chose littéraire.*

28. Not all scholars of the history of madness agree with Foucault's interpretation. For example, Allen Thiher's far-ranging study examines history of intersections of madness, medicine, and literature from Athenian drama to the postmodern. Throughout, he demonstrates that, in contrast to Foucault's argument, human confrontation with madness is characterized by continuity rather than rupture: "There has been a great unity on our tradition's understanding of madness, in spite of failed attempts during the Renaissance to recast medical thought and in spite of a tendency during the Enlightenment to reductively explain madness as a question of dysfunctional, mechanical physiology" (161).

29. For more on the exchange between Derrida and Foucault, see Downing 31 and Veit-Wild 1.

30. See Still and Velody for responses to Foucault's work.

31. This manuscript is held at the Beinecke Rare Book and Manuscript Library at Yale University. It is missing pages 1–10, 14, and 18–29.

32. Conrad edited this version by hand. It consists of thirty-five sheets, covering pages 1–58 out of the more than two hundred pages of the manuscript and is held in the Berg Collection of the New York Public Library. Two additional copies of the completed typescript, one sent to Robert McClure for copyright purposes and the other revised by Conrad before publication, have not survived.

33. This quote appears on page 227 of the manuscript and page 648 of the serial publication in *Blackwood's Edinburgh Magazine.* I have chosen to use the Beinecke's pagination rather than Conrad's own, as the latter was somewhat erratic.

34. Manuscript page 228; serial page 648.

Chapter 2

1. The best history of the colonial period in the region is Brocheux and Heméry's *Indochina: An Ambiguous Colonization.*

2. In addition to the clear parallels between *La voie royale* and *Heart of Darkness*, Malraux may also have been inspired by historical events: in 1888, a Frenchman named Marie-Charles David de Mayréna had declared himself king of Sedang in what is now southern Vietnam. Brocheux and Hémery give a summary of King Marie's brief reign.

3. In her memoir, Clara Malraux writes: "My daydreaming [about Cambodia] remembered (or did it foresee?) *Heart of Darkness*: we too were going to push up the river and go back into ourselves. And then again how could one fail to dream, more or less consciously, of one's childhood games, filled with cruelty, savages with spears, ritual feasts, slavery, torture, and of endowing oneself with strange powers?" (*Memoirs* 124).

4. For more on this possible ailment, see Todd, *Une vie* 21, 184, and Cate 6.

5. I have altered Howard Curtis's translation in order to be more specific. He renders "elle était phtisique, avec indifférence" as "she was consumptive, but neglected herself" (*La voie* 38).

6. While original estimates of attendance were based on the actual number of entrance

tickets sold (almost thirty-four million), later researchers have concluded that the number of actual attendees was lower (perhaps eight million). See Andrew and Ungar 305.

7. See the "Échelle comparative des 10 principales affections traité dans les hôpitaux d'Indochine en 1929" (Comparative scale of the ten principal afflictions treated in Indochinese hospitals in 1929) in Gaide n.p.

8. This translation is my own, as Stephen Becker's 1976 translation omits this section.

9. I have altered the first sentence of this translation to reflect Malraux's French more accurately.

10. Two statistics make the comparison clear: Dr. James A. B. Hobson wrote in 1867, "Not only has the European on leaving home a melancholy foreboding of a speedy termination of his existence but his relatives and friends also reckon him, from the day of his embarkation as amongst the dead; and to what extent these forebodings have been realized I leave the death-rate of the few Europeans who visit the coast to tell" (qtd. in Balfour and Scott 77). In contrast, according to Dr. L. Gaide, a campaign of "preventive quininization" was conducted in an uninterrupted fashion from 1922 to 1929 in Indochina, during which the number of people receiving quinine treatments increased threefold. While malaria continued to be the most common cause of death among hospital patients, the ratio of deaths to diagnosed cases of malaria declined overall during the same period (283, 298).

11. Clara Malraux notes in her autobiography that she and her husband were careful to use protective clothing and gear such as mosquito nets to guard against infection (*Nos vingt ans* 300).

12. In this translation, I have altered Howard Curtis's "retarded" to "senile" to reflect Malraux's *gâtisme* (senile decay).

13. See Joyeux 267–68 for more on the gradual debilitation caused by liver abscess in the tropics.

14. Stoler points out the ostensible link between sex and moral weakness in French society at the time: "It was through sexual contact with women of color that French men 'contracted' not only disease but debased sentiments, immoral proclivities and extreme susceptibility to decivilized states" ("Making" 647).

15. The French reads, "Le besoin d'aller jusqu'au bout de ses nerfs" (*La voie* 20).

16. I have altered Curtis's translation of this segment to highlight Malraux's wordplay.

17. I have translated Malraux's *langage de chair* (*La voie* 122) as "language of the flesh." Curtis does not translate the phrase at all.

18. The Association Amicale Santé Navale et d'Outre-Mer (Naval and Overseas Health Association) keeps an informative though biased record of the colonial French health corps' activities in Indochina and Africa during the first half of the twentieth century. The translations from ASNOM in this book are mine.

19. The Association Amicale Santé Navale et d'Outre-Mer (ASNOM) relates that throughout the nineteenth century, numerous authors attributed cases of "madness"—of mental alienation and psychological trouble—to malaria. In 1902, Comméléran dedicated his entire thesis to the subject of "Neurosis and Malaria." According to ASNOM, "Some patients, exhausted from a difficult stay and beset by frequent bouts of fever, showed periods of irritability followed by apathy. The malarial origin, according to the old authors, could be recognized by the fact that everything goes back to normal after a quinine treatment. The modern era, while confirming the parasitic impact of malaria on the brain, nevertheless discounts the notion that malaria causes madness."

20. Dr. Paul Hartenberg wrote in his treatise on neurasthenia: "Malaria frequently creates a neurasthenic state, common in colonials, and sometimes persisting for months after return home.... Syphilis, particularly in the secondary stage, is equally accompanied by asthenic symptoms" (54–55).

21. The presence of this doctor, clearly trained in Western medicine, reflects the historical record: in 1926, the colonial health services in Francophone colonies began permitting indigenous residents into French-run medical schools, most often training them in Hanoi (Gaide 5).

Chapter 3

1. See also Leonidas Morales, qtd. in Eyzaguirre 81. In more recent decades, *La vorágine* has undergone a critical revival. For examples, see Molloy; Alonso; and Sommer, *Foundational Fictions.*

2. There have been very few scholarly articles that focus on Cova's madness. Mauro Torres reads the novel as an oedipal struggle between Cova and Narciso Barerra that is resolved in the latter's demise. Sylvia Molloy's far superior "Contagio narrativo y gesticulación retórica en *La vorágine*" (Narrative contagion and rhetorical gesticulation in *The Vortex*) examines the novel as a *texto enfermo* (sick text) without the benefit of historical background. Luis Eyzaguirre explores Rivera's pathology in the context of Rivera's Romanticism.

3. See González Echevarría, *Myth* 142–53, and Alonso 139–54.

4. Sommer argues that national novels "fueled desire for domestic happiness that runs over into dreams of national prosperity; and nation building projects invested private passions with public purpose" (*Foundational Fictions* 7). She rightly recognizes that "the most daunting obstacle to heroic patriotism is Cova himself" (267).

5. The important exception to this general neglect is Gabriella Nouzeilles's *Ficciones somáticas.* While our books share a focus on medical and corporeal imagery, Nouzeilles's study analyzes late nineteenth century Argentine novels, and my work examines twentieth century fears of degeneration.

6. See Neale Silva 445 for an account of rumored diagnoses, and Charria Tobar 117.

7. This and most of the biographical information recounted here is taken from Eduardo Neale Silva's *Horizonte humano* (Human horizon), still the best work on Rivera's life.

8. It is unclear if this Gabriel Camargo Pérez is related to the Dr. Gabriel Pérez of Sogamoso mentioned by Rosselli. Camargo Pérez's mention of neurasthenia makes it seem that he had some sort of medical training in his background.

9. See Chapter 1 for my discussion of tropical neurasthenia (as compared to general neurasthenia).

10. Neale Silva corroborates that on his way to the United States, Rivera stopped off in Panama to see Javier Morán in order to "resolve any doubts about his state of health. There he received various documents and prescriptions" (415).

11. Freudian thought was introduced in Latin America by Víctor Raúl Haya de la Torre, the Peruvian doctor and politician who later distanced himself from Freud's ideas. Freud had a significant impact on popular psychological culture in Argentina during the middle of the twentieth century, but his influence on the rest of Latin American psychology has been less than in Europe and the United States.

12. "La selva de anchas cúpulas, al sinfónico giro / de los vientos, preludia sus grandiosos maitines; / y el gemir de dos ramas como finos violines / lanza la móvil fronda su profundo suspiro" (Rivera, *Promised Land/Tierra de promisión* 16).

13. The *Bulletin de l'Amerique Latine* was published in Paris, the center of medical knowledge for Latin Americans in the nineteenth and early twentieth centuries. Articles in the *Bulletin* were read by doctors in both Europe and the Americas and gave their authors an international prestige.

14. For more on these specific diseases, see Stepan, *Hour* 24 and 43.

15. For the link between patriotism and eugenics, see Stepan, *Hour* 36.

16. Alonso has noted, however, that the crimes Rivera denounced had all but ceased ten years before the publication of *The Vortex* (157).

17. See, for example, Alonso 139.

18. While it is clear that Rivera is tapping into both literary and medical lexicons in describing Cova's madness, I disagree with Ernesto Mächler Tobar when he states that Cova's madness is simulated for poetic purposes and is a result of Cova having witnessed the gruesome deaths of his compatriots (such as the decapitation of Millán earlier in the novel) (205).

19. In several instances, I have altered Earle K. James's translation (1935) for lexical clarity.

20. Dr. Antonio Gómez Calvo compiled a catalog of illnesses suffered by patients at the Asilo of Bogotá between 1900 and 1906 (Rosselli 246–47). It is notable that many of the conditions Rivera mentions in his novel are classified together as "neurosis" in Gómez Calvo's report: "Epilepsia, Histeria, Catalepsia, Neurasthenia" (qtd. in Rosselli 247).

21. For an excellent account of the Colombian literary climate of the time, see Neale Silva 166–70.

22. The Nicaraguan poet Rubén Darío was the founder of Latin American *modernismo*, an avant-garde literary movement of Latin America that fused symbolism with French Parnassianism. Seeking a pure aesthetic ideal, *modernista* writers often fetishized foreign art objects in their poetry. Darío established this practice in poems such as "Sonatina" in *Prosas profanas* (1896).

23. The Real Academia Española defines *catalepsia* as an "accidente nervioso repentino, de índole histérica, que suspende las sensaciones e inmoviliza el cuerpo en cualquier postura en que se le coloque" (a sudden nervous attack of the hysterical type that deadens sensation and immobilizes the body in whatever position it is placed).

24. I have altered James's translation to more closely reflect the Spanish here (*La vorágine* 131).

25. Miguel de Unamuno, author of *San Manuel Bueno, mártir* (1930) and one of the most prolific Spanish intellectuals of the twentieth century, was steeped in the positivist tradition. Like Arguedas, he discussed social and political problems using medical language.

26. I have altered James's translation here to reflect the Spanish original.

27. This is similar to Cabeza de Vaca's powers as a *curandero*, which he describes in his *Narrative*.

28. This scene evokes—perhaps unintentionally—the end of Arthur Conan Doyle's *The Lost World*, in which Professor Challenger, a preeminent renegade scientist, enters the wilderness of Venezuela and meets an ape that bears a resemblance to him in its features, carriage, and gestures. The scene is an ironic play on Darwinian theory and questions the superiority of the white race presented in the rest of the novel by creating resonances between the two supposedly divergent races.

29. Stepan points out that "the belief that many of the diseases rife among the poor—tuberculosis, syphilis, alcoholism, mental illness—were hereditary merely fueled the

fear of social decay" (24) and that Latin American eugenicists were predominantly concerned with "the Indians, the indigenous masses whose poverty and marginalization the eugenicists recognized" (150). Sexual relations between lighter and darker segments of the population were therefore thought to imperil the sexual health of both parties and their offspring (45).

30. I have again altered James's translation to reflect more precisely the Spanish original.

31. As Doris Sommer notes, Zoraida's "unproductive eroticism is unnatural, immoral, unpatriotic" (*Foundational Fictions* 266).

32. The phrase "witchery of the jungle" appears as "embrujamiento de la montaña" in the Spanish original (*La vorágine* 294).

33. The phrase "the jungle giddiness" appears as "el mareo de las espesuras" in the Spanish original (*La vorágine* 294).

34. Roberto González Echevarría wrote about this first in *Alejo Carpentier: The Pilgrim at Home* 28.

Chapter 4

1. As I explained in "A Note on Translations" at the start of this book, all page citations for *Canaima* in this chapter refer to the English-language translation by Will Kirkland unless otherwise noted. Likewise, all page citations for *Doña Barbara* refer to the translation by Robert Malloy.

2. As Carpentier would do later, Gallegos often capitalizes nouns in *Canaima* to infuse each object or person with a mythical, archetypal aura.

3. As Arturo Uslar Pietri states, "It was not a purely Comtian positivism that came to Colombia, but rather a hybrid mix of influences, as was the case in all of Latin America, and here, as in other countries, it was linked to Darwinism, atheism, anticlericalism, and literary naturalism and realism" (qtd. in Luna 33–34).

4. A clear and concise description of Zola and the advent of literary naturalism can be found in Brian Nelson's introduction to *The Cambridge Companion to Émile Zola*.

5. Other Latin American novels that demonstrate a debt to French naturalism include Eugenio Cambaceres's *Música sentimental* (1884) and Federico Gamboa's *Santa* (1903), the latter of which bears many affinities to Zola's *Nana* (1880).

6. All these stories are included in book 1 of *Obras Completas*.

7. I have altered translator Robert Malloy's rendering of Gallegos's *rictus* as "leer" and *fisiológico* as "physical" to keep them closer to the Spanish original (571), in order to illustrate the medical cast of the language.

8. See Arguedas's *El pueblo enfermo* (1909) and Zúmeta's *El continente enfermo* (1899).

9. Once more, I have altered Malloy's translation of "una personificación del alma de la raza, abierta como el paisaje a toda acción mejoradora" to better reflect the Spanish original (624).

10. For example, Gallegos was chair of psychology at the normal school in Caracas in 1912. According to Liscano, Gallegos obtained the post by answering the question, "How would you describe a hill to your students?" Liscano also tells us that Gallegos "was the only candidate" (67).

11. James was familiar with late nineteenth-century European and North American scientists' interest in South American indigenous groups, degeneration, and racial typing. While a student at Harvard in 1865, James went to Brazil with Dr. Louis Agassiz, professor of geology at Harvard and a preeminent anti-Darwinist who maintained that

human races, like plant species, were distinct. As Nancy Leys Stepan explains in *Picturing Tropical Nature*, Agassiz took photographs intended to "provide accurate visual evidence of the character of racial *hybrids*, or mixed race types, especially of evidence of the supposed degenerations caused by the mixtures which seemed so pervasive in the sensual climate of the tropics" (27). The issue of racial intermixing, particularly in Brazil, posed a problem to his theory that he sought to resolve by photographing "racial hybrids" and demonstrating their inferiority to "pure" racial specimens. Tellingly, he never published any demonstration of the inferiority of Brazilian subjects. Stepan's revision of his diaries shows that James was a skeptical member of the expedition. While his later writings on psychology would have a great impact on Gallegos, there is no evidence that James's trip influenced his *Principles of Psychology*.

12. Victoria Ocampo demonstrates this interest in *El viajero y una de sus sombras (Keyserling en mis memorias)* (The traveler and one of his shadows [Keyserling in my memories], 1951). As one of Argentina's wealthiest philanthropists and patrons of the arts, Ocampo significantly influenced intellectual currents in Latin America by funding publications such as *Sur* in addition to her own writings.

13. See Chapter 3 for more on degeneration and eugenics in Latin America in the first half of the twentieth century.

14. González Echevarría was the first to note this, in "*Canaima* and the Jungle Books" (337).

15. The original Spanish reads: "Como ocurre a su protagonista, Carpentier descubre que la selva está hecha de libros" (González Echevarría, "Introducción" 46).

Chapter 5

1. I have altered Harriet de Onís's excellent translation here in order to retain the idea of an encampment defended by stakes, rather than her "stockaded settlement." The Spanish text reads, "Se decía que [El Adelantado ...] se había hecho el rey de un palenque de negros huidos al monte hacía trescientos años, y que, según afirmaban algunos, tenían un pueblo defendido por estacadas, donde siempre retumbaba un trueno de tambores" (190).

2. John Incledon maintains that this passage was added later because it goes against much of the other descriptions in the novel (65). While it certainly does mark a departure from the narrator's other descriptions of the forest, there is no other evidence to suggest that it was a later insertion.

3. Roberto González Echevarría also analyzes this topic in his introduction to the novel ("Introducción" 50).

4. For more on the links between surrealism and mental and physical illness, see Matthews and Orban.

5. Lautréamont's *Chants de Maldoror* (1869) inspired Breton, who popularized the phrase "La recontre fortuite sur une table de dissection d'un parapluie et d'une machine à coudre" (qtd. in Caplán 157).

6. Carpentier consistently capitalizes the word *hechicero* in *Los pasos perdidos*, and I do so here so that the word retains the monumental and symbolic quality capitalization connotes.

7. Breton was able to read Freud even before his work was translated into French; see Matthews 34.

8. On Artaud and Carpentier, see Birkenmaier 177, 185, 190–92.

9. See Birkenmaier 155 and González Echevarría, *Alejo Carpentier* ch. 2.

10. "El estudiante" is frequently difficult to find, so I reproduce the Spanish version of this excerpt here: "Prendido a la mesa de metal por diez afilerazos helados, el paciente había sabido de guantes de caucho paseándose por sus vísceras, y, en menos de 22 segundos, su vientre había sido zurcido, con el gesto favorito de los sastres agazapados en sus mesas, mientras el hilo recorría ovillos de carne, y la aguja relucía, entre el pulgar y el índice, a la luz de las bombillas." According to Foucault, the Hôtel-Dieu was used as an insane asylum in the eighteenth century (*History of Madness* 103). I have been unable to ascertain whether Carpentier was aware of this coincidence.

11. Carpentier notes: "For Plato, free will had almost no effect on the bards' songs. Their inspiration was of a divine sort, and it was a kind of unknown flow that, coming from above, simply used a subject in order to transform itself into stanzas. Socrates affirmed that poets wrote by instinct, just as the seers, without any knowledge of what they were saying. The wry Cicero went further, saying, 'One must be demented to write good poetry'" ("El arte" 12).

12. In an additional article, "Médico y poeta" (Poet and doctor), published in his column "Letra y solfa" in *El nacional* on 27 October 1953, Carpentier further shows that he was well aware of the close relationship between medical matters and surrealist art. In this brief piece, he describes the "double life" lived by many artists and writers in order to make ends meet; in addition to writing, Carpentier worked for French radio and for an advertising agency in Caracas, so this issue was close to his heart. Carpentier mentions the life of the surrealist and psychologist Pierre Mabille as an exemplar of this dual path. Carpentier's veneration of Mabille shows that he was clearly mindful of the multiple intersections of surrealism and science, of art and medicine. These two disciplines were thus closely aligned in Carpentier's fiction of the time; the association between Western art and medicine would be equally as strong in *The Lost Steps* as it was in his "Letra y solfa" column.

13. In his later prologue to the novel, Carpentier admitted that the work bore too heavily the traces of the *vanguardia*, so much so that he had disowned it for many years. The Cuban critic Juan Marinello called the novel "a great unkept promise," lacking "an epic dimension" (174). The heart of the matter was that Carpentier had failed to make the Cué family fully realized characters; they remained sympathetically portrayed archetypes of Afro-Cuban culture. Carpentier recognized his own limitations in the novel: "I thought I knew my characters, but with time I saw that, by observing them superficially, from the outside, I had lost the deep soul, the biting pain" (*¡Écue-Yamba-O!* 8). Carpentier also laments his *vanguardismo* in the novel, particularly in the first chapter, which is reminiscent of surrealist and futurist description in passages such as the evocation of the great sugar mill (8). Indeed, Birkenmaier shows that in this first novel Carpentier "is still experimenting with the idea of using surrealist imagery to call attention to the poetic potential of the Afro-Cuban world" (79).

14. Perhaps the strongest and most persistent influence on his work from the avant-garde of the thirties, especially from his collaborations in *Documents*, is the refusal to privilege Western culture above non-Western culture. In one of the volumes of *Documents*, Leiris maintained that ethnography was a science "that is magnificent because it places all civilizations on the same footing and does not consider any of them as more valuable than any other" (qtd. in Birkenmaier 56).

15. For example, Birkenmaier states, "There exists a surrealist pattern which belies his later statements about the movement" (35). According to Raúl Caplán, "It is easy to see" in

The Lost Steps "how the critique of surrealism is accompanied by the recovery of a few of its themes, such as the idea of the chance encounter, but with the purpose of giving it a meaning that is not merely the fruits of the unconscious" (158).

16. Patricio Rizzo-Vast demonstrates the similarities between the fourth edition of *VVV* (1944) and Carpentier's reference to fantastical art in *Los pasos perdidos* (467). Birkenmaier also mentions the radio as example of importance of surrealism in the novel.

17. Celia Rabinovitch has written that in Bosch, "the surrealists found a sympathetic vision whose grotesque and secret iconography was, by definition, a surrealist form of painting" (61).

18. Carpentier coined the term *lo real maravilloso* (the marvelous real) to describe his unique literary style. He first mentioned the term in the article "Lo real maravilloso de América," but it became more widely known when the article was reprinted as the prologue to his novel *The Kingdom of This World.*

19. See Bataille's lectures for the Collège de Sociologie, particularly his two "Attraction et repulsion" articles in Hollier *Collège*. Michel Leiris studied the Dogon language of West Africa and possession rights in Ethiopia (Rabinovitch 109).

20. See López-Baralt 81–92. I will return to López-Baralt's insights on Carpentier shortly.

21. As González Echevarría has noted: "The topic of racial mixing was debated by Latin American intellectuals of the 1920s and 30s, in books such as *The Cosmic Race* (1925) by the Mexican José Vasconcelos. Against those who sought the Europeanization of Spanish America—like Sarmiento—many intellectuals of the modern era saw racial mixing as a possibility of cultural rejuvenation that was not available to Europe" ("Introducción" 147).

22. Harriet de Onís renders this description of Rosario as "her attire was of no period" (*Lost Steps* 83), but I have rendered *fuera del tiempo* (*Los pasos* 148) here as "outside of time" to emphasize that this characterization applies to more than simply her clothing.

23. In his article "A Detective Story: The Influence of Mircea Eliade on Alejo Carpentier's *Los pasos perdidos*," Tusa outlines the similarities between Carpentier's novel and Eliade's 1952 article "Symbolisme indien de l'abolition du temps" (Indian symbolism of the abolition of time). He perhaps overstates his case by arguing that the article "not only determined the structure, plot, and characters of *Los pasos perdidos* but also caused Carpentier to emphasize an aspect of his philosophical position which is unique in his oeuvre" (45).

24. Eliade's book *Le chamanisme et les techniques archaïques de l'extase* (*Shamanism: Archaic Techniques of Ecstasy*) was published in Paris in 1951 by Payot.

25. The English translation of *The Lost Steps* does not include this postscript to the novel. The original text reads: "Los indios descritos en la jornada 23 son Shirishanas del Alto Caura. Un explorador grabó fonográficamente—en disco que obra en *los archivos del folclore venezolano*—el Treno del Hechicero" (331).

26. Carpentier's description of the shaman is based on his research and involvement with the Servicio de Investigación de Folklore Nacional (SIFN) of Venezuela during his residency in Caracas. For more on his ethnographic activities, see Rogers "El órifco ensalmador."

27. In "Anthropologists and Other Frauds," Graham Huggan also notes the affinities between *Tristes tropiques* and *The Lost Steps*. However, he interprets Carpentier's work as a response to Lévi-Strauss's, because he mistakenly believes that *Tristes tropiques* antedates *The Lost Steps*.

28. I have translated Carpentier's "elogios de la locura" as "praise of madness" rather than Onís's "madness" to make the resonance with the author's earlier work clear. Roberto González Echevarría was the first to observe that this "King" is André Breton ("Introducción" 309).

29. Carpentier's uneasy negotiation between Old and New World cultures has led González Echevarría to state that Carpentier is "unable to be autochthonous at the moment of writing" (*Alejo Carpentier* 154). For example, even in his later *Explosion in a Cathedral* (*El siglo de las luces*), Carpentier perhaps unwittingly evokes the activities of the surrealists with a sense of wonder. With a conviction that echoes Breton, Dr. Ogé (a "doctor" and "*curandero*") states: "What we claim to do ... is to release the transcendental powers dormant in man" (*Explosion* 71). Furthermore, while in the Foreigner's Lodge, a gathering place for Freemasons in the novel, the main character Esteban is reminded of Ogé when he hears stories of miraculous cures through magnetism, people put into trances, and various forms of divination: "Extremes of subtlety had been attained in the interpretation of dreams, and, by means of automatic writing, they had held converse with the basic 'ego,' conscious of previous existences, which lies concealed within every one of us" (*Explosion* 103; *Siglo* 133). This list of activities, in particular automatic writing's contact with the ego ("*yo profundo*") is much more reminiscent of Carpentier's involvement with the surrealists than of the Enlightenment he purports to depict in the novel. These elements formed an essential part of Carpentier's aesthetic formation, along with his previously mentioned interest in the occult. Thus, even when the action of the literary works is transplanted to Europe, Haiti, or Venezuela, or set several centuries earlier, the psychological and literary results of Carpentier's years in Paris permeate his creations.

30. M. Ian Adams views the novel as an exploration of how the protagonist's alienation results in artistic creation.

Conclusion

1. In *The Green House*, Vargas Llosa explores the lawless, brutal side of the wilderness, particularly the exploitation and abuse of natural and human resources.

2. While I do not agree with McWatt that Mariella is also transformed into the Arawak woman (79), it is clear that here, as in other tropical novels, women's sexuality is explicitly linked to place: both are penetrated by the protagonists of these narratives.

3. Graham Huggan shows that Harris's postcolonial revision of the river voyage of *Heart of Darkness* seeks to move beyond "the prescribed limits of an imperial discourse" ("Anxieties" 2–3). Harris attains this postmodern accomplishment through the fantastical, allegorical nature of the novel in which the ultimate point of the journey is not a previous historical or geographical point, but rather the site of birth and death—the "Palace."

4. Regarding Schomburgh, Benítez Rojo acutely points out that this character is a nod to Richard Schomburgk's *Travels in British Guyana*, a book that heavily influenced Carpentier when he was writing *The Lost Steps* (188).

5. In this sense, *Palace of the Peacock* presents a strong contrast to *The Lost Steps*. As Jean-Pierre Durix argues, Harris's work differs from previous Caribbean novels because it "does not suggest that a return to a previous historical stage might constitute a radical step in the right direction" (86). Nevertheless, I disagree with Durix's assertion that Harris "offers no alternative utopia" to Caribbean realities. In Harris's postmodern novel, that utopia occurs only

in the deaths of the protagonists, which allows them to reach the Palace of the Peacock in the final pages of the book.

6. *The Storyteller* is often read within the context of Vargas Llosa's 1990 bid for the presidency of Peru. Kokotovic and Sommer (the latter in "About Face") both frame their readings of the novel within the broader scope of Vargas Llosa's role in defining contemporary Peruvian culture.

7. Misha Kokotovic points out the cultural hollowness of the chapters narrated by Saúl: "The narrative structure of *The Storyteller* privileges the narrator's position by making him the ultimate authority in the text, suggesting that his statements are indeed to be taken as authoritative.... The Machiguenga chapters, rather than constituting an autonomous narrative in an indigenous voice, are revealed to be the product of the Western narrator and therefore structurally subordinate to the Western narrative.... *El hablador* is based on ventriloquism, not dialogue, or even a tension between two genuine cultural alternatives" (453–54). The great irony of the novel is that the chapters in which Vargas Llosa's narrator purports to re-create the words of the storyteller only serve to underscore the impossibility of the task, as many critics (and indeed the narrator himself) point out. Vargas Llosa's novel is thus a self-reflexive tropical tale that, in the broadest interpretation, narrates the failure of the protagonist to bring Machigenga storytelling into the mainstream of Latin American literature.

8. The only possible exception to this is Carpentier, who was involved with Venezuelan ethnographic activities while he lived in Caracas. Yet, as I showed in Chapter 5, this interest in ethnography brought its own crisis of representation to the novel.

9. In this respect, *Mark and Olly* is similar to *The Vortex*, in that Rivera maintained that much of the novel was a faithful reproduction of events that transpired in the Vichada in the 1920s.

10. In May 2011, anthropologist Glenn H. Shepard Jr. published an exposé in *Anthropology News* called "The Mark and Olly Follies" condemning the show as a fabricated hoax. He also noted that the presence of the foreign film crew resulted in a dangerous cold epidemic in which four Machigenga died of respiratory infections (Shepard). In Anglophone anthropological circles the group's name is now rendered Matsigenka, while the Spanish transliteration is Machiguenga. I have used the more popular anglicized spelling Machigenga.

Bibliography

Achebe, Chinua. "An Image of Africa." *Massachusetts Review* 18.4 (1977): 782–94.

Acosta Cruz, María Isabel. "Writer-Speaker? Speaker-Writer? Narrative Cultural Intervention in Mario Vargas Llosa's *El hablador*." *Inti: Revista de literatura hispánica* 29–30 (Spring 1989): 133–45.

Adams, M. Ian. *Three Authors of Alienation: Bombal, Onetti, Carpentier.* Austin: U of Texas P, 1975.

Adorno, Rolena. *The Polemics of Possession in Spanish American Narrative.* New Haven: Yale UP, 2008.

Adorno, Rolena, and Patrick Charles Pautz, eds. and trans. *The Narrative of Cabeza de Vaca.* 1542. Lincoln: U of Nebraska P, 2003.

Aínsa, Fernando. "¿Infierno verde o Jardín del Edén? El *topos* de la selva en *La vorágine* y *Los pasos perdidos*." *Espacios del imaginario latinoamericano: Propuestas de geopoética.* Havana: Arte y Literatura, 2002. 103–48.

Alberdi, J. B. *Bases y puntos de partidos para la organización política de la República Argentina.* Buenos Aires, 1852.

Allaby, Ailsa, and Michael Allaby. "Köppen climate classification." *A Dictionary of Earth Sciences.* 1999. *Encyclopedia.com.* 10 July 2010.

Allan, Derek. "An Inhuman Transcendence: Perken, in Malraux's *La voie royale*." *Journal of European Studies* 25.2 (June 1995): 109–22.

Alonso, Carlos. *The Spanish American Regional Novel: Modernity and Autochthony.* Cambridge: Cambridge UP, 1990.

Andrew, Dudley, and Steven Ungar. *Popular Front Paris and the Poetics of Culture.* Cambridge: Harvard UP, 2005.

Araujo, Orlando. *Lengua y creación en la obra de Rómulo Gallegos.* 1956. 3rd ed. Caracas: En la Raya, 1977.

Arendt, Hannah. "The Imperialist Character (On Kipling)." *Reflections on Literature and Culture.* Ed. Susannah Young-Ah Gottlieb. Stanford: Stanford UP, 2006. 167–71.

Arguedas, Alcides. *Pueblo enfermo.* 1909. La Paz: Gisbert, 1975.

Arnold, David. "Illusory Riches: Representations of the Tropical World." *Singapore Journal of Tropical Geography* 21.1 (2000): 6–18.

Artaud, Antonin. "Lettre aux médecins-chefs des asiles de fous." *La révolution surréaliste* 3 (15 Apr. 1925): 29.

Ash, Beth Sharon. *Writing in Between: Modernity and Psychosocial Dilemma in the Novels of Joseph Conrad*. New York: St. Martin's, 1999.

ASNOM. *L'oeuvre humanitaire du corps de santé colonial français (1890–1968)/The Humanitarian Work of the French Naval and Colonial Health Services (1890–1968)*. Association Amicale Santé Navale et d'Outre-Mer, 2001–2011. *www.asnom.org*. 27 July 2011. Site in French and English.

Azuela, Mariano. *Los de abajo*. Ed. Marta Portal. Mexico City: Red, 1987.

Balfour, Andrew, and Henry H. Scott. *Health Problems of the Empire*. Glasgow: Collins, 1924.

Balza, José. "¿Se es o no se es?" Gallegos, *Canaima* (Minguet) xv–xvi.

Barceló Sifontes-Abeu, Lyll, ed. *Canaima ante la crítica*. Caracas: Monte Avila, 1995.

Beard, George M. *A Practical Treatise on Nervous Exhaustion* (*Neurasthenia*). New York: Putnam, 1883.

Bederman, Gail. *Manliness and Civilization: A Cultural History of Gender and Race in the United States, 1880–1917*. Chicago: U of Chicago P, 1995.

Bellini, Giuseppe. "Viaje al alto orinoco: Un posible antecedente de *Los pasos perdidos*." Meyran 17–27.

Bello, Andrés. *Selected Writings of Andrés Bello*. Trans. Frances M. López-Morillas. Ed. Iván Jaksic. New York: Oxford UP, 1997.

Benítez Rojo, Antonio. *The Repeating Island: The Caribbean and the Postmodern Perspective*. Trans. James Maraniss. Durham: Duke UP, 1996.

Benjamin, Walter. *Walter Benjamin: Selected Writings*. Ed. Marcus Bullock and Michael W. Jennings. Vol. 3. Cambridge: Belknap-Harvard, 2002.

Bernard, Claude. *An Introduction to the Study of Experimental Medicine*. Trans. Henry Copley Greene. Birmingham, AL: Classics of Medicine Library, 1980.

Bessiere, Jean. "Que l'on peut lire ensemble Conrad, Leiris, Cendrars, Butor: Le 'primitivisme' et son anachronisme; D'une pensée de l'histoire, de la littérature, et de son archéologie." McIntosh-Varjabédian 215–37.

Biasin, Gian-Paolo. *Literary Diseases: Theme and Metaphor in the Italian Novel*. Austin: U of Texas P, 1975.

Birkenmaier, Anke. *Alejo Carpentier y la cultura del surrealismo en América Latina*. Frankfurt: Vervuert, 2006.

Bloch, Oscar, and Walther von Wartburg, eds. *Dictionnaire étymologique de la langue française*. 6th ed. 4 vols. Paris: PUF, 1975.

Bock, Martin. *Joseph Conrad and Psychological Medicine*. Lubbock: Texas Tech UP, 2002.

Boddam-Whetham, J. W. *Roraima and British Guiana: With a glance at Bermuda, the West Indies, and the Spanish Main*. London: Hurst, 1879.

Borges, Jorge Luis. "The Ethnographer." *Collected Fictions*. Trans. Andrew Hurley. New York: Penguin, 1998. 334–35.

———. "El etnógrafo." *Elogio de la sombra*. Buenos Aires: Emecé, 1969. 59–61.

"Boys to Men." *Mark and Olly: Living with the Machigenga*. Travel Channel, 2009.

Breton, André. "Manifeste du surréalisme." 1924. *Oeuvres complètes* 311–46.

———. "Manifesto of Surrealism." 1924. *Manifestoes of Surrealism*. Trans. Richard Seaver and Helen R. Lane. Ann Arbor: U of Michigan P, 1969.

———. *Nadja*. 1928. Trans. Richard Howard. New York: Grove, 1960.

———. *Nadja*. 1928. *Oeuvres complètes* 645–753.

———. *Oeuvres complètes*. Paris: Gallimard, 1988.

Bristow, Joseph. *Empire Boys: Adventures in a Man's World*. London: Harper, 1991. Reading Popular Fiction.

Brocheux, Pierre, and Daniel Hémery. *Indochina: An Ambiguous Colonization, 1858–1954*. Trans. Ly Lan Dill-Klein, with Eric Jennings, Nora Taylor, and Noémi Tousignant. Berkeley: U of California P, 2009.

Brooks, Peter. *Reading for the Plot: Design and Intention in Narrative*. New York: Knopf, 1984.

Brushwood, John Stubbs. *The Spanish American Novel: A Twentieth-Century Survey*. Austin: U of Texas P, 1975.

Bueno, Salvador. "Alejo Carpentier y el fundador de ciudades." *Escritura* 9.17–18 (Jan.–Feb. 1984): 127–35.

Burroughs, Edgar Rice. *Tarzan of the Apes*. New York: McClurg, 1914.

Cabeza de Vaca, Álvar Núñez. *The Narrative of Cabeza de Vaca*. 1542. Ed. and trans. Rolena Adorno and Patrick Charles Pautz. Lincoln: U of Nebraska P, 2003.

Caldwell, Roy Chandler, Jr. "Mascarita's Metamorphosis: Vargas Llosa and Kafka." *Comparatist* 25 (May 2001): 50–68.

Camargo Pérez, Gabriel. "Rincones secretos de Rivera." *Cultura* (June 1946): 11–18.

Cameron, Douglas M. "Vargas Llosa and *The Storyteller:* The Failure of Ethnography and the Recuperation of Writing." *MACLAS* 6 (1992): 135–45.

Campbell, Joseph. *The Hero with a Thousand Faces*. Princeton: Princeton UP, 1971.

Caplán, Raúl. "Types et stereotypes dans *Los pasos perdidos*." *Le representation de l'espace dans le roman hispanoaméricain: "Los pasos perdidos" de Alejo Carpentier, "La vorágine" de José Eustasio Rivera*. Ed. Néstor Ponce. Nantes: Editions du Temps, 2002. 153–67. Lectures d'une oeuvre.

Carpentier, Alejo. "André Malraux, o el anhelo de la evasión." *Social* 16.5 (May 1931): 37, 74, 78–79.

———. "El arte de los locos." *Carteles* 14.30 (28 July 1929): 12, 50.

———. *¡Écue-Yamba-O!* 1933. Madrid: Alianza, 2002.

———. "El estudiante." 1929. *La gaceta de Cuba* Dec. 1989: 3.

———. *Explosion in a Cathedral*. Trans. John Sturrock. Boston: Little, 1963.

———. "En la extrema avanzada: Algunas actitudes del 'surrealismo.'" *Social* 13.12 (Dec. 1928). Rpt. in *Obras completas* 9: 125–31.

———. *The Kingdom of This World*. Trans. Harriet de Onís. New York: Farrar, Straus and Giroux, 1949.

———. "El Kodacrome y la etnografía." 1947. *Obras completas* 16: 99–103.

———. *The Lost Steps*. 1953. Trans. Harriet de Onís. New York: Noonday-Farrar, 1989.

———. "Médico y poeta." *El nacional* 27 Oct. 1953: 24.

———. *Obras completas*. 17 vols. Ed. Felix Baez-Jorge. Mexico City: SigloXXI, 1994.

———. *Los pasos perdidos*. 1953. Ed. Roberto González Echevarría. Madrid: Cátedra, 1985.

———. "Lo real maravilloso de América." *El nacional* 8 Apr. 1948: 8.

———. *El reino de este mundo*. Mexico City: Edición y Distribución Ibero-Americana de Publicaciones, 1949.

———. *El siglo de las luces*. 1962. Havana: Instituto del Libro, 1968.

Carreras González, Olga. "Tres fechas, tres novelas, un tema: Estudio comparativo de *La vorágine, Canaima y Los pasos perdidos*." *Explicación de textos literarios* 2 (1974): 169–78.

Castellanos, Jesús. "Rudyard Kipling." *Los optimistas*. Madrid: América, 1914. 71–114.

"Catalepsia." 21st ed. Madrid: Espasa Calpe, 1992.

Cate, Curtis. *André Malraux: A Biography*. London: Hutchinson, 1995.

Céline, Louis-Ferdinand. *Journey to the End of the Night*. Trans. Ralph Manheim. New York: New Directions, 1983.

———. *Voyage au bout de la nuit*. Paris: Noël, 1932.

Charria Tobar, Ricardo. *José Eustasio Rivera en la intimidad*. Bogotá: Tercer Mundo, 1963.

Cheng, Yuan-Jung. *Heralds of the Postmodern: Madness and Fiction in Conrad, Woolf, and Lessing*. New York: Peter Lang, 1999.

Chiampi, Irlemar. *El realismo maravilloso*. Caracas: Monte Ávila, 1983.

Clifford, James, and George E. Marcus, eds. *Writing Culture: The Poetics and Politics of Ethnography*. Berkeley: U of California P, 1986.

Collits, Terry. *Postcolonial Conrad: Paradoxes of Empire*. London: Routledge, 2005. Routledge Research in Postcolonial Literatures.

Columbus, Christopher. *The "Diario" of Christopher Columbus's First Voyage to America*. Abstracted by Bartolomé de Las Casas. Trans. Oliver Dunn and James E. Kelley Jr. Norman: U of Oklahoma P, 1989.

———. "Primer viaje a las Indias." *Diario de abordo*. Ed. Luis Arranz Márquez. Madrid: Dastin, 2000.

Comaroff, Jean, and John Comaroff. *Of Revelation and Revolution*. Vol. 1. Chicago: U of Chicago P, 1991.

Conley, Katharine. *Robert Desnos, Surrealism, and the Marvelous in Everyday Life*. Lincoln: U of Nebraska P, 2003.

Conrad, Joseph. *Almayer's Folly*. 1895. New York: Doubleday, 1923.

———. *The Collected Letters of Joseph Conrad*. Ed. Frederick R. Karl and Laurence Davies. 9 vols. Cambridge: Cambridge UP, 1983–2007.

———. "Congo Diary." *Congo Diary and Other Uncollected Pieces*. Ed. Zdzislaw Najder. New York: Doubleday, 1978.

———. *Heart of Darkness*. 1899. Oxford: Oxford U P, 2002.

———. "The Heart of Darkness." [1899.] TS. Berg Collection of English and American Literature, New York Public Library.

———. "The Heart of Darkness." MS Conrad 899h. Beinecke Rare Book and Manuscript Library, Yale University, New Haven.

———. Letter to the managing director of the expedition led by Mssrs. Walfords and Co. 4 November 1889, in French. Manuscript pasted into the first edition of Conrad, *Youth*, at Beinecke Rare Book and Manuscript Library, Yale University, New Haven. A typed copy of the English translation published in Jean-Aubry, *Joseph Conrad in the Congo* 27–28, is also pasted into this volume.

———. *Lord Jim*. 1900. Project Gutenberg, 2006. 25 Aug. 2010. *www.gutenberg.org*.

———. "An Outpost of Progress." *Complete Short Stories*. New York: Barnes and Noble, 2007. 31–49.

———. *Youth: A Narrative, and Two Other Stories*. Edinburgh: Blackwood, 1902.

Cooppan, Vilashini. *Worlds Within: National Narratives and Global Connections in Postcolonial Writing*. Stanford: Stanford UP, 2009.

Cornick, Martyn. "Malraux and Conrad: Imagery of Confrontation in *La voie royale* and *Heart of Darkness*." *Mélanges Malraux Miscellany* 15.1–2 (Spring–Fall 1983): 7–15.

Corominas, Juan. *Diccionario crítico etimológico de la lengua castellana*. 4 vols. Bern: Francke, 1954.

Cosgrove, Denis. "Tropics and Tropicality." Driver and Martins 197–216.

Cronon, William. "The Trouble with Wilderness; or, Getting Back to the Wrong Nature." Cronon, *Uncommon Ground* 69–90.

———, ed. *Uncommon Ground: Toward Reinventing Nature.* New York: Norton, 1995.

Curtin, Philip D. *Disease and Empire: The Health of European Troops in the Conquest of Africa.* Cambridge: Cambridge UP, 1998.

Cuvardic García, Dorde. "El hecho aventurero en *Los pasos perdidos.*" *Revista de filología y lingüística de la Universidad de Costa Rica* 26.1 (Jan.–June 2000): 15–26.

Darío, Rubén. 1896. *Prosas profanas.* Madrid: Espasa Calpe, 1964.

de Ferrari, Guillermina. "Enfermedad, cuerpo y utopía en *Los pasos perdidos* de Alejo Carpentier y en *Pájaros de la playa* de Severo Sarduy." *Hispanic Review* 70.2 (Spring 2002): 219–41.

Defoe, Daniel. *Robinson Crusoe.* 1719. Ed. Michael Shinagel. New York: Norton, 1975.

De Lange, Attie, Gail Fincham, and Wieslaw Krajka. *Conrad in Africa: New Essays on "Heart of Darkness."* Dublin: Social Science Monographs, 2002.

DeLoughrey, Elizabeth M., Renée K. Gosson, and George B. Handley, eds. *Caribbean Literature and the Environment: Between Nature and Culture.* Charlottesville: U of Virginia P, 2005. New World Studies.

de Onís, Harriet, trans. *The Lost Steps.* By Alejo Carpentier. 1953. New York: Noonday-Farrar, 1989.

Díaz, Nancy Gray. "The Metamorphoses of Maldoror and Mackandal: Reconsidering Carpentier's Reading of Lautréamont." *Modern Language Studies* 21.3 (Summer 1991): 48–56.

Dobrinsky, Joseph. *The Artist in Conrad's Fiction: A Psychocritical Study.* Ann Arbor: U of Michigan Research P, 1989.

Downing, Lisa. *The Cambridge Introduction to Michel Foucault.* Cambridge: Cambridge UP, 2008.

Doyle, Arthur Conan. *The Lost World.* London: Hodder, 1912.

Driver, Felix, and Luciana Martins, eds. *Tropical Visions in an Age of Empire.* Chicago: U of Chicago P, 2005.

Durán Luzio, Juan. "Alexander von Humboldt y Andrés Bello: Etapas hacia una relación textual." *Escritura* 12.23–24 (1987): 139–52.

Durix, Jean-Pierre. "Origins in *Palace of the Peacock.*" *Theatre of the Arts: Wilson Harris and the Caribbean.* Ed. Wilson Harris and Hena Maes-Jelinek. Amsterdam: Rodopi, 2002.

Echavarría, Arturo. "La confluencia de las aguas: La geografía como configuración del tiempo en *Los pasos perdidos* de Carpentier y *Heart of Darkness* de Conrad." Vásquez 159–86.

Edmond, Rod. "Home and Away: Degeneration in Imperialist and Modernist Discourse." *Modernism and Empire.* Ed. Howard J. Booth and Nigel Rigby. Manchester: Manchester UP, 2000. 39–63.

———. "Returning Fears: Tropical Disease and the Metropolis." Driver and Martins 175–96.

Eliade, Mircea. *Le chamanisme et les techniques archaïques de l'extase.* Paris: Payot, 1951.

———. *Shamanism: Archaic Techniques of Ecstasy.* 1951. Trans. Willard R. Trask. Fwd. Wendy Doniger. Princeton: Princeton UP, 2004. Bollingen Series 76.

Ellis, Elizabeth A. *André Malraux et le monde de la nature.* Paris: Lettres Modernes, 1975.

"End of the Affair." *Mark and Olly: Living with the Machigenga.* Travel Channel, 2009.

Esonwanne, Uzoma. "'Race' and Reading: A Study of Psychoanalytic Criticisms of Joseph Conrad's *Heart of Darkness*." De Lange, Fincham, and Krajka 271–98.

Ette, Ottmar. *Literature on the Move*. Amsterdam: Rodopi, 2003.

Exposition Coloniale Internationale. *Guide officiel*. Text by A. Demaison. Paris, 1931.

Eyzaguirre, Luis B. "Patología en *La vorágine* de José Eustasio Rivera." *Hispania* 56.1 (1973): 81–90.

Fabian, Johannes. *Out of Our Minds: Reason and Madness in the Exploration of Central Africa*. Berkeley: U of California P, 2000.

Fallaize, Elizabeth. *Malraux: La voie royale*. London: Grant, 1982.

Fanon, Frantz. *Black Skin, White Masks*. Trans. Charles Lam Markman. New York: Grove, 1967.

Felman, Shoshana. *La folie et la chose littéraire*. Paris: Editions du Seuil, 1978.

———. *Writing and Madness* (*Literature/Philosophy/Psychoanalysis*). Trans. Martha Noel Evans and the author, with the assistance of Brian Massumi. Appendix trans. Barbara Johnson. Palo Alto: Stanford UP, 2003.

Fernández de la Cuesta, Ismael. "La música, elemento natural de lo fantástico en la pintura de El Bosco." *El Bosco y la tradición pictórica de lo fantástico*. Madrid: Galaxia Gutenberg, 2006. 127–66.

Figueira, Dorothy M. *The Exotic: A Decadent Quest*. Albany: State U of New York P, 1994.

Foucault, Michel. *The Birth of the Clinic: An Archaeology of Medical Perception*. Trans. A. M. Sheridan Smith. New York: Pantheon, 1973.

———. *Folie et déraison: Histoire de la folie à l'âge classique*. Paris: Plon, 1961.

———. *History of Madness*. Ed. Jean Khalfa. Trans. Jonathan Murphy and Jean Khalfa. London: Routledge, 2006.

———. *Naissance de la clinique: Une archéologie du regard médicale*. Paris: PUF, 1963.

French, Jennifer. *Nature, Neocolonialism, and the Spanish American Regional Writers*. Hanover: UP of New England, 2005.

Frye, Northrop. *Anatomy of Criticism: Four Essays*. 1957. Fwd. Harold Bloom. Princeton: Princeton UP, 2000.

Gaide, L. *L'assistance médicale et la protection de la santé publique*. Hanoi: Imprimerie d'Extrême-Orient, 1931. Exposition Coloniale Internationale.

Gallagher, Thomas E. "Vargas Llosa, *The Storyteller*, and the Premature Demise of Ethnography." *MACLAS* 6 (1992): 121–33.

Gallegos, Rómulo. *Canaima*. 1935. Barcelona: Araluce, 1936.

———. *Canaima*. 1935. Trans. Will Kirkland. Ed. Michael J. Doudoroff. Pittsburgh: U of Pittsburgh P, 1996.

———. *Canaima*. 1935. Ed. Charles Minguet. 2nd ed. Nanterre: ALLCA XX, 1996. Colección Archivos.

———. *Doña Bárbara*. 1929. *Obras completas* 1: 493–806.

———. *Doña Barbara*. 1929. Trans. Robert Malloy. New York: Peter Smith, 1948.

———. "La necesidad de valores culturales." *El cojo ilustrado* 15 Aug. 1912: 439–42.

———. *Obras completas*. 2nd ed. 2 vols. Prologue by José López Pacheco. Madrid: Aguilar, 1959.

———. "Las tierras de Dios." 1931. *Una posición en la vida*. Caracas: Centauro, 1977. 1: 112–45.

Galton, Francis. *Hereditary Genius: An Inquiry into Its Laws and Consequences.* London: Macmillan, 1869.

Garelick, Rhonda K. "*La voie royale* and the Double Time of Art." *André Malraux.* Ed. Harold Bloom. New York: Chelsea, 1989. 181–92.

Gates, Barbara. "Kurtz's Moral Insanity." *Victorians Institute Journal* 11 (1982): 53–59.

Gaviria Alvarez, Germán. "Viaje y visión del ser en *Los pasos perdidos.*" *Cuadernos hispano-americanos* 649–50 (July–Aug. 2004): 61–68.

Geddes, Jennifer L. "A Fascination for Stories: The Call to Community and Conversion in Mario Vargas Llosa's *The Storyteller.*" *Literature and Theology* 10.4 (Dec. 1996): 28–41.

Gerbi, Antonello. *Nature in the New World: From Christopher Columbus to Gonzalo Fernández de Oviedo.* 1975. Trans. Jeremy Moyle. Pittsburgh: U Pittsburgh P, 1985.

Gilbert, Sandra M., and Susan Gubar. *The Madwoman in the Attic: The Woman Writer and the Nineteenth-Century Literary Imagination.* New Haven: Yale UP, 1979.

Gilman, Charlotte Perkins. *The Charlotte Perkins Gilman Reader.* Ed. Jane A. Lane. New York: Pantheon, 1980.

González, Eduardo. "*Los pasos perdidos*, el azar y la aventura." *Revista iberoamericana* 38.81 (1972): 585–613.

González Echevarría, Roberto. *Alejo Carpentier: The Pilgrim at Home.* Ithaca: Cornell UP, 1977.

———. "*Canaima* and the Jungle Books." Gallegos, *Canaima* (Kirkland) 331–48.

———. "*Canaima* y los libros de la selva." *Casa de las Américas* 201 (1995): 22–31. Rpt. in *Literatura y cultura venezolanas: Ponencias del Coloquio literatura y cultura venezolana.* Centre d'Etudes de Littérature Vénézuelienne, Paris, 11, 12, and 13 May 1995. Caracas: Bello, 1996. Rpt. in Gallegos, *Canaima* (Minguet) 503–17.

———. "Introducción." *Los pasos perdidos.* Ed. Roberto González Echevarría. Madrid: Cátedra, 1985.

———. *Myth and Archive: A Theory of Latin American Narrative.* 1990. 2nd ed. Durham: Duke UP, 1998.

———. *The Voice of the Masters: Writing and Authority in Modern Latin American Literature.* Austin: U of Texas P, 1985.

Gosse, Edmund. "Rudyard Kipling." *Century* 42 (Oct. 1891): 901–10. R. L. Green 105–24.

Gould, Peter, and Rodney White. *Mental Maps.* 2nd ed. New York: Routledge, 1986.

Gouru, Pierre. *Les pays tropicaux.* Paris: PUF, 1947.

———. *The Tropical World: Its Social and Economic Conditions and Its Future Status.* Trans. S. H. Beaver and E. D. Laborde. New York: Wiley, 1966.

Green, Martin Burgess. *The Adventurous Male: Chapters in the History of the White Male Mind.* University Park: Pennsylvania State UP, 1993.

———. *Dreams of Adventure, Deeds of Empire.* London: Routledge, 1980.

Green, Robert Lancelyn, ed. *Kipling: The Critical Heritage.* New York: Barnes and Noble, 1971.

Greene, Graham. *Journey without Maps.* London: Heinemann, 1978.

Greenfeld, Anne Miriam. "Malraux's *La voie royale* as a Royal Road of Regression." *LittéRéalité* 13.2 (Autumn–Winter 2001): 23–36.

Griffith, John W. *Joseph Conrad and the Anthropological Dilemma: "Bewildered Traveller."* Oxford: Clarendon, 1995.

Grove, Richard H. *Green Imperialism: Colonial Expansion, Tropical Island Edens, and the Origins of Environmentalism, 1600–1860.* Cambridge: Cambridge UP, 1995.

Guerard, Albert J. *Conrad the Novelist.* New York: Atheneum, 1967.

Guerrero, Gustavo. "De las notas a la novela: El memorándum de Gallegos y la génesis de *Canaima*." Gallegos *Canaima* (Minguet) 359–76.

Güiraldes, Ricardo. *Don Segundo Sombra*. Madrid: Espasa Calpe, 1934.

Gutiérrez-Vega, Zenaida. "El mundo de los personajes en *La vorágine*. *Revista de estudios hispánicos* 5.2 (May 1971): 131–46.

Hampson, Robert. "'Heart of Darkness' and 'The Speech That Cannot Be Silenced.'" *English: Journal of the English Association* 39.163 (Spring 1990): 15–31.

Harris, Wilson. *Palace of the Peacock*. London: Faber, 1988.

Hartenberg, Paul. *Treatment of Neurasthenia*. Edinburgh: Frowde, 1914. Oxford Medical Publications.

Harvey, Sally. "Alejo Carpentier: Travel and Perspective." *Travellers' Tales, Real and Imaginary, in the Hispanic World and Its Literature*. Ed. Alun Kenwood. Melbourne: Voz Hispánica, 1993. 75–90.

Hawkins, Hunt. "The Issue of Racism in *Heart of Darkness*." *Conradiana* 14.3 (1982): 163–71.

Headrick, Daniel R. *The Tools of Empire: Technology and European Imperialism in the Nineteenth Century*. New York: Oxford UP, 1981.

"Heaven or Hell." *Mark and Olly: Living with the Machigenga*. Travel Channel, 2009.

Hegel, Georg W. F. *The Philosophy of History*. Kitchener, Canada: Batoche, 2001.

Hernández de López, Ana María, ed. *Mario Vargas Llosa: Opera omnia*. Madrid: Pliegos, 1994.

Hills, Elijah Clarence, ed. *The Odes of Bello, Olmedo, and Heredia*. New York: Putnam, 1920.

Hollier, Denis. *Le Collège de Sociologie, 1937–1939*. Paris: Gallimard, 1979.

———, ed. *Documents, 1929–1930*. Paris: Jean-Michel Place, 1992.

———, ed. *A New History of French Literature*. Cambridge: Harvard UP, 1989.

Hudson, W. H. *Green Mansions*. 1904. New York: Dover, 1989.

Huggan, Graham. "Anthropologists and Other Frauds." *Comparative Literature* 46.2 (Spring 1994): 113–28.

———. "Anxieties of Influence: Conrad in the Caribbean." *Commonwealth* 11.1 (1988): 1–12.

Humboldt, Alexander von. *Personal Narrative of Travels to the Equinoctial Regions of the New Continent*. 1807–1834. Abridged edition. Ed. and trans. Jason Wilson. Introd. Malcolm Nicolson. New York: Penguin, 1996.

Hunter, Allan. *Joseph Conrad and the Ethics of Darwinism: The Challenges of Science*. London: Croom Helm, 1983.

Incledon, John. "The Writing Lesson in *Los pasos perdidos*." *Siglo XX/Twentieth Century* 8.1–2 (1990–1991): 55–68.

"Interviews with Mark and Olly." *Mark and Olly: Living with the Machigenga*. Travel Channel, 2009.

Isaacs, Jorge. *María*. 1867. Ed. Donald McGrady. Madrid: Cátedra, 1986.

Jacobs, Robert G. "Comrade Ossipon's Favorite Saint: Lombroso and Conrad." *Nineteenth Century Fiction* 23.1 (June 1968): 74–84.

James, William. *Principles of Psychology*. Vol. 1. 1890. Cambridge, MA: Harvard UP, 1981.

———. *Talks to Teachers on Psychology and to Students on Some of Life's Ideals*. New York: Holt, 1899.

Jean-Aubry, G. *Joseph Conrad in the Congo*. Boston: Little, 1926.

———. *Joseph Conrad: Life and Letters*. London: Heinemann, 1927.

Johnson, A. James M. "Into Africa: 'The Black Savages and the White Slaves' in Joseph Conrad's 'An Outpost of Progress.'" *English Language Notes* 334 (June 1996): 62–70.

———. "Victorian Anthropology, Racism, and *Heart of Darkness*." *Ariel* 28.4 (October 1997): 111–31.

Joyeux, Charles. *Précis de médicine coloniale*. Paris: Masson, 1927.

"Jungle." *Oxford English Dictionary*. 2nd ed. 1989.

"Jungle fever." *Oxford English Dictionary*. 2nd ed. 1989.

Karl, Frederick R. "Introduction to the Danse Macabre: Conrad's *Heart of Darkness*." *Heart of Darkness*. By Joseph Conrad. Ed. Ross C. Murfin. Boston: St. Martin's, 1989. 123–38.

———. *Joseph Conrad: The Three Lives*. New York: Farrar, 1979.

Karl, Frederick R., and Laurence Davies, eds. *Collected Letters of Joseph Conrad*. 9 vols. Cambridge: Cambridge UP, 1983–2007.

Keller, Richard C. *Colonial Madness: Psychiatry in French North Africa*. Chicago: U of Chicago P, 2007.

Kennedy, Dane. "The Perils of the Midday Sun: Climatic Anxieties in the Colonial Tropics." *Imperialism and the Natural World*. Ed. John MacKenzie. Manchester: Manchester UP, 1990. 118–40.

Keyserling, Hermann. *Meditaciones suramericanas*. Trans. Luis López-Ballesteros y de Torres. Madrid: Espasa Calpe, 1933.

———. *South American Meditations*. New York: Harper, 1932.

Kipling, Rudyard. *The Jungle Books*. 1894–1895. Ed. Lisa Makman. New York: Barnes and Noble, 2004.

———. *Plain Tales from the Hills*. Garden City: Doubleday, 1899.

Klein, Ernest D. *A Comprehensive Etymological Dictionary of the English Language*. 2 vols. New York: Elsevier, 1996.

Kokotovic, Misha. "Mario Vargas Llosa Writes Of(f) the Native: Modernity and Cultural Heterogeneity in Peru." *Revista canadiense de estudios hispánicos* 25.3 (2001): 445–67.

Kristal, Efraín. *The Temptation of the Word: The Novels of Mario Vargas Llosa*. Nashville: Vanderbilt UP, 1998.

Kucich, John. *Imperial Masochism: British Fiction, Fantasy, and Social Class*. Princeton: Princeton UP, 2007.

Kutzinski, Vera M., and Ottmar Ette, eds. *Political Essay on the Island of Cuba*. By Alexander von Humboldt. Trans. J. Bradford Anderson, Vera M. Kutzinski, and Anja Becker. Chicago: U of Chicago P, 2011.

Langlois, Walter G. *André Malraux: The Indochine Adventure*. New York: Praeger, 1966.

Leask, Nigel. *Curiosity and the Aesthetics of Travel Writing, 1770–1840*. Oxford: Oxford UP, 2002.

Lefebvre, Henri. *The Production of Space*. Oxford: Blackwell, 1991.

Lévi-Strauss, Claude. *Tristes tropiques*. Paris: Plon, 1955.

Lewis, Pericles. *Modernism, Nationalism, and the Novel*. Cambridge: Cambridge UP, 2000.

Liscano, Juan. *Rómulo Gallegos y su tiempo*. Caracas: Monte Avila, 1980.

López-Baralt, Mercedes. "Los pasos encontrados de Lévi-Strauss y Alejo Carpentier: Literatura y antropología en el siglo veinte." *Revista del Centro de Estudios Avanzados de Puerto Rico y el Caribe* 7 (July–Dec. 1988): 81–92.

Lost. ABC, Sept. 2004–May 2010.

Lüken, Otto. "Joseph Conrad and the Congo." *London Mercury* 22.130 (Aug. 1930): 350.

Luna, José Ramón. *El positivismo en la historia del pensamiento venezolano.* Caracas: Arte, 1971.

Mächler Tobar, Ernesto. "El hombre enfrenta la selva: De *La vorágine* a *Los pasos perdidos* por *La voie royale.*" Vásquez 199–212.

Makman, Lisa. Introd. and notes. *The Jungle Books.* By Rudyard Kipling. 1894–1895. New York: Barnes and Noble, 2004.

Malraux, André. *La condition humaine.* Paris: Gallimard, 1933.

———. *Les conquérants.* Paris: Grasset, 1928.

———. *The Conquerors.* Trans. Stephen Becker. New York: Holt, 1976.

———. *Man's Fate.* Trans. Haakon M. Chevalier. New York: Modern Library, 1961.

———. *La voie royale.* 1930. Preface, commentary, and notes by Christiane Moatti. Paris: Grasset, 1992.

———. *Way of the Kings.* Trans. Howard Curtis. London: Hesperus, 2005.

Malraux, Clara. *Memoirs.* New York: Farrar, 1967.

———. *Nos vingt ans.* Paris: Grasset, 1966.

Manson, Patrick. *Tropical Diseases.* New York: William Word, 1898.

Marcone, Jorge. "Cultural Criticism and Sustainable Development in Amazonia: A Reading from the Spanish-American Romance of the Jungle." *Hispanic Journal* 19.2 (Fall 1998): 281–94.

———. "Jungle Fever: Primitivism in Environmentalism: Rómulo Gallegos's *Canaima* and the Romance of the Jungle." *Primitivism and Identity in Latin America: Essays on Art, Literature, and Culture.* Ed. Erik Camayd-Freixas and José Eduardo González. Tucson: U of Arizona P, 2000. 157–72.

Marinello, Juan. "Una novela cubana." *Literatura hispanoamericana: Hombres y meditaciones.* Mexico City: Ediciones de la Universidad Nacional de México, 1937. 167–78.

Mark and Olly: Living with the Machigenga. Travel Channel, 2009.

Martínez-San Miguel, Yolanda. "Una lectura del origen en el Nuevo Mundo: La re-escritura de la crónica en *Los pasos perdidos.*" *Lucero* 3 (Spring 1992): 19–27.

Mason, Peter. *Infelicities: Representations of the Exotic.* Baltimore: Johns Hopkins UP, 1998.

Matthews, J. H. *Surrealism, Insanity, and Poetry.* Syracuse: Syracuse UP, 1982.

McClure, John A. *Kipling and Conrad: The Colonial Fiction.* Cambridge: Harvard UP, 1981.

McIntosh-Varjabédian, Fiona, ed. *Discours sur le primitif.* Paris: Université Charles-de-Gaulle, 1992. Collection UL3 travaux et recherches.

McKusick, James. *Green Writing: Romanticism and Ecology.* New York: St. Martin's, 2000.

McWatt, Mark. "Libidinous Landscapes: Sexual Inscriptions of Place in Guyanese Literature." *Commonwealth Essays and Studies* 25.2 (Spring 2003): 73–82.

Meyran, Daniel, ed. *La représentation de l'space hispano-américain: "Los pasos perdidos" de Alejo Carpentier et "La vorágine" de José Eustasio Rivera.* Perpignan: CRILAUP, 2002.

Michael, Marion, and Wilkes Berry. "The Typescript of 'The Heart of Darkness.'" *Conradiana* 12.2 (1980): 147–55. Rpt. in *Joseph Conrad's Heart of Darkness: A Casebook.* Ed. Gene M. Moore. London: Oxford UP, 2004.

Mikkonen, Kai. "'It is Not the Fully Conscious Mind Which Chooses West Africa in Preference to Switzerland': The Rhetoric of the Mad African Forest in Conrad, Céline, and Greene." *Comparative Critical Studies* 5.2–3 (2008): 301–15.

Minguet, Charles, ed. *Canaima.* By Rómulo Gallegos. 1935. 2nd ed. Nanterre, France: ALLCA XX, 1996. Colección Archivos.

Molloy, Sylvia. "Contagio narrativo y gesticulación retórica en *La vorágine*." *La vorágine: Textos críticos.* Ed. Monserrat Ordóñez. Bogotá: Alianza, 1987.

Mongia, Padmini. "The Rescue: Conrad, Achebe, and the Critics." *Conradiana* 33.2 (2001): 153–63.

Montesquieu. *De l'esprit des lois.* 1748. Paris: Garnier Frères, n.d.

———. *The Spirit of the Laws.* 1748. Trans. and ed. Anne M. Cohler, Basia Carolyn Miller, and Harold Samuel Stone. Cambridge: Cambridge UP, 1989.

Morel, Bénédict-Augustin. *Traité des degenerescences physiques, intellectuelles et morales de l'espece humaine.* Paris: Masson, 1857.

Morin, Henry G. S. *Sur la lutte contre le paludisme dans les collectivités ouvrières (Est Cochinchine et Sud-Annam): Essai de prophylaxie rationnelle et pratique à l'usage des exploitations agricoles, industrielles et forestières des chantiers de travaux publics et de chemin de fer, etc. . . .* Hanoi: Imprimerie d'Extrême Orient, 1931. Exposition Coloniale Internationale, Indochine Française, Section des Services D'Intérêt Social, Inspection Générale du Travail de l'Indochine.

Moura, Jean-Marc. "Le primitive selon André Breton: Le mythe et l'humour." McIntosh-Varjabédian 153–66.

Muller, Gregor. *Colonial Cambodia's "Bad Frenchmen": The Rise of French Rule and the Life of Thomas Caraman, 1840–1887.* New York: Routledge, 2006.

Mutis, Álvaro. *Amirbar.* Bogotá: Norma, 1980.

———. *La nieve del almirante.* Madrid: Alianza, 1986.

Myers, Gerald E. "Introduction: The Intellectual Context." *Principles of Psychology.* By William James. Vol. 1. Cambridge, MA: Harvard UP, 1981.

Najder, Zdzislaw, ed. *Heart of Darkness with The Congo Diary and Up-River Book by Joseph Conrad.* London: Hesperus, 2002.

Napier, A. David. *Foreign Bodies: Performance, Art, and Symbolic Anthropology.* Berkeley: U of California P, 1992.

Neale Silva, Eduardo. *Horizonte humano: Vida de José Eustasio Rivera.* Madison: U of Wisconsin P, 1960.

Nelson, Brian. *The Cambridge Companion to Émile Zola.* Cambridge: Cambridge UP, 2007.

The New Oxford Annotated Bible. Ed. Bruce M. Metzger and Roland E. Murphy. New York: Oxford UP, 1991. New Revised Standard Version.

Nicolson, Malcolm. "Alexander von Humboldt and the Geography of Vegetation." *Romanticism and the Sciences.* Ed. Andrew Cunningham and Nicholas Jardine. Cambridge: Cambridge UP, 1990. 169–85.

Nordau, Max. *Degeneration.* New York: Appleton, 1895. Trans. of *Entartung.*

Nouzeilles, Gabriela. *Ficciones somáticas: Naturalismo, nacionalismo y políticas médicas del cuerpo (Argentina 1880–1910).* Rosario: Beatriz Viterbo, 2000.

Nyman, Jopi. *The Postcolonial Animal Tale from Kipling to Coetzee.* New Delhi: Atlantic, 2003.

Obregón Torres, Diana. *Sociedades científicas en Colombia: La invención de una tradición, 1859–1936.* Bogotá: Colección Bibliográfica Banco de la República, 1992.

Ocampo, Victoria. *El viajero y una de sus sombras (Keyserling en mis memorias).* Buenos Aires: Sudamericana, 1951.

Ogede, Ode S. "Phantoms Mistaken for a Human Face: Race and the Construction of the African Woman's Identity in Joseph Conrad's *Heart of Darkness*." *The Foreign Woman in British Literature.* Westport: Greenwood, 1999. 127–38.

O'Hanlon, Redmond. *Joseph Conrad and Charles Darwin: The Influence of Scientific Thought on Conrad's Fiction*. Edinburgh: Salamander, 1984.

Orban, Clara. *Surrealist Case Studies: Literature, the Arts and Medicine*. New Orleans: UP of the South, 2001.

Ordoñez Vila, Montserrat, ed. *La vorágine: Textos críticos*. Bogotá: Alianza, 1987.

Paris, Bernard J. *Conrad's Charlie Marlow: A New Approach to "Heart of Darkness" and Lord Jim*. New York: Palgrave Macmillan, 2005.

Parrinder, Patrick. *"Heart of Darkness*: Geography as Apocalypse." *Fin de Siècle, Fin du Globe*: Fears and Fantasies of the Late Nineteenth Century. Ed. John Stokes. New York: Macmillan, 1992. 85–101.

Parry, Benita. "The Content and Discontents of Kipling's Imperialism." *Postcolonial Studies: A Materialist Critique*. London: Routledge, 2004.

Pauly, Véronique. "The Logic of Delirium in *Lord Jim*." *L'epoque conradienne* 30 (Jan. 2004): 171–83.

Pedlar, Valerie. *"The Most Dreadful Visitation": Male Madness in Victorian Fiction*. Liverpool: Liverpool UP, 2006.

Perés, Ramón D., trans. *El libro de las tierras vírgenes*. 3rd ed. Barcelona: Guinart, 1918. Trans. of Kipling *Jungle Books*.

Pérez Firmat, Gustavo. *"Ese Idioma*: Alejo Carpentier's Tongue Ties." *Symposium* Fall 2007: 183–97.

Plato. *Phaedrus*. Ed. and trans. Christopher Rowe. New York: Penguin, 2005.

Porter, Roy. *Madness: A Brief History*. Oxford: Oxford UP, 2002.

Pratt, Mary Louise. *Imperial Eyes: Travel Writing and Transculturation*. London: Routledge, 1992.

Prodoscimi, María del Carmen. *"The Storyteller*, Mario Vargas Llosa's Two Tales of the Amazon." *Américas* 41.2 (Mar. 1989): 22–27.

Quiroga, Horacio. *Cuentos completos*. Ed. Leonardo Garet. Tomo 2. Buenos Aires: Cruz del Sur, 2002.

———. *Cuentos de amor de locura y de muerte*. 1917. Palencia: Menoscuarto, 2004.

———. *Cuentos de la selva*. 1918. Barcelona: Muchnik, 1999.

———. *The Decapitated Chicken and Other Stories*. Trans. Margaret Sayers Peden. Austin: U of Texas P, 1988. Pan American Series.

Rabinovitch, Celia. *Surrealism and the Sacred*. Boulder: Westview, 2002.

Raleigh, Walter. *The Discoverie of the Large, Rich, and Bewtiful Empyre of Guiana*. Ed. Neil L. Whitehead. Norman: U of Oklahoma P, 1997.

Ramírez, Liliana. *La vorágine: Estudio literario*. Bogotá: Panamericana, 2001.

Ray, Carina. "African Humanity under Siege: A Long History." *Zeleza Post: Informed News and Commentary on the Pan African World*, 3 May 2008. *www.zeleza.com/blog/carina-ray*. 15 January 2010.

"Reserva Comunal Machiguenga." Parks Watch. *Parkswatch.org*. 14 October 2011.

Rey, Alain, ed. *Dictionnaire culturel en langue française*. Paris: Dictionnaires Le Robert, 2005.

Rhys, Jean. *Wide Sargasso Sea*. New York: Norton, 1966.

Rieger, Branimir M., ed. *Dionysus in Literature: Essays on Literary Madness*. Bowling Green, OH: Bowling Green State U Popular P, 1994.

Rigney, Barbara. *Madness and Sexual Politics in the Feminist Novel: Studies in Brontë, Woolf, Lessing, and Atwood*. Madison: U of Wisconsin P, 1978.

Rivera, José Eustasio. *Promised Land/Tierra de promisión*. 1921. Trans. Carl W. Cobb.
　　Lewiston: Edwin Mellen, 1999. Hispanic Literature 45.

———. *La vorágine*. Bogotá: Cromos-Tamayo, 1924.

———. *The Vortex*. Trans. Earle K. James. New York: Putnam, 1934.

Rizzo-Vast, Patricio. "Paisaje e ideología en *Los pasos perdidos*." *La torre* 5.17 (July 2000):
　　463–77.

Rodó. *Ariel*. Ed. Raimundo Lazo. Mexico City: Editorial Porrua, 1997.

Rodríguez, Ileana. *Transatlantic Topographies: Islands, Highlands, Jungles*. Minneapolis:
　　U of Minnesota P, 2004. Cultural Studies of the Americas 17.

Rodríguez Monegal, Emir. *Narradores de esta América*. Vol. 1. Montevideo: Alfa, 1969.

Rogers, Charlotte. "Medicine, Madness, and Writing in *La vorágine*." *Bulletin of Hispanic
　　Studies* 87.1 (Jan. 2010): 89–108.

———. "*El órfico ensalmador*: Ethnography and Shamanism in Alejo Carpentier's *Los pasos
　　perdidos*." *Revista canadiense de estudios hispánicos* 30.2 (Sept. 2011): 351–72.

Romero Beltrán, Arturo. *Historia de la medicina colombiana, siglo XIX*. Antioquia:
　　Conciencias y Universidad de Antioquia, 1996.

Romeu, Raquel. "Influence of Climate on the Cultures of the Jungle as Perceived by Two
　　Latin American Novelists." *Climate and Literature: Reflections of Environment*. Ed. Janet
　　Pérez and Wendell Aycock. Lubbock: Texas Tech UP, 1995. 107–13.

Rosman, Silvia. *Dislocaciones culturales: Nación, sujeto y comunidad en América Latina*.
　　Rosario: Beatriz Viterbo, 2003.

Ross, Jack. "Wilson Harris, Joseph Conrad, and the South American 'Quest' Novel."
　　Landfall: New Zealand Arts and Letters 46.4 (Dec. 1992): 455–68.

Rosselli, Humberto. *Historia de la psiquiatría en Colombia*. Book 1. Bogotá: Horizontes,
　　1968.

Rothenberg, Albert. *Creativity and Madness: New Findings and Old Stereotypes*. Baltimore:
　　Johns Hopkins UP, 1990.

Rozelle, Lee. *Ecosublime: Environmental Awe and Terror from New World to Oddworld*.
　　Tuscaloosa: U of Alabama P, 2006.

Ruiz, Juan. *The Book of Good Love*. Trans. Elisha Kent Kane. Introd. John Esten Keller.
　　Chapel Hill: U of North Carolina P, 1968.

Sandison, Alan. *The Wheel of Empire: A Study of the Imperial Idea in Some Late Nineteenth
　　and Early Twentieth-Century Fiction*. London: St. Martin's, 1967.

Sarduy, Severo. *Colibrí*. Barcelona: Argos Vergara, 1984.

Sarmiento, Domingo Faustino. *Civilización i barbarie: Vida de Facundo Quiroga i aspecto
　　físico, costumbres y ámbitos de la República Argentina*. Santiago de Chile, 1845.

Sartre, Jean Paul. *No Exit, and Three Other Plays*. New York: Vintage, 1989.

Sass, Louis A. *Madness and Modernism: Insanity in the Light of Modern Art, Literature, and
　　Thought*. New York: Basic, 1992.

Saunders, Corinne, and Jane Macnaughton, eds. *Madness and Creativity in Literature and
　　Culture*. New York: Palgrave Macmillan, 2005.

Segalen, Victor. *Essay on Exoticism: An Aesthetics of Diversity*. Trans. and ed. Yael Rachel
　　Schlick. Fwd. Harry Harootunian. Durham: Duke UP, 2002.

"Selva." *Diccionario de la lengua española*. 21st ed. Madrid: Espasa Calpe, 1992.

Sepúlveda, Luis. *Un viejo que leía novelas de amor*. Barcelona: Tusquets, 1989.

Shepard, Glenn H., Jr. "The Mark and Olly Follies." *Anthropology News*. May 2011.
　　assets.survivalinternational.org. 5 February 2012.

Shields, Rob. *Places on the Margin: Alternative Geographies of Modernity*. London: Routledge, 1991.

Showalter, Elaine. *The Female Malady: Women, Madness, and English Culture, 1830–1980*. New York: Pantheon, 1985.

Siganos, André. "Le mythe amazonien: De quelques precautions théoriques et opératoires." *Iris: Les cahiers du Gerf* 27 (2004): 89–96.

"Silva." *Oxford Latin Dictionary*. Oxford: Clarendon, 1982.

Silva, José Asunción. *De sobremesa*. 1896. Prologue by Gabriel García Márquez. Madrid: Hiperión, 1996.

Skeat, Walter W. *An Etymological Dictionary of the English Language*. Oxford: Clarendon, 1910.

Skurski, Julie. "Ambiguities of Authenticity in Latin America: *Doña Bárbara* and the Construction of National Identity." *Poetics Today* 15.4 (Winter 1994): 605–42.

Slater, Candace. "Amazonia as Edenic Narrative." Cronon *Uncommon Ground* 114–31.

———. *Entangled Edens: Visions of the Amazon*. Berkeley: U of California, 2002.

Sommer, Doris. "About Face: The Talker Turns." *Reading the Shape of the World: Toward an International Cultural Studies*. Ed. Henry Schwartz. Boulder: Westview, 1996.

———. *Foundational Fictions: The National Romances of Latin America*. Berkeley: U of California P, 1991.

Sontag, Susan. *Illness as Metaphor; and, AIDS and Its Metaphors*. New York: Picador, 2001.

Spengler, Oswald. *The Decline of the West*. Trans. Charles Francis Atkinson. New York: Oxford UP, 1991.

Spitta, Silvia. *Misplaced Objects: Migrating Collections and Recollections in Europe and the Americas*. Austin: U of Texas P, 2009.

Stepan, Nancy Leys. *"The Hour of Eugenics": Race, Gender, and Nation in Latin America*. Ithaca: Cornell UP, 1991.

———. *Picturing Tropical Nature*. Ithaca: Cornell UP, 2001.

Stephens, Doris T. "The Symbolic Spiritual Quest in *Los pasos perdidos*." *Romance Quarterly* 29.2 (1982): 155–65.

Still, Arthur, and Irving Velody, eds. *Rewriting the History of Madness: Studies in Foucault's "Histoire de la folie."* London: Routledge, 1992.

Stoekl, Allan. "1937, March. Three Former Surrealists Found the Collège de Sociologie. The Avant-Garde Embraces Science." Hollier, *New History* 931.

Stoler, Ann Laura. *Carnal Knowledge and Imperial Power: Race and the Intimate in Colonial Rule*. Berkeley: U of California P, 2002.

———"Making Empire Respectable: The Politics of Race and Sexual Morality in 20th-Century Colonial Cultures." *American Ethnologist* 16.4 (1989): 634–60.

"Strangers in the Rainforest." *Mark and Olly: Living with the Machigenga*. Travel Channel, 2009.

Street, Brian V. *The Savage in Literature: Representations of "Primitive Society" in English Fiction, 1858–1920*. London: Routledge, 1975.

Suárez-Galbán Guerra, Eugenio. "Del Congo de Conrad al Orinoco de Carpentier." Vásquez 187–98.

Surya, Michel. *Georges Bataille: An Intellectual Biography*. Trans. Krzysztof Fijalkowski and Michael Richardson. London: Verso, 2002.

Swift, Jonathan. "On Poetry: A Rhapsody." *Jonathan Swift: The Complete Poems*. Ed. Pat Rogers. New Haven: Yale UP, 1983.

Terrón de Bellomo, Herminia. "El discurso sobre América Latina en un texto fundador: *La vorágine* de E. Rivera." *Alba de América: Revista literaria* 21.39–40 (July 2002): 407–15.

Thiher, Allen. *Revels in Madness: Insanity in Medicine and Literature.* Ann Arbor: U of Michigan P, 1999.

Thompson, Brian. "From Fascination to Poetry: Blindness in Malraux's Novels." *Witnessing André Malraux: Visions and Re-Visions.* Ed. Brian Thompson and Carl A. Viggiani. Middletown: Wesleyan UP, 1984. 159–68.

Thompson, Krista A. *An Eye for the Tropics: Tourism, Photography, and Framing the Caribbean Picturesque.* Durham: Duke UP, 2006.

Thornberry, Robert S. "Malraux, Stevenson, and Rivière: *La voie royale* and the Novel of Adventure." *André Malraux: Across Boundaries.* Ed. Geoffrey T. Harris. Amsterdam: Rodopi, 2000. 1–15.

Tobin, Beth Fowkes. *Colonizing Nature: The Tropics in British Art and Letters, 1760–1820.* Philadelphia: U of Pennsylvania P, 2005.

Todd, Olivier. *André Malraux: Une vie.* Paris: Gallimard, 2001.

———. *Malraux: A Life.* New York: Knopf, 2005.

Todorov, Tzvetan. "Knowledge in the Void: *Heart of Darkness.*" Trans. Walter C. Putnam III. *Conradiana* 21.2 (1989): 161–72.

Toms, H. W. "European Women and Children in the Tropics." *British Medical Journal* 1.3676 (20 June 1931): 1091–92.

Torgovnick, Marianna. *Gone Primitive: Savage Intellectuals, Modern Lives.* Chicago: U of Chicago P, 1990.

Torres, Mauro. *Dialéctica de los sueños seguida de una interpretación psicoanalítica de "La vorágine."* Bogotá: Universidad Libre de Colombia, 1962.

"Trouble in Paradise." *Mark and Olly: Living with the Machigenga.* Travel Channel, 2009.

Tusa, Bobs M. "A Detective Story: The Influence of Mircea Eliade on Alejo Carpentier's *Los pasos perdidos.*" *Hispanófila* 88 (Sept. 1986): 41–65.

Van Gennep, Arnold. *The Rites of Passage.* Trans. Monika B. Vizedom and Gabrielle L. Caffee. Introd. Solon T. Kimball. Chicago: U of Chicago P, 1960.

Vargas Llosa, Mario. *La casa verde.* Barcelona: Seix Barral, 1965.

———. *El hablador.* Barcelona: Seix Barral, 1987.

———. *The Storyteller.* Trans. Helen Lane. New York: Picador; Farrar, 1989.

———. *El sueño del celta.* Madrid: Alfaguara, 2010.

Vasconcelos, José. *La raza cósmica: Misión de la raza iberoamericana; Notas de viajes a la América del Sur.* Barcelona: Agencia Mundial de Librería, 1925.

Vásquez, Carmen. *Alejo Carpentier et "Los pasos perdidos."* Paris: Indigo, 2003. Publication of the Centre d'Études Hispaniques d'Amiens.

Vázquez de Parga, Salvador. *Héroes de la aventura.* Barcelona: Planeta, 1983.

Veit-Wild, Flora. *Writing Madness: Borderlines of the Body in African Literature.* Oxford: Currey; Harare: Weaver; Johannesburg: Jacana; Hollywood: African Academic-Tsehai, 2006.

Wakefield, Steve. *Carpentier's Baroque Fiction: Returning Medusa's Gaze.* Woodbridge: Tamesis-Boydell, 2004.

Watts, Cedric. "'A Bloody Racist': About Achebe's View of Conrad." *Joseph Conrad: Critical Assessments.* Ed. Keith Carabine. Sussex: Helm, 1992. 2: 405–18.

White, Andrea. *Joseph Conrad and the Adventure Tradition: Constructing and Deconstructing the Imperial Subject*. Cambridge: Cambridge UP, 1993.

White, Hayden. "The Forms of Wildness: Archaeology of an Idea." *The Wild Man Within: An Image in Western Thought from the Renaissance to Romanticism*. Ed. Edward Dudley and Maximillian E. Novak. Pittsburgh: U of Pittsburgh P, 1972. 3–38.

Whitehead, Neil L. *Dark Shamans: Kanaimà and the Poetics of Violent Death*. Durham: Duke UP, 2002.

Wiesenthal, Chris. *Figuring Madness in Nineteenth-Century Fiction*. New York: St. Martin's, 1997.

Woodruff, Charles Edward. *The Effects of Tropical Light on White Men*. New York: Rebman, 1905.

———. "Tropical Subjects." *Philadelphia Medical Journal* 7 Apr. 1900: 773.

Woolf, Virginia. *The Voyage Out*. 1915. Introd. Michael Cunningham. New York: Modern Library, 2000.

Wurgaft, Lewis W. *The Imperial Imagination: Magic and Myth in Kipling's India*. Middletown: Wesleyan UP, 1983.

Wyers, Frances. "Carpentier's *Los pasos perdidos*: Heart of Lightness, Heart of Darkness." *Revista hispanica moderna* 45.1 (June 1992): 84–95.

Wylie, Lesley. "Hearts of Darkness: The Celebration of Otherness in the Latin American *novella* [sic] *de la selva*." *Romance Studies* 23.2 (July 2005): 105–16.

Yerena, Jesús A. *La medicina en la obra literaria de Rómulo Gallegos*. Caracas: Presidencia de la República, 1977.

Zins, Henryk. *Joseph Conrad and Africa*. Nairobi: Kenya Literature Bureau, 1982.

Zúmeta, César. *El continente enfermo*. New York, 1899. Caracas: Rescate, 1961.

Zweig, Paul. *The Adventurer*. New York: Basic, 1974.

Index

Achebe, Chinua, 46, 47, 192n5
Adams, M. Ian, 203n30
Adorno, Rolena, 183
adventure novels
  quest romance and, 10–11
  tropical quest narratives and, 10–13,
    19–20, 144–45, 146–47, 171–72
*The Adventurous Male: Chapters in the History
  of the White Male Mind* (Green),
  188n25
Africa
  colonial medicine and, 33–34
  Hegel on, 6–7
  in *Journey to the End of the Night*, 15–16
"African spleen," 35, 36–37. *See also* tropical
  neurasthenia
Agassiz, Louis, 199–200n11
aging, 75
Aguirre, Wrath of God (movie), 2
Ahrimán, 129
Aínsa, Fernando, 186n8
Alberdi, J. B., 101
alcohol and alcoholism
  delirium tremens, 109, 131
  as hereditary disease, 198–99n29
  racial degeneration and, 108–9
  as racial poison, 104
  tropical neurasthenia and, 37
  in *The Vortex*, 101, 102, 108–9
  warm climates and, 22
Alejo Carpentier: The Pilgrim at Home
  (González Echevarría), 156

Alejo Carpentier y la cultura del surrealismo
  (Birkenmaier), 152
Almayer's Folly (Conrad), 39
Alonso, Carlos J., 107, 114–15, 198n16
Americas, 7–9. *See also* Latin America; *specific
  countries*
Amirbar (Mutis), 2, 174
"André Malraux, o el anhelo de la evasión"
  (Carpentier), 27–28, 145, 159, 163
Anstice, Mark, 178–82, 184
"Anthropologists and Other Frauds"
  (Huggan), 202n27
anthropology
  Carpentier and, 155, 165–67
  Gallegos and, 122–23, 128, 135
  Mark and Olly and, 180–81
  See also ethnography
Apocalypse Now (movie), 2, 29–30
Araujo, Orlando, 137
Arendt, Hannah, 189n30
Argentina
  eugenics in, 101, 102
  medical knowledge in, 26–27
  naturalist novel in, 191n54
  psychology in, 125, 197n11
Arguedas, Alcides, 101–2, 103, 109, 123–25
Ariel (Rodó), 120, 126
Arnold, David, 185n4
Around the World in Eighty Days (Verne), 11
arsenic, 22, 97–98
Artaud, Antonin, 57, 149, 150–51
  "El arte de los locos" (Carpentier), 154